THE CHARTER OF RIGHTS

Ian Greene

With a Foreword by Peter H. Russell

James Lorimer & Company, Publishers
Toronto, 1989

Front cover photo: Supply and Services Canada, Photocentre; photo by Paul Couvrette

---

Canadian Cataloguing in Publication Data

Greene, Ian
The Charter of Rights
Bibliography: p.
Includes index.
ISBN 1-55028-187-9 (bound) ISBN 1-55028-185-2 (pbk.)

1. Canada. Canadian Charter of Rights and Freedoms. 2. Civil rights — Canada. 3. Canada — Constitutional law — Amendments. I. Title.

KE4381.5.G74 1989 342.71'085 C89-093556-4
KF4483.C519G74 1989

James Lorimer & Company, Publishers
Egerton Ryerson Memorial Building
35 Britain Street
Toronto, Ontario M5A 1R7

Printed and bound in Canada

6 5 4 3 2 1 89 90 91 92 93 94

To Helen and John
from whom I have learned
that interpersonal respect
is the basis of rights

Contents

Foreword

Communist China may seem an odd place to look for lessons in the rule of law. Although that regime may not rely very much on formal rules of law as a basis for freedom and order, it does do one thing with new laws that is sorely lacking in Western "rule of law" countries like Canada. When a new law is promulgated, public education sessions are held so that ordinary citizens can learn what the new law is all about.

But we in the West take the "trickle down" approach to legal knowledge. We expect knowledge of the laws, old and new, to trickle down to the public — mainly through the lawyers who are paid to tell us what they think we need to know.

This is certainly true of the Canadian Charter of Rights and Freedoms. While most Canadians have heard about it, they have only the foggiest idea of what is in it. News reports make them aware that the Charter is being dealt with in the courts, but they really do not have an overall perspective on how the judiciary is interpreting it or how these court rulings are influencing Canadian life.

It is not the public's fault that they lack this knowledge, for until now no book has provided an overview of the Charter, setting out its background, analyzing its contents, explaining how its key terms have been treated by the judges and pointing out the practical consequences of these decisions.

This is precisely the gap which Ian Greene's book so admirably fills. In a clear, concise and engaging manner he makes the Charter accessible to the non-lawyer. The chapters in which he unravels the reasoning of the judges in the leading Charter decisions are especially valuable. Here Canadians who are interested in learning about the real Charter will discover an essential truth — the constitution means what the judges say it means.

Whether Canadians will like what they discover the judges have been doing with the Charter is another matter. Greene himself maintains a healthy perspective on the Charter. He sees it as a mixed blessing but recognizes that it is here to stay. In his final chapter he makes some imaginative suggestions on how we might get more out of the Charter by relying less exclusively on our judges to give meaning to its contents.

By making it possible for many more Canadians to become knowledgeable about the Charter, Ian Greene's book contributes substantially to movement in the direction he advocates.

Peter H. Russell
University of Toronto
February 1989

Acknowledgements

I am grateful to so many people for their help and support in the preparation of this book that it is hard to know where to begin. Professor Donald Smiley, Professor Peter Russell, Timothy Endicott and Curtis Fahey, my editor at Lorimer, read through the entire manuscript and provided me with some very helpful comments. Judith Turnbull, the copy editor, went far beyond the call of duty with her assistance. It is impossible for me to thank them all enough, not only for the benefit of their insights, but for their good humour and encouragement. The following people read parts of the manuscript, and I am indebted to them for their suggestions: Doris Annear, Richard Cullen, Fred Fletcher, Marc Gold, Chief Judge C.A. Kosowan, Chief Justice J.H. Laycraft, Peter McCormick, Eilonwy Morgan, Stephen Newman, Leo Panitch, Rob Shropshire, Christine Sypnowich, George Szablowski, Martin Thomas, Ellen Turley and Reg Whitaker. I would also like to thank colleagues from whom I have learned much about human rights through informal discussions over the past few years. They include Carl Baar, Robert Drummond, Peter Hogg, Ninette Kelley, Rainer Knopff, Samuel LaSelva, Patrick Monahan, Ted Morton, Sidney Peck, David Shugarman and Brian Slattery. I am especially grateful for having had the opportunity to participate in the Constitutional Law Group at Osgoode Hall Law School which was organized first by Professor Peter Hogg, and then by Professor Marc Gold. All of the persons mentioned above have contributed towards improving the manuscript, but I take full responsibility for its shortcomings.

I have received helpful comments from undergraduate and graduate students too numerous to mention, and I am especially thankful to Andy Knight and Michael Bobkowitz. There are many others who have provided assistance in various forms, including Margaret Bertram, Peter Gabor, Munyonzwe Hamalengwa, Betty Knapp, Linda Kuttis, Edward Low, Bob MacDermid, Diane McCallum, Helen Morgan, Joanna Morgan, John Morgan, Angie Ritter, Anne

Stretch, Judy Wolever and Pat Vadacchino. Most importantly, I am indebted to my wife, Eilonwy Morgan, without whose good cheer and tolerance for my unusual working hours the project would never have been completed.

Preface

*The protection of human rights is the final end of govern-
ment and ... the degree to which human rights are
safeguarded is the final test by which any polity should be
judged. — Donald Smiley (2)*

Most Canadians would likely agree with the above quote from
one of Canada's leading political scientists. According to
public opinion polls, however, 80 per cent of Canadians would dis-
agree with the main argument in the essay in which the quote appears:
that a constitutional charter of rights is *not* the best way to protect
human rights in Canada.

We have had the Charter since 1982. While the question of whether
we should have had a constitutional bill of rights is now irrelevant,
other questions have replaced it: Has the Charter been a success?
What has its impact been? How might it affect our lives in the future?
This book is intended to provide readers with the raw materials to
reach their own conclusions about these questions.

A few words about the plan of the book are in order. Chapters 1
and 2 provide a background to understanding Charter decisions.
Chapter 1 considers the nature of human rights or civil liberties. It
also recounts some human rights issues in Canada prior to the Charter
era, including some leading Canadian Bill of Rights decisions. In
chapter 2, the events leading to the creation of the Charter are summarized, and the links between the Charter and other human rights
legislation (such as the Bill of Rights) are pointed out. Chapter 2 also
summarizes the hopes of the Charter's supporters, and the fears of its
opponents.

Chapters 3 to 8 comment on specific cases and controversies arising from the Charter. Chapter 3 focuses on the section of the Charter
that encompasses the "fundamental freedoms": freedom of religion,
expression, assembly and association. The Supreme Court's decisions
regarding Sunday-closing legislation and the right to strike are dis-

cussed, along with the two decisions on the validity of provisions for French-only commercial signs in Quebec's Bill 101.

Chapter 4 deals with judicial decisions regarding the "democratic rights" — for example, whether prisoners and the mentally handicapped can vote, whether the Charter might force a more equitable distribution of voters between urban and rural ridings, and what constitutes fair regulation of the elections process. These democratic rights cases have so far been decided in the lower courts; none of them have reached the Supreme Court of Canada.

The Supreme Court's controversial decision to strike down Canada's abortion law is reviewed in chapter 5, which centres on the "legal rights" sections of the Charter. Also considered in this chapter are Supreme Court decisions concerning the right to an independent judge, the right to counsel (especially with regard to drinking drivers), police powers of search and seizure, the presumption of innocence, and whether cruise missile testing violates security of the person. As well, the 1985 Supreme Court decision confirming a refugee claimant's right to an oral hearing — a decision that led to chaos in the unprepared Immigration Department — is analyzed.

Chapter 6 deals with the Charter's "equality rights." The Supreme Court's first decision about this section (the *Andrews* case, 1989) is highlighted. In addition, the *Borowski* case, in which the Supreme Court was asked to decide whether the fetus should have an equal right to life, is considered. The Roman Catholic high school funding issue in Ontario is cited to illustrate the relation between equality rights and other parts of the Charter.

Chapter 7 reviews the Charter's effect on the status of the official languages of Canada and minority language education rights. The chapter focuses on the six Supreme Court decisions that interpret language rights inside and outside of the Charter. These cases deal with the "Quebec clause" in Bill 101, language rights in New Brunswick, Manitoba and Saskatchewan, and whether Manitoba and Quebec courts must issue bilingual summonses.

In total, nineteen Supreme Court of Canada decisions on the Charter are considered in detail, as well as four other recent Supreme Court decisions that affect human rights. These decisions represent only about a third of the judgments the Court has rendered on the Charter up to early 1989. The cases chosen are those that seem to best illustrate how the Supreme Court is interpreting the Charter. (A number of lower court decisions are also mentioned, as well as about thirty other Supreme Court Charter decisions.) What the book tries to explain is the reasoning process the judges followed, so that readers can enter into the debate about the interpretation of the rights and freedoms listed in the Charter. From this perspective, a fair amount of attention is given to dissenting opinions, since they represent alternative viewpoints. Readers are encouraged to read the judicial decisions for themselves. The book contains references not only to the judicial decisions in the law reports, but also to the edited and more readable versions of these decisions in the series *Leading Decisions of the Supreme Court of Canada* and in the casebook by Peter Russell, Rainer Knopff and F.L. Morton, *Federalism and the Charter: Leading Constitutional Decisions* (5th ed.).

In the text, cases are referred to with numbers in square brackets; these numbers correspond to a list of cases at the end of the book. Bibliographic references are contained in a separate list. Numbers in round brackets refer to specific articles or books if an author has more than one entry in the list of references.

The final chapter assesses the effect of the Charter on the general respect for human rights in Canada. It argues that while the Charter itself has had little success in promoting more interpersonal respect — which is what rights are all about — its impact has been felt in other ways. It has provided politicians with a new means of discarding political hot potatoes and has offered new challenges for lawyers and judges. Nevertheless, the Charter does have a positive potential for promoting human rights. I suggest some strategies that may help to nurture this potential and at the same time strengthen our democratic institutions.

Ian Greene
Toronto, May 1989

1

Setting the Stage: Civil Rights in Canada and the Pre-Charter Era

Ronald Dworkin, a contemporary legal theorist, has described the basis of rights in a liberal society as follows: "We might say that individuals have a right to equal concern and respect in the design and administration of the political institutions that govern them . . . . [T]hey possess [this right] not by virtue of birth or characteristic or merit or excellence but simply as human beings with the capacity to make plans and give justice" (3). Four scholars (Paul Sniderman, Frederick Fletcher, Peter Russell and Phillip Tetlock) have conducted research into the thinking of Canadians about human rights and have concluded that those who are committed to civil liberties show "a generalized commitment to tolerance." As well, these authors argued that a commitment to *individual* rights can coexist with a commitment to the larger community.

Building on these approaches, I adopt the position that at the basis of the concept of human rights or civil liberties is the belief that every human being deserves — and owes to others — respect and fair treatment. Human beings deserve these things simply because they are human beings.

This definition of rights-consciousness emphasizes that rights are not simply claims that individuals can demand with no responsibilities attached. In order to have rights, rights-bearers have a coincidental responsibility towards others to tolerate their rights. Some, like Canadian political philosopher C.B. Macpherson, would go further and argue that rights-bearers also have a responsibility to take action to ensure that others have the *opportunity* to exercise their rights, that is, to pursue self-realization.

Controversies about rights often involve the question of whether individuals' personal claims or their responsibilities to others should be given priority. Such issues can rarely be resolved through applying "correct" legal reasoning. Rather, what is involved is human rights policy-making.

Civil Rights

Rights and Freedoms

The phrases "human rights" and "civil liberties" are often used interchangeably, as they are in this book. However, a distinction can be made between rights and liberties that helps to shed some light on the content of the more general concept of civil rights. (See Hohfeld, Lederman (1) and Hart.)

A "liberty" can be thought of as the ability to do something without constraints imposed or permitted by the state. For example, freedom of expression and freedom of religion can be considered as liberties in this sense.

A "right" can be regarded as the consequence of a duty that is placed on an individual or on the state either by law or by some higher authority. For example, some of the legal rights and language rights in the Charter can be regarded in this way. They are rights owed to individuals because of duties imposed by law on the state. Section 10(a) of the Charter gives to the state the duty of informing "promptly" persons who are arrested or detained of "the reasons therefor." As a result of the state's legal duty, "everyone" has a "right." Similarly, section 18(1) of the Charter provides that Parliament "shall" print and publish in English and French all "statutes, records and journals." Because of this duty, Canadians have a right to certain bilingual documents. However, if the legal duty were ever repealed, the right would cease to exist.

According to those who adhere to one of the schools of "natural law" (for example, Plato, Aristotle, St. Thomas Aquinas, Locke and Rousseau), a law of nature can impose certain duties on the state regardless of whether these duties are enshrined in a government's laws. The laws of nature that give rise to natural rights may derive from correct reasoning or from a deity.

However, according to "judicial positivists" (like Jeremy Bentham, John Austin and H.L.A. Hart), only laws made by legislatures can impose duties on governments. The positivists take this position because, among other reasons, the natural law theorists themselves do not agree about the content of the supposed "laws of nature."

Approaches to rights based on natural law theories have been more influential among jurists in the United States and the continent of Europe than among jurists in the Anglo-Canadian tradition. Even so, it is possible that judges may draw from natural law concepts of rights when interpreting the general phrases in the Charter.

Whether a person adheres to a positivist or natural law conception of rights may depend to some extent on whether government is viewed as friend or enemy. For some, government in a democracy represents community interests. From this perspective, a government's role in the human rights field is primarily to ensure that optimum conditions exist for citizens to use their rights and freedoms. These people are likely to view rights from a positivist standpoint because government, as an instrument of the people, can generally be trusted to take appropriate action. For others, those who control government — even in a democracy — tend to run it in their own self-interest or for the wrong interests. Thus, government itself is the major threat to human rights, and a legal fence needs to be erected to keep governments within bounds. These people may tend to believe in natural rights.

The fact that the Charter refers to both rights and liberties is reflected in its full title — the Charter of Rights and Freedoms. Yet it is not always possible to distinguish easily between a right and a liberty. For example, it is not clear whether the right to retain counsel in section 10(b) means a *right* that is a result of a duty imposed on the state to ensure the provision of counsel, or that persons who are arrested or detained are *at liberty* to choose a lawyer, or both. As a result, I have not attempted to distinguish in any systematic way between rights and freedoms when describing the Charter. Supreme Court judges have on occasion referred to this distinction when interpreting the Charter, as noted in chapter 7.

The terms "human rights" and "civil liberties" are emotionally charged. Some feel strongly that they are entitled to certain "natural rights," and they become very zealous about protecting them. In addition, both Thomas Pocklington and Cynthia Williams have noted a tendency in recent years to frame what were formerly called political demands as human rights claims. For example, we now hear about a shopper's right to shop on Sunday, a student's right to a student loan, or non-smokers' rights. Donald Smiley (3) has suggested translating the term "right" into "claim upon the state" in order to promote clearer thinking about the appropriateness of such claims without the emotional overtones.

Rights in Liberal Democracies

In societies in which interpersonal respect, self-worth and fairness are considered important either for religious or secular reasons, these values have been promoted in culturally specific ways. In Western liberal societies, civil rights claims have traditionally involved one or more of three elements:

- Individual citizens should have a wide range of freedom to think and do as they please, subject to some limits intended to prevent harm to others or to promote particular social goals. This element has two implications: first, that governments must *refrain* from acting so as to restrict freedom unnecessarily, and second, that governments must sometimes *act* to ensure the protection of freedom. For example, governments must refrain from interfering with religious ceremonies but should act to protect worshippers who are physically threatened by their opponents.
- In situations in which it is acceptable either for the state or another citizen to restrict an individual's freedom, certain principles of fairness must be followed that are intended to ensure that freedom is not restrained unnecessarily. For example, those accused of criminal activity are presumed innocent until proven guilty before an independent and impartial judge.
- The same standards of freedom and acceptable restraints should apply equally to everyone unless there is a valid reason why they should not. This is because all people are considered as equally deserving of respect.

A recent example will help to illustrate these elements. In 1988 the Supreme Court struck down section 251 of the Criminal Code, the law that prohibited abortions unless they endangered a woman's life or health and unless they had been approved in advance by a hospital abortion committee (*Regina v. Morgentaler* [100]). Newspaper headlines on the day the decision was announced proclaimed that the

Supreme Court had declared that the Charter provided a right to abortions. These headlines were misleading. What the Supreme Court had actually decided was that Parliament had restricted abortions in an unjust manner. For example, Chief Justice Brian Dickson noted that a woman who wanted an abortion had to prove that the continued pregnancy would endanger her "life or health," but no definition of "health" was given in the legislation. Unfairness was created here, as the woman wanting an abortion would not know what standards of proof she would have to meet. Furthermore, five judges criticized section 251 because it condoned unequal access to abortions. As a result of the procedural barriers the law had erected, only 20 per cent of Canadian hospitals could or would perform abortions. Therefore, in many areas of Canada, abortions could not be obtained at all. The Supreme Court decision meant that if Parliament wanted to regulate abortions, it would have to do so in a way that respected the guarantees of procedural fairness, or "fundamental justice," in section 7 of the Charter.

The Supreme Court's decision about the abortion law illustrates two of the three elements included in the liberal democratic concept of civil liberties or human rights. With respect to the second element — procedural fairness — the Court decided that the limits to a pregnant woman's "liberty" and "security of person" must meet specific standards of procedural fairness. In relation to the third element — equality — the Court held that the same freedoms, restraints, and standards of procedural fairness should apply to all women in Canada who are contemplating an abortion. (The Court did not rely on section 15, the equality rights section of the Charter, but on the general notion that rights apply equally to everyone.) The Supreme Court did not consider the issue related to the first civil liberties element — optimal freedom — specifically, whether the Charter rights to liberty and security of the person include a right for pregnant women to decide whether to have abortions. This is because judges usually prefer to decide cases on the narrowest and simplest grounds, and in this case, the procedural question was the easiest to decide. This important decision will be discussed in more detail in chapter 5.

In many countries, a controversy over whether women have a right to obtain abortions would not arise. Canada is among a minority of countries that proclaim an important place for civil rights in their systems of government. We share this viewpoint with the citizens of other countries that adhere to the liberal-democratic tradition. The liberal democracies tend to place a higher value on civil rights because of the heritage of their religious, ideological, economic and political traditions, which stress the importance of individual initiative and which regard most persons as capable of making prudent decisions about how to use their freedom.

The belief in individualism, which is so much a part of our political culture, is not shared by a great many of the world's governments. Some governments with a Marxist ideology, for example, claim that the logic of capitalism prevents the owners of capital from making economic decisions that will benefit the entire community. From this perspective, the capitalist economic system compels the owners of capital to exploit labour. Economic freedom for capitalists necessarily results in economic servitude for labour.

In an authoritarian state like Singapore, civil liberties are viewed by the government as an impediment to stability and economic growth. A prominent government supporter recently asked, "How many Singaporeans really want free speech, anyway? They want orderliness, a decent living . . . . We must keep [sensitive issues like race, religion and language] under control." In even more repressive authoritarian states like South Africa, where the government can stave off the majority only with military force, permitting civil liberties would only intensify the problems of holding on to power. In a fundamentalist religious state like Iran, ideas and activities that vary from the government's interpretation of the official religion are considered to be wrong; to permit them would be to condone evil.

Limits to Rights

Even in the liberal democracies, individual freedom is far from absolute, and inequality in treatment is often acceptable. The following are several examples of generally accepted restrictions on liberty, procedural fairness or equality in Canada:

- Inequality of treatment is practised in numerous cases of relevant differences in ability. We also tolerate a very unequal distribution of wealth, which contributes to social inequality.
- Freedom of expression does not include the right to disseminate false information. Thus, it is possible to sue for libel, and there are laws against misleading advertising and perjury. In 1988 Toronto publisher Ernst Zundel was convicted of the Criminal Code offense of spreading false news. Zundel had persistently written that the Holocaust was a hoax. The

Court considered that the prohibition against distributing false news was a "reasonable limit" to freedom of expression.

- The government's desire to promote public order gives rise to another set of restrictions. Individuals cannot carry a handgun unless they are police officers or otherwise licensed to do so. It is an offence to promote hatred against a recognizable group. Furthermore, civil liberties can be suspended, within limits, to punish or rehabilitate criminal offenders, or to keep them from creating additional disorder.

- Emergencies, such as wars, epidemics or forest fires, sometimes cannot be dealt with effectively unless certain human rights are temporarily curtailed. Canada's new federal Emergencies Act, which received unanimous consent from the House of Commons in 1988 and replaced the old War Measures Act, outlines the situations in which the federal government would consider itself justified in assuming emergency powers.

- The unrestricted practice of some rights results in a violation of other rights. There is perhaps no clearer example of this conflict of rights than the abortion issue: an unborn child's right to life versus a pregnant woman's right to liberty and security of the person. Another example consists of the "gag orders" judges sometimes place on the publication of information pertinent to a controversial trial. There is a conflict between the accused person's right to a fair trial and the freedom of the media. In such cases of conflict between two incompatible rights, one or both will have to be limited in order for the conflict to be resolved.

- There are numerous restrictions on our freedom so that important public policy goals can be promoted. For example, Canadians are forced to contribute towards the cost of health-care services, whether or not they use them, and doctors are not allowed to extra-bill. Our federal and provincial governments claim to support free enterprise, but intervene regularly in the marketplace in the name of fair competition, consumer protection and labour peace.

- Although we are a relatively tolerant society, accepting a diversity of moral standards, there are nevertheless certain moral prohibitions that restrict our liberty. According to public opinion polls, the majority of Canadians support the laws that restrict prostitution and hard-core pornographic films and videos.

It is obvious, then, that our commitment to freedom and equality in Canada is not absolute. We value these principles but within what we consider to be reasonable limits. Our beliefs about the balance between rights and limits are the product of our religious, philosophic, economic and political convictions. If there are diverse opinions about these matters — as there obviously are in Canada — there is bound to be disagreement about the appropriate border between rights and limits.

John Stuart Mill, the nineteenth-century English philosopher, claimed that restrictions on our liberties were justifiable only to prevent harm to others. Many of the restrictions noted above could be considered as measures to prevent individuals from harming others. With regard to limits designed to promote public policy goals, however, the harm principle is not always clearly evident. Concerning the legislation on morality issues, the harm principle is the least evident. Nevertheless, it is possible that indulgence in pornography is associated with the tendency to commit various crimes; the scientific evidence here is inconclusive. It is also arguable that prostitution encourages relationships of exploitation and subservience, but it is not clear to what extent this "harm" has a ripple effect beyond the willing participants. Plainly, there is no easy solution to the problem of where to draw the line between rights and limits.

The thinking of Canadians about rights and limits depends on the nature of their rights-consciousness. There are four major sources of rights-consciousness in our society: the liberal political ideology, the emergence of democratic values, the impact of the American Bill of Rights on our thinking, and Canada's bilingual and bireligious heritage.

The Origins of Rights-Consciousness

Liberalism

The political philosophy of liberalism, which stresses individual self-determination and equality, developed in the context of a number of events that occurred in Europe several centuries ago. First, the Renaissance, which spread across Europe in the fifteenth century, celebrated with new vigour "the dignity of man." Second, the Protestant Reformation of the sixteenth century led to rebellion against the rigidly hierarchical structure of church and state. Luther's theology —that human beings could establish individual relations with God and that the church authorities were not necessary as intermediaries — set the stage for the further development of individualist ideals, especially in an England beset by civil wars in the seventeenth century.

In these wars, the traditional order was pitted against the new ideals of individualism: the traditional hierarchical church against the individualist reformers, the absolute authority of the monarch against the supremacy of Parliament, judicial subservience to the crown against judicial independence, the economic privilege of the nobility against the rising merchant class. In the "Glorious Revolution" of 1688, the new order triumphed. The revolution resulted in the supremacy of Parliament and provided for the impartial application of the law, new economic freedom for the merchant class and somewhat greater religious toleration. John Locke, who wrote his *Second Treatise on Government* in 1690, became the chief philosopher of the age.

Locke attempted to convince his readers of the inherent rationality of the new political system. He began with the premise that human beings are basically reasonable. If they could wipe the slate of history clean and negotiate a new social contract, they would agree on the need for creating a government. This government would provide the necessary social order so that people could pursue their own individual goals in life. It follows that government must exist only by the consent of the governed and for the benefit of the governed.

To give all people an equal chance to pursue their goals, an elected legislature should enact laws that would be equally applicable to all citizens. As Locke put it, the laws are "not to be varied in particular Cases, but [there should be] one Rule for the Rich and Poor, for the Favourite at Court, and the Country Man at Plough." So that the laws could be administered without favouritism, administrative officials and judges should act impartially. In other words, the state would be ruled by equally applicable, impartially administered laws, not by the arbitrary whims of government officials. This principle became known as the rule of law. The preamble to the Canadian Charter of Rights and Freedoms proclaims that Canada is founded on "principles that recognize . . . the rule of law."

Locke's political philosophy became known as liberalism. During the eighteenth century, the ideals of liberalism took a firm hold on the property-owning classes in the United Kingdom. Judicial independence — an essential precondition for the rule of law — was guaranteed by an act of Parliament in 1701. Certain human rights, such as freedom of speech, religion, assembly and association, became accepted as constitutional principles. These principles were respected to the extent that politicians and public servants had the knowledge and integrity to observe them, and to the extent that voters would not re-elect governments that violated them.

The ideals of liberalism had an important influence on the courts in England. Since the twelfth century, whenever Parliament had not provided a law to define how a dispute should be settled, the courts would settle the dispute according to what the judges believed to be the community standards. The decisions of the higher courts became precedents for the deciding of future cases. The whole body of this judge-made law became known as "the common law." With the advent of the ideology of liberalism, the judiciary expanded the common law to reflect liberal ideals.

The most important method the courts developed to protect individual freedom was to pay strict attention to the principle of the rule of law. Pursuant to the rule of law, government officials may act only if authorized to do so by a law enacted by the legislature, and the law is presumed to apply equally to all. A good example of the application of this principle is the case of *Entick v. Carrington* [36] in 1765. A British cabinet minister had signed a search warrant that no law had given him the power to sign. The person who had been searched illegally was successful in suing the crown for trespass.

Another principle developed through the common law to prevent unnecessary restrictions of a person's liberty when confronted with the power of the state in court was *mens rea* (guilty mind). Pursuant to this doctrine, a court will refuse to convict unless it can be shown that an accused person *intended* to commit the act of which he or she is accused or that the person acted recklessly. Other safeguards developed through the common law include the principle that the crown must prove its case beyond a reasonable doubt in a criminal prosecution, that confessions will not be accepted by judges unless they are given freely, that an accused person cannot be compelled to testify and that no one can be forced to incriminate himself or herself. In addition, the courts developed procedures known as "prerogative writs," which are court orders intended to help remedy unlawful violations of public liberties by government officials. The best known of these is the writ of *habeas corpus*, which is intended to determine whether a person who has been imprisoned has been dealt with according to law.

These common-law principles and procedures are all reflected in the Canadian Bill of Rights and the Charter of Rights and Freedoms.

It should be noted that the liberal ideology has a number of variants. There is the rationalist approach characteristic of the Enlightenment and American liberalism, which claims that correct reasoning can accurately describe natural rights. In contrast, there is Burkean liberalism (also known as conservatism), which is skeptical about the ability of human beings to devise "correct" solutions through the reasoning process and is more inclined to trust the lessons of history. Peter Russell (9) claims that Canadian liberalism has more in common with the Burkean tradition. Liberals like Ronald Dworkin stress the respect that each individual is *owed* — and this is particularly true of American liberalism — while other liberals place more weight on the respect that is owed *to* others and the community as a whole. Patrick Monahan maintains that Canadian liberalism has a more communitarian flavour than the highly individualistic American liberalism.

The Development of Democratic Values

After the Glorious Revolution, the people who could elect the members of the House of Commons were those with newly established economic power — property owners. The franchise remained extremely limited; because of property qualifications, only the wealthiest 5 per cent of the population could vote. Thus, as C.B. Macpherson (2) has pointed out, the United Kingdom became liberal long before it became democratic.

Adam Smith became the philosopher of economic liberalism during the eighteenth century, emphasizing the overall benefits that would accrue to society if individuals had as much freedom as possible to pursue their economic goals. The emphasis that liberalism placed on equality — equal access to the marketplace, equal application of the law — eventually caused the disenfranchised propertyless classes to demand equality in the right to vote. Thomas Paine became their spokesperson, and his famous book, *The Rights of Man*, became their rallying cry. Yet the extension of the franchise was slow to be accepted, both in the United Kingdom and Canada. This was because of the fear that the poor might take advantage of democracy to limit the freedom of the upper classes.

In Canada, since property qualifications limited the franchise in 1867, and since women were disenfranchised, the country at that time could not be considered democratic. But the logic of the liberal ethic of equality proved too strong for the privileged classes to resist, and by 1920 the franchise had been extended to most non-native adults in federal and provincial elections, except in Quebec, where women were not granted the right to vote until 1940. Native people who lived on reserves were not enfranchised until 1960. Adults who are still sometimes excluded from voting today include prisoners, the mentally incompetent and judges (to promote their impartiality and independence). It was not until the Charter came into effect that the right to vote received recognition in the formal constitution. The Charter challenges to the remaining restrictions on the right to vote will be discussed in chapter 4.

Thus, while the right to vote and to participate in the political life of the country is recognized today as an important human right, it was slow to be accepted. By 1960 the almost-universal adult franchise had achieved the status of a constitutional principle in every part of the country.

The U.S. Bill of Rights

The American Declaration of Independence of 1776 reflected the liberal ideals of individual freedom and equality:

> We hold these truths to be self-evident, that all men are created equal, that they are endowed by their Creator with certain unalienable Rights, that among these are Life, Liberty and the pursuit of Happiness. That to secure these rights, Governments are instituted among Men, deriving their just powers from the consent of the governed.

Much of the impetus behind the American Revolution was the idea that an independent America could protect human rights more effectively than had the British colonial administration. The more influential framers of the U.S. constitution, such as James Madison and Alexander Hamilton, thought that the checks and balances built into the 1787 constitution would be sufficient to protect civil liberties, especially with regard to the Congress, which was granted a limited list of powers. However, some state leaders were not so trusting. In order to secure the ratification of the constitution by the states, a bill of rights was added in 1789 consisting of the first ten amendments to the constitution.

The bill enumerated the civil rights the newly independent Americans were most worried about losing, based on the experience of their colonial heritage. It prohibited the U.S. Congress from restricting freedom of speech, of the press and of assembly, and from adopting an official state religion. It protected certain procedural rights: not to be subjected to unreasonable searches or seizures, not to have to testify against oneself, not to be punished twice for the same offence, not to be deprived of life, liberty or property except through the due process of law, and not to be subjected to cruel and unusual punishment. It also contained some positive legal rights: to a speedy trial, to a jury in more serious cases and to reasonable bail. There were also rights that might seem odd to us today but were of particular concern to Americans because of abuse suffered at the hands of British soldiers: a right not to provide accommodation to soldiers and a right to bear arms.

Three amendments added after the civil war abolished slavery, extended the guarantee of due process and equal protection to the state jurisdictions, and prohibited racial discrimination concerning the right to vote. Three more amendments added in this century gave women the right to vote, abolished the poll taxes that some states had been using to disenfranchise blacks, and set a uniform voting age of eighteen years. The history of the American Bill of Rights indicates that a society's approach to rights evolves over time.

Most of the human rights the Americans placed in their constitution had been recognized as constitutional principles in the United Kingdom during the eighteenth century or had developed as principles of common law to protect the rule of law and individual freedom. Yet the British authorities had been far more careful to ensure that these principles were observed at home than in the colonies. The Americans were therefore not impressed with entrusting their rights to constitutional principles or the common law. Converting these human rights tenets to prose, and then placing them in a written constitution that could not easily be amended, was an experiment in devising a more effective means of protecting rights and liberties. It is a procedure Canada initially rejected but has now adopted.

Canada's Bilingual and Bireligious Heritage

The two most important cleavages in the colonies that were to become Canada were language and religion. An agreement to create a new federation could be secured only if there were minimal constitutional guarantees for the linguistic and religious minorities in each of the new provinces and for the francophone minority in federal institutions. The minorities in the provinces overlapped each other, but not perfectly. Although francophones tended to be Roman Catholic and anglophones Protestant, there were also anglophone Catholics in each colony. Thus, the constitution contains separate guarantees of minority language rights and minority religious education rights.

Section 133 of the British North America Act (BNA Act) states that either English or French may be spoken by anyone in Parliament or in the Quebec legislature and that both languages must be used in the records, journals and enactments of both legislatures. Further, either language may be used in courts of Quebec or in any courts established by Parliament (today these latter are the Supreme Court of Canada, the Federal Court and the Tax Court). Section 133 was thus intended to protect the anglophone minority in Quebec and the francophone minority in federal institutions. When Manitoba gained provincehood in 1870, after Louis Riel's failed rebellion, franco-Manitobans were granted similar language guarantees in the Manitoba Act. The francophone minority in the North-West Territories was provided with similar language rights in a federal statute. These provisions continued in Alberta and Saskatchewan when they were created in 1905, subject to change by the provincial legislatures.

The denominational school rights are contained in the somewhat complex section 93 of the BNA Act. Section 93 gives the provincial legislatures the power to make laws in relation to education, except that no law can "prejudicially affect any Right or Privilege with respect to Denominational Schools which any Class of Persons" had in a province when it was admitted to Canada. If a province attempts to reduce the denominational school rights of a religious minority, those affected can appeal to the federal government, not only to request protection of rights granted at the time of entry into Canada, but also to request the protection of rights granted since that time. If the government decides that the grievance is legitimate, then the federal Parliament may enact legislation to remedy the situation. The federal Parliament's power to enact remedial legislation has never been used, although in 1896 the federal Conservative government drafted remedial legislation to protect Roman Catholic schools in

Manitoba. An election intervened, however, and it was won by the Liberals. The new prime minister, Wilfrid Laurier, negotiated a settlement with the Manitoba government instead of intervening with federal legislation.

The language and denominational school rights in the BNA Act have been called a "small bill of rights" by Peter Hogg (1). They were so important to the creation of Canada that they were the only substantive rights written into our original constitution. The Fathers of Confederation did not regard this "small bill of rights" as a bill of rights in the American sense, but simply as a practical necessity to bring about the union of the British North American colonies. The constitutional rights in Canada resulted more from duties owed by governments as a result of political compromises than from the idea that there are natural liberties which governments are prohibited from interfering with. The U.S. Bill of Rights concentrated more on rights in the latter sense.

In fact, Canada's political elite was very much opposed to the concept of an American-style bill of rights. The Fathers of Confederation preferred the parliamentary form of government that had evolved in the United Kingdom. One of the working principles behind the parliamentary system is legislative supremacy, and this principle has overshadowed the entire debate about how civil liberties should be protected in Canada. Fears about losing legislative supremacy hampered judicial enforcement of the civil liberties principles before 1960. With one exception, the Supreme Court's view of legislative supremacy also prevented the judiciary from striking down statutes that conflicted with the Canadian Bill of Rights. The same principle continues to trouble the Supreme Court in its search for an acceptable interpretation of the Charter. For these reasons, it is necessary to take a closer look at the concept.

Legislative Supremacy

At first glance, legislative supremacy may seem like a straightforward legal concept that has no obvious connection with civil liberties. After the Glorious Revolution of 1688, it was accepted that the legislative branch of government could determine the powers of the other two branches: the executive (which became known as the cabinet and the public service) and the judiciary. Canada inherited the principle of legislative supremacy pursuant to the preamble of the BNA Act, which stated that Canada would have a constitution "similar in principle to that of the United Kingdom."

Legislative supremacy could not apply to Canada in exactly the same way as it applied to the United Kingdom for three reasons. First, since Canada was a federal country, there was no single legislature that was "supreme." Instead, each of the legislatures, federal or provincial, was supreme within its own jurisdiction. Second, since Canada was until 1931 subservient to the British government with regard to external relations, no legislature in Canada was supreme in this field. Third, since the British North America Act did not contain an amending formula, the British Parliament, until 1982, had legal responsibility for amending Canada's constitution. (After 1867, however, the British Parliament always amended Canada's constitution according to the wishes of the relevant Canadian authorities.) In sum, legislative supremacy in Canada meant simply that the federal and provincial legislatures, within the bounds of their jurisdictions, could determine the powers of the other two branches and of subordinate administrative bodies.

The usefulness of the principle of legislative supremacy in a legal sense is that it provides judges with a guide for ranking legal rules. If a judge encounters a conflict between a statute and a cabinet order, or between a statute and the common law, the statute takes precedence in both cases because legislatures, which create statutes, are superior to cabinets and the judiciary. If there is a conflict between two statutes, the more recent one takes precedence because a current legislature is legally supreme at any given time. Clearly, judges need rules to assist them in distinguishing between valid and invalid laws, and legislative supremacy is helpful in this regard.

The principle of legislative supremacy, however, took on an aura far in excess of these straightforward implications. From the late eighteenth century until very recently, legislative supremacy was thought of as having almost sacrosanct properties. Canadian judges between 1960 and 1982 were reluctant to give priority to the Canadian Bill of Rights over other statutes because they feared that in doing so they would negate legislative supremacy. In large measure, this expansion of the principle was the result of the writings of the late-nineteenth-century British constitutional lawyer A.V. Dicey. In 1885 Dicey published a comprehensive analysis of the British constitution entitled *Introduction to the Study of the Law of the Constitution*. The book has had an enormous impact on the thinking of British and Canadian lawyers and judges. Dicey declared that legislative supremacy was "the dominant characteristic of [British] political institutions."

Dicey wrote during the time of the ascendancy of notions of British political and cultural superiority, and a major purpose of his analysis seems to have been to prove the excellence of British constitutional principles compared to those of other world powers, such as France, Germany and the United States. Dicey praised legislative supremacy for its promotion of popular sovereignty — the legislative branch, controlled by the (property-owning) people, is supreme — for enabling governments to react quickly to crises, and for facilitating flexible constitutional adaptation to changing circumstances. Contrasting the virtues of legislative supremacy with some of the problems that he identified with the U.S. constitution, he pointed out that the U.S. constitution was so difficult to amend that it could be considered practically unamendable. (Amendments require the assent of three-quarters of the state legislatures, all except one of which are bicameral, and two-thirds of each House of Congress.) Thus, instead of having popular sovereignty in any real sense, Americans lived under a regime of constitutional supremacy. Because judges decide the meaning of the constitution, constitutional supremacy really meant judicial supremacy. Dicey also claimed that the U.S. constitution limits the ability of governments to respond to crises and prevents adaptation to changing times.

The process judges follow when they compare lower-status laws with higher-status laws (such as a constitution), with a view to striking down lower-status laws that are incompatible with the higher laws, is known as "judicial review." Dicey considered that judicial review of legislative enactments cannot coexist with legislative supremacy. He thought that one of the legal implications of legislative supremacy — that a legislature must be considered free to change previous legislation — should be broadened to become a *political* principle of the constitution — that a legislature cannot set limits on itself, even limits it can amend. This Diceyan thinking had a predominant impact on the way in which Canadian courts approached the Canadian Bill of Rights. But even before the Bill of Rights, Canadian judges were often reluctant to tamper with government decisions affecting human rights.

Civil Liberties Cases Prior to the Canadian Bill of Rights

The record of the courts in protecting civil liberties during the first nine decades after Confederation is mixed. As a rule, judges felt that, because of legislative supremacy, they had no power to stop violations of human rights unless the law that caused the violation offended the federal division of powers. In 1899 the Judicial Committee of the Privy Council in London (which served as Canada's highest appeal court until 1949) struck down a British Columbia law that prohibited anyone of Chinese origin from working in mines [131]. The committee found that this provincial law interfered with federal jurisdiction over "naturalization and aliens." In 1902, however, the Judicial Committee upheld British Columbia legislation that denied the vote to Canadians of Asiatic origin as being within the proper bounds of provincial jurisdiction [30]. This legislation remained in effect until after the Second World War. The Judicial Committee commented, in accord with the principle of legislative supremacy, that the judges could not consider "the policy or impolicy of such enactment."

Some judges were of the opinion that the liberal ideal of equality applied to all private facilities that had a government licence. As an illustration, in 1899 a black man successfully sued a Montreal theatre in the Quebec Superior Court for refusing to allow him and his female companion to occupy the better seats in the house [43]. This approach did not win many fans among the judges, however. In 1921 the Quebec Court of Appeal found that racial segregation in theatres was acceptable as an exercise of the private rights of theatre owners [49]. The Supreme Court of Ontario in 1924 dismissed a suit by a black man against a restaurant owner who would not serve blacks [38]. Similarly, in 1939 the Supreme Court of Canada dismissed a suit by a black man who was refused service in the tavern at the Montreal Forum. The majority on the Court stated that "[a]ny merchant is free to deal as he may choose with any individual member of the public," unless a specific law creates restrictions [25].

In 1914 the Supreme Court upheld Saskatchewan legislation that forbade those of Chinese origin to employ white women. The chief justice actually applauded the legislation for protecting the "bodily health" and "morals" of white women [67]. During this era, federal immigration laws made it almost impossible for Chinese women to enter Canada; these laws remained in place until the 1950s.

It was not until 1930 that women were recognized as legal "persons." In 1928 the Supreme Court was asked whether the word "persons" in section 24 of the BNA Act — the section that defined eligibility for Senate appointments — included women. The Supreme Court gave the standard legal answer up to that time: no. The appeal to the Judicial Committee produced a different result [35]. The Judicial Committee likened the Canadian constitution, the BNA Act, to a "living tree" that should be interpreted in the light of changing social circumstances. The committee noted that attitudes towards the position of women had changed, and that the constitution should take this into account. It declared that women should now be included in the term "persons" in section 24.

Beginning in the 1930s, some judges attempted to establish a new route to protect civil liberties claims, over and above the established rules of common law. This approach was rooted in the preamble to the BNA Act. The preamble to the 1867 constitution states that the provinces forming the new country "[d]esire to be federally united ... with a Constitution similar in Principle to that of the United Kingdom." These words imply that the civil liberties principles that had developed in the United Kingdom before 1867 (being part of that country's unwritten constitution) became an essential feature of our constitution. The question arises, however, whether legislative enactments that violate the U.K.'s human rights principles are subject to judicial review in this country.

The Supreme Court of Canada was faced with this question in 1938. The previous year, the Social Credit legislature in Alberta enacted a package of legislation that was intended to put Social Credit theory into effect, and thus to bring the province out of the Depression. The federal government referred the legislation to the Supreme Court of Canada. (The Supreme Court Act permits the federal government to send "references," which are often questions about the constitutionality of legislation, directly to the Supreme Court.)

The package of legislation referred to the Court included the Accurate News and Information Act, better known as the "Alberta Press Bill." This legislation gave a government agency, the Social Credit Board, the power to prohibit the publication of a newspaper, force a newspaper to print corrections of articles that the board considered inaccurate, and prohibit newspapers from publishing articles written by certain blacklisted persons. The reason that the bill was included with the Social Credit legislation was that the government thought that the monetary reforms would only work if the people *believed* in them. Leading Alberta newspapers had ridiculed Social Credit theory, thus diminishing the theory's credibility.

The Court unanimously found the Alberta Press Bill *ultra vires* (beyond the powers of the legislature) [76]. It viewed the bills as closely connected to the other Social Credit bills that it had declared *ultra vires* because they invaded the central government's jurisdiction over banking, interest and legal tender. However, three judges, led by Chief Justice Lyman Duff, saw the Alberta Press Bill as so contrary to the constitutional principle of freedom of the press that they felt compelled to give additional reasons.

Duff based his civil liberties argument on two points. First, as noted earlier, the preamble to the BNA Act has the effect of implanting in Canada the civil liberties principles of the U.K., which included freedom of the press and freedom of speech. Second, because the BNA Act stipulates that the House of Commons must be elected and that its members must represent the provinces proportionately according to their populations, then the House is a "representative" body. Both of these features mean that the constitution "contemplates a parliament working under the influence of public opinion and public discussion . . . . [I]t is axiomatic that the practice of this right of free public discussion of public affairs, notwithstanding its incidental mischiefs, is the breath of life for parliamentary institutions." In other words, freedom of the press is essential to democracy. (The almost universal adult franchise achieved by 1937 gave somewhat more weight to Duff's argument than it would have had in 1867.)

This reasoning became known as the "Duff Doctrine." Had it ever been adopted by the majority of the Supreme Court, it is possible that there might have been less public demand for a charter of rights and freedoms because the Duff Doctrine would have been there to protect rights. Duff's approach raised issues the Court was never able to resolve, and thus a majority never endorsed it until the Charter era. The most important of these issues is the question of whether Duff's approach can be squared with legislative supremacy.

If Canada did have a legally enforceable implied bill of rights, then what had been constitutional principle in the U.K., as enforced through the political process, would become part of a rigid constitution in Canada, as enforced by judges. This judicial enforcement of civil liberties could limit the powers of legislatures and thus would call legislative supremacy into question. Moreover, because the implied bill of rights would consist of abstract principles and judicial decisions about these abstractions, it would be even less clear than a written bill of rights. As a result, legislative powers would not only be limited, but limited in a very imprecise fashion. Judges understandably were reluctant to impose such a major change on the Canadian political system.

Neither the implied bill of rights nor any of the other procedures the courts had developed to protect civil liberties were of much use to Japanese Canadians during and immediately after the Second World War. In one case, a 1945 deportation order issued against British subjects of Japanese origin was upheld by the Judicial Committee [28]. (In the United States, the judiciary allowed the detention of Japanese Americans in spite of the Bill of Rights.) The total suspension of human rights for Canadians of Japanese origin, the confiscation of their property, and their forced internment during the war marked one of the low points for civil liberties in Canada. Although Prime Minister Mackenzie King had personal doubts about the necessity for this treatment of Canada's Japanese citizens, he realized that the majority of Canadians were suspicious and distrustful of the Japanese Canadians and wanted "tough" action. The measures taken may have been carried out more to boost the morale of the average Canadian for the war effort than for security reasons.

Another major civil liberties issue prominent around the same time concerned the Gouzenko affair. Igor Gouzenko, a Soviet cipher clerk who defected, provided Canadian authorities with a list of Soviet "spies" in Canada. As a result, twenty-six persons were arrested and held incommunicado. The usual procedural rights were suspended under the authority of the War Measures Act, and secret trials were held in 1945. Detainees and many witnesses were not allowed to consult counsel and were not informed that their testimony might be used as evidence against them. When these abuses became public knowledge in 1946, many concluded that the government had unnecessarily restricted basic legal rights. According to Cynthia Williams, the civil liberties section of the Canadian Bar Association viewed such measures as "totally unacceptable in peacetime and a threat to Canadian democracy and the rule of law."

The Supreme Court did succeed to some extent in protecting civil liberties in Quebec during the infamous Duplessis era. During the 1950s, the Court was challenged by seven cases in which individuals claimed that their civil rights had been unfairly restricted. In all of these cases, the Supreme Court decided in favour of the civil liberties claim and against the submissions of the Quebec government.

Three cases are particularly interesting. The *Saumur* case involved a Jehovah's Witness who had been distributing literature on the streets of Quebec City [123]. Both provincial and municipal authorities had been active in restricting the activities of the Jehovah's Witnesses, whose doctrine was highly insulting to the Roman Catholic Church. The Quebec City Council had enacted a by-law, ostensibly to keep the streets free of litter, which prohibited the distribution of literature on sidewalks without a permit from the chief of police. The chief, of course, would give permits to anyone except Jehovah's Witnesses. Saumur appealed his conviction under the by-law all the way to the Supreme Court. He claimed that his freedom of religion and of speech, as protected by Canada's implied bill of rights pursuant to the Duff Doctrine, had been violated. The Supreme Court struck down the Quebec City by-law in a 5-4 decision, but the majority could not agree on their reasons. Two judges cited the Duff Doctrine, interpreting it to include freedom of religion as well as freedom of speech and the press, while two others claimed that only the federal Parliament could restrict freedom of religion under its criminal-law power. A fifth judge found that the by-law conflicted with a provincial statute that protected freedom of worship.

In 1937 the Quebec legislature enacted a law, commonly known as the "padlock law," which allowed the police to lock up any premises that were used to distribute information on communism. A tenant named John Switzman had been distributing Communist litera-ture from his apartment in 1949, and he was duly locked out of his home as a result. His landlady, Freda Elbling, sued for cancellation of the lease. Switzman claimed that the padlock law was *ultra vires*, both because of the Duff Doctrine and because it trenched on the federal criminal power. Eight years after Switzman was locked out of his home, the Supreme Court struck down the padlock law on the grounds that it violated the federal Parliament's criminal jurisdiction. Five of the eight judges in the majority relied on the criminal power argument. Only three judges invoked the Duff Doctrine in their reasoning [128].

Because of the many instances of harassment of Jehovah's Wit-nesses by Quebec authorities in the 1950s, the Witnesses were fre-quently in court and often had to post bail to stay out of jail until their trials. A wealthy Montreal restaurateur by the name of Frank Ron-carelli would often post bail for the Witnesses, much to the annoyance of the authorities. Premier Duplessis tried to bring Roncarelli to heel by ordering the cancellation of his liquor licence. Frank Scott, the well-known civil liberties lawyer and professor, represented Ron-carelli in his suit to regain the licence. Scott argued that Duplessis had violated the rule of law in that the premier had no statutory authority to order the cancellation of Roncarelli's licence. Moreover, by singling out Roncarelli, the premier had acted in an arbitrary fashion, thus violating the principle of the equal application of the law. The Supreme Court agreed, and Roncarelli regained his licence [119].

The Duplessis era, along with the early Social Credit period in Alberta, the early civil liberties abuses in B.C. and Saskatchewan, legalized discrimination against blacks, and the treatment of Japanese Canadians during the Second World War, had taught important lessons about civil liberties. Legislatures, cabinets and the majority of voters, it was clear, could not always be trusted to enforce human rights. As well, the mechanisms developed by the common-law courts to protect civil liberties, while spectacularly effective in a case like *Roncarelli*, were not as effective as might have been hoped. Finally, the Duff Doctrine of an implied bill of rights seemed incapable of winning the support of the majority of the Supreme Court.

The Canadian Bill of Rights Era

John Diefenbaker was a Prairie populist who was concerned about the potential that the rapidly expanding federal and provincial bureaucracies had for limiting individual freedoms and procedural safeguards. That concern, coupled with an abhorrence of racial discrimination, convinced him that Canada needed a bill of rights. He also realized the potential that a Canadian bill of rights could have for promoting the concept of "one Canada." According to Diefenbaker, the bill could become a symbol that would transcend regional identities and apply to "all, including the poor, the dispossessed, the ignored and the shut-out."

Diefenbaker was familiar with the Saskatchewan Bill of Rights, which had been enacted by the provincial CCF (Co-operative Commonwealth Federation) government in 1947. The Saskatchewan bill was the first written bill of rights to be enacted in any Canadian jurisdiction. It applied only within the province, and it contained no enforcement mechanism. There was very little litigation concerning the Saskatchewan bill, in part because lawyers were not used to a bill of rights and were therefore uncomfortable with pursuing claims under its authority. However, the bill was popular with the voters, and it did have some educational value.

There is evidence from Diefenbaker's own writing that he preferred a Canadian bill of rights that would have a superior status over other laws. In other words, the bill would be entrenched into the constitution through an amendment to the BNA Act. The BNA Act, as a British imperial statute, took priority over the enactments of federal and provincial legislatures.

Diefenbaker was unable to obtain the broad consent of the provincial governments that was needed for such an amendment. He therefore settled for a bill of rights that was just an ordinary enactment of Parliament. As such, it lacked the constitutional authority of the BNA Act. Moreover, it could apply only to matters under the jurisdiction of the federal government. Nevertheless, as W.H. McConnell (2) has shown, Diefenbaker and his party thought they had created a bill of rights the courts could use to nullify federal legislation that conflicted with it.

The Bill of Rights is relatively simple in its format. Its central provisions cover only one and one-half pages. This compares with seven equivalent pages for the Canadian Charter of Rights and Freedoms.

Section 1 of the Bill declares that several rights and freedoms "have existed and shall continue to exist." They include the following: the right to "life, liberty, security of the person and enjoyment of property," unless deprived thereof "by due process of law"; the right to "equality before the law and the protection of the law"; and the freedoms of religion, speech, assembly, association and the press. These rights and freedoms are "to exist without discrimination by reason of race, national origin, colour, religion or sex."

Section 2 protects a number of rights that Canadians have when confronted with the legal-judicial system. These rights are based on the procedures developed by judges through the common law to protect civil liberties. They include the right not to be arbitrarily detained or imprisoned or to be subjected to "cruel and unusual treatment or punishment." Moreover, no one can be arrested or detained without knowing the reason, and detainees have a right to retain a lawyer "without delay." Section 2 affirms the *habeas corpus* remedy. Furthermore, it states that individuals cannot be forced to give evidence without their lawyer being present, or forced to give evidence that would incriminate them.

Section 2 also confirms the right to "a fair hearing in accordance with the principles of fundamental justice for the determination of ... rights and obligations, the right to be presumed innocent until proven guilty in a fair and public hearing by an independent and impartial tribunal, the right to reasonable bail and the right to an interpreter."

Section 2 of the Bill contains a controversial "notwithstanding" clause, which reads as follows: "Every law of Canada shall, unless it is expressly declared ... that it shall operate notwithstanding the Canadian Bill of Rights, be so construed and applied as not to abrogate . . . any of the rights or freedoms herein recognized." Some may wonder what use a bill of rights is if Parliament can override it through a notwithstanding clause. Yet, upon closer examination, the clause provides some benefits. For one thing, it clearly indicates that the Bill was intended to take priority over other ordinary statutes. If the Bill was not intended to be superior to other statutes that contradicted it, there would be no need for the notwithstanding clause. It must also be kept in mind that if Parliament utilizes the notwithstanding clause, it is not necessarily overriding a right in the abstract, but rather the Supreme Court's *interpretation* of a right. As the Court decisions discussed below will show, since judicial reasoning about rights can sometimes leave much to be desired, an "escape clause" for legislatures can be more than justified on this ground alone.

The major legal hurdle involving the new Bill of Rights was how, in a system with legislative supremacy, an ordinary statute like the Bill could take precedence over other ordinary statutes, particularly those enacted after it. According to legislative supremacy, a current legislature is always supreme and cannot be prevented from amending laws by the enactments of a previous legislature. Diefenbaker and his supporters were never clear on how this difficulty could be overcome. They seemed simply to have faith that judges would somehow find a solution.

Canadian judges did not find the solution to the apparent constraints of legislative supremacy. In a 1985 Charter case, Mr. Justice Gerald Le Dain commented on the reason the Supreme Court had failed to give the Bill of Rights the broad and liberal interpretation that the Court gave to the Charter [109]:

[A] court cannot, in my respectful opinion, avoid bearing in mind an evident fact of Canadian judicial history, which must be squarely and frankly faced: that on the whole, with some notable exceptions, the courts have felt some uncertainty or ambivalence in the application of the Canadian Bill of Rights because it did not reflect a clear constitutional mandate to make judicial decisions having the effect of limiting or qualifying the traditional sovereignty of Parliament.

The Supreme Court's first major decision on the Canadian Bill of Rights, *Robertson and Rosetanni v. The Queen* [117], was one of those decisions in which the Court demonstrated the "uncertainty or ambivalence" referred to by Le Dain. The issue was whether the federal Lord's Day Act violated the guarantee of freedom of religion in the Bill. Robertson and Rosetanni operated a bowling alley in Hamilton and kept it open on Sundays in violation of the Lord's Day Act. They argued that the guarantee of freedom of religion in the Bill of Rights should take priority over the Lord's Day Act. Their position was that the act violated freedom of religion because it forced them to comply with a religious practice — the observance of a religious holy day — against their will.

A panel of five judges heard the case, and Mr. Justice Roland Ritchie wrote the opinion for the majority of four. Ritchie contended that the Bill was not intended to protect rights and freedoms in the abstract, but rather rights and freedoms as they existed in 1960. He referred to section 1 of the Bill, which stated that the rights in the Bill "have existed and shall continue to exist." (This phrase had been inserted into the Bill to allay the perception that the Bill was giving Canadians *new* rights that had not previously existed in convention or the common law.) He argued that the Bill therefore referred to freedom of religion as it existed in Canada in 1960.

Ritchie concluded that freedom of religion in 1960 implied an "absence of disabilities." In other words, governments ought not to *prevent* people from participating in their preferred religious practices, but they are free to *promote* certain religious practices. The Lord's Day Act, he claimed, merely promoted the observance of the Christian holy day. It did not prevent members of other religions from practising their religions — it simply resulted in a minor inconvenience for them. According to Ritchie, "the practical result of this law on those whose religion requires them to observe a day of rest other than Sunday is a purely secular and financial one in that they are required to refrain from carrying on or conducting their business on Sunday as well as on their own day of rest."

Ritchie acknowledged that the Lord's Day Act had a clearly religious purpose. He claimed, however, that in determining an infringement of freedom of religion, it was the effect rather than the purpose of the legislation that counted. For Ritchie, the effect of the act was purely secular. It merely established a weekly holiday. (In a 1985 Charter case known as *Big M* [82], the Supreme Court rejected Ritchie's interpretation of freedom of religion. This case is reviewed in chapter 3.)

This narrow interpretation of the Bill of Rights allowed the Court's majority to avoid the appearance of interfering with legislative supremacy. Mr. Justice John Cartwright dissented, however, claiming that the Lord's Day Act plainly violated the Bill. He disagreed with Ritchie that the purpose of legislation is irrelevant in determining an infraction of freedom of religion. "[T]he purpose and the effect of the Lord's Day Act are to compel under the penal sanctions of the criminal law, the observance of Sunday as a religious holy day by all the inhabitants of Canada . . . . In my opinion a law which compels a course of conduct, whether positive or negative, for a purely religious purpose infringes the freedom of religion."

Cartwright was also of the opinion that the Bill of Rights authorized judges to strike down laws that violated rights. Some lower-court judges and academics had argued that the Bill should be treated as a mere aid to interpretation in order to protect legislative supremacy. If the Bill were treated as an aid to interpretation, or "rule of construction," it would mean that judges would apply the Bill only in cases where it was unclear whether Parliament had intended a particular law to violate a right. In cases where a law clearly violated a right, the Bill would be of no use. Cartwright disagreed with this rule-of-construction approach. He pointed to the notwithstanding clause in the Bill and contended that if Parliament had intended the Bill to be simply a rule of construction, the notwithstanding clause would have been unnecessary.

The only case prior to 1982 in which the Supreme Court applied the Bill in such a way that a discriminatory statute became inoperative — the most famous of the "notable exceptions" referred to by Le Dain above — was the *Drybones* decision [86]. During the seven years between *Robertson and Rossetani* and *Drybones*, the Supreme Court had been subjected to a great deal of criticism from civil libertarians, who saw the judges as slaves to the theory of legislative supremacy. Whether because of sensitivity to this criticism or for some other reason, the majority in the *Drybones* decision applied the Bill so as to render inoperative a section of the Indian Act. The section in question created a liquor offence that applied specifically to Indians and created harsher penalties than the equivalent offence for the general public.

Ritchie, who wrote the majority decision, found that the Indian Act resulted in racial discrimination, since it denied Drybones equality before the law as guaranteed by the Bill of Rights. In explaining why the Bill of Rights gave the Court the power to declare inoperative the discriminatory section of the Indian Act, he followed the same line of reasoning that Cartwright had used in *Robertson and Rosetanni* to hold that the Bill of Rights was more than a rule of construction.

Ritchie summarized his judgment with the following words: "[In] a situation in which, under the laws of Canada, it is made an offence punishable at law on account of race for a person to do something which all Canadians who are not members of that race may do with impunity," that person has been denied equality before the law. It is ironic that in the *Drybones* decision, Mr. Justice Cartwright dissented. He declared that his decision in *Robertson and Rosetanni* had been wrong. He had now concluded that it would be dangerous for the courts to usurp the legislature's role by striking down statutes that conflict with the Bill of Rights.

Within a few years, the majority on the Court came around to an approach approximating that of Cartwright's dissent in *Drybones*. In the *Lavell* and *Bédard* decisions of 1974, the Court again adopted the *Robertson and Rosetanni* style of interpreting the Bill so as to avoid declaring statutes inoperative [4]. The issue was whether section 12 of the Indian Act, which defines a status Indian and at that time treated Indian men more favourably than Indian women, violated the Bill. Section 12 declared that if an Indian woman married a non-Indian, she automatically forfeited her Indian status. However, if an Indian man married a non-Indian, he not only retained his Indian status, but his wife gained Indian status as well.

The cases were brought forward by two Indian women who had married non-Indians, thereby losing their Indian status. They claimed that section 12 discriminated against them on the basis of sex and that therefore they had been denied equality before the law.

This time the judges were split 5-4, with the majority finding no violation of sexual equality. Once again, Mr. Justice Ritchie wrote the opinion for the majority. Ritchie identified the central issue in the case as the meaning of the phrase "equality before the law" in the Bill of Rights. The influence of Dicey in deciding this issue is evident:

"[E]quality before the law" as recognized by Dicey as a segment of the rule of law, carries the meaning of equal subjection of all classes to the ordinary law of the land . . . and in my opinion the phrase "equality before the law" as employed in section 1(b) of the Bill of Rights is to be treated as meaning equality in the administration or application of the law by the law enforcement authorities and the ordinary courts of the land . . . . The fundamental distinction between the present case and that of *Drybones*, however, appears to me to be that the impugned section in [*Drybones*] could not be enforced without denying equality of treatment in the administration and enforcement of the law before the ordinary courts of the land to a racial group, whereas no such inequality of treatment between Indian men and women flows as a necessary result of the application of s.12(1)(b) of the *Indian Act*.

Legal experts have been puzzling over this passage since it was written. Perhaps Ritchie was drawing attention to the fact that nothing *compels* Indian women to marry non-Indians, let alone to marry, so that discrimination based on sex is not a "necessary result" of section 12. However, the general consensus among legal commentators is that Ritchie did not convincingly distinguish between the discrimination in *Drybones* and that in *Lavell* and *Bédard*. Mr. Justice Bora Laskin, who had been appointed to the Supreme Court in 1971, wrote in his dissenting opinion that "unless we are to depart from what was said in *Drybones*," Lavell and Bédard were discriminated against contrary to the Bill. It seems likely that the Court had buckled under the strain of continued worry over the possible abandonment of legislative supremacy.

After *Lavell* and *Bédard*, the Supreme Court continued to find no inconsistency between the Bill of Rights and discriminatory provisions in federal legislation. A good example of this is the *Bliss* case, in which the Court considered whether the provisions of the Unemployment Insurance Act that related to pregnant women violated the Bill of Rights [19]. In the 1970s the Unemployment Insurance Act stipulated a longer qualifying period for unemployment insurance benefits for pregnant women than for others to ensure that no pregnant woman could claim unemployment insurance benefits unless she was already working when she became pregnant. The majority on the Supreme Court could find no discrimination based on sex in these provisions; rather, the discrimination was based on pregnancy (notwithstanding that, barring new developments in medical science, only women can be pregnant).

Other Civil Liberties Cases

Not only did the Supreme Court interpret the Canadian Bill of Rights narrowly during this period, it also tended to dismiss civil liberties claims that arose outside of the Bill. It should be remembered that the Bill applied only to federal laws and administrative activities. Therefore, civil liberties claims that did not challenge a federal law or administrative action tended to rely on the twin claims of the Duff Doctrine: that Canada inherited the conventional civil liberties of the

United Kingdom in a judicially enforceable form and that freedom of expression is the "life and breath" of a democracy.

One such case arose in British Columbia in the early 1960s. In 1960 the Social Credit government of Premier W.A.C. Bennett was seriously threatened by the New Democratic Party (NDP) in a provincial election. Alarmed at gains made by the social democratic party, the right-wing Socreds determined to weaken the position of the NDP. The government realized that the NDP received most of its financial support from contributions by unions and that most unions received their funds from compulsory deductions from workers' paychecks (known as the "union check-off"). In 1961 the Social Credit legislature enacted a law forbidding unions to donate money to any political party — federal or provincial — if that money had been collected through the union check-off procedure. However, no similar ban was placed on business donations to political parties. This move effectively cut off the NDP's funding, while the Social Credit party's funding was left intact.

The issue of the validity of the B.C. labour legislation came to the Supreme Court of Canada in 1963 in the *Oil, Chemical and Atomic Workers Union* case [59]. The unions argued that the legislation violated the Duff Doctrine, since it prevented freedom of expression. In other words, funds were needed to fight an election campaign, and unless unions could spend their funds in the same way that businesses could during an election, they would be effectively muzzled.

The majority on the Supreme Court panel, four of seven judges, not only upheld the B.C. legislation, but praised it for protecting the right of workers not to have to contribute indirectly to a political campaign. The three dissenting judges, however, applied the Duff Doctrine. One of these judges, Mr. Justice Cartwright, noted that since unions in B.C. received 99.8 per cent of their funds from the union check-off, the new labour legislation had the practical effect of preventing unions from participating in political campaigns. (The issue of whether unions may contribute funds to political parties has led to several Charter cases. Most notable is the *Lavigne* case, in which Merv Lavigne, a college teacher, sought a declaration that union political contributions financed through the check-off violate "freedom of association" as protected by the Charter [72]. Lavigne lost in the Ontario Court of Appeal but has appealed to the Supreme Court of Canada.)

Another civil liberties case involved the Hutterites. During the Second World War, there was a great deal of resentment against the communities of Hutterites in Alberta. The Hutterites (a Christian sect formed during the Reformation), being pacifist, refused to join the Canadian armed forces. They believe in communal living and operate a number of communal farms in Alberta. In response to public pressure, Alberta's Social Credit legislature enacted the Communal Property Act, which restricted the growth of the Hutterite communities. This discriminatory legislation was upheld by the Supreme Court in 1969 as a valid exercise of provincial jurisdiction over property [134]. The legislation was eventually repealed by the Conservative legislature in 1972 because it violated the spirit of the Alberta Bill of Rights, enacted in 1971.

Then there was the case of the journalist who in the 1970s challenged the constitutional validity of Nova Scotia's film censorship law [58]. The provincial censorship board had banned *Last Tango in Paris*, which the journalist wanted to see. When the case reached the Supreme Court of Canada in 1978, the Court's majority upheld the censorship laws as coming within provincial jurisdiction over "matters of a merely local or private nature" (section 92[16] of the Constitution Act, 1867). (Under the Charter, provincial film censorship laws will survive a court challenge only if the government can demonstrate that they are "reasonable limits" to freedom of expression.)

The last major case in which the Supreme Court considered the Duff Doctrine before the Charter era was a case involving the right to hold a demonstration. In November 1969 the Montreal City Council passed a by-law permitting the Executive Committee of the city to ban all public demonstrations for thirty-day periods. Shortly after the by-law was passed, the Executive Committee issued an ordinance prohibiting demonstrations for a month. This was a time of frequent demonstrations in Montreal — by students for changes in the universities, by supporters of Quebec independence and by those against the war in Vietnam. There had been about one hundred demonstrations in the first nine months of the year. The police were seriously concerned about terrorists taking advantage of the police preoccupation with demonstrations. With the police busy watching the crowds, it would be easier for a terrorist to slip a bomb into a mailbox or a public building.

The validity of the by-law was challenged in court by Claire Dupond, and the case eventually made its way to the Supreme Court of Canada in 1978 [1]. Dupond argued that the by-law offended the Duff Doctrine because it restricted freedom of speech. Demonstrations were considered to be "speech in action." Civil rights promoters throughout the Western world had learned that in order to increase public awareness of human rights, it is important to get media attention, and demonstrations are a very effective way of doing this. Demonstrations can also provide a rough indication of the level of public support for the ideas of the demonstrators.

Mr. Justice Jean Beetz wrote the opinion for the majority. He not only rejected all of Dupond's arguments but dismissed the claim based on the Duff Doctrine with a vigour that disturbed many civil liberties advocates in Canada. He wrote that "none of the freedoms referred to is so enshrined in the constitution as to be above the reach of competent legislation." As Peter Russell (7) has commented, this decision appeared "to be virtually the final nail in the coffin of [the Duff Doctrine's contention that there are] constitutional limits on provincial laws affecting fundamental rights and freedoms."

Furthermore, Beetz scoffed at the idea that demonstrations could be considered "speech in action":

Freedoms of speech, of assembly and association, of the press and of religion are distinct and independent of the faculty of holding assemblies, parades, gatherings, demonstrations or processions on the public domain of a city . . . . Demonstrations are not a form of speech but of collective action.

Mr. Justice Laskin wrote a strongly worded dissent, which was concurred in by Justices Spence and Dickson:

Here [in the Montreal by-law], persons who might seek to associate or gather for innocent purposes are to be barred . . . because of a desire to forestall the violent or the likely violent. This is the invocation of a doctrine which should alarm free citizens even if it were invoked and applied under the authority of the Parliament of Canada.

Surprisingly, the reasonable presumption that the Duff Doctrine died in the *Dupond* decision has turned out to be highly exaggerated. In the case of *OPSEU v. A.-G. for Ontario* [62] (a 1987 case discussed in chapter 4), the Duff Doctrine was resurrected — by Mr. Justice Beetz. But in 1978 few would have predicted such an event.

Judicial Protection of Civil Liberties to 1982

It is clear that by the late 1970s the Supreme Court had adopted the view that if a particular law violated a human right, it was the responsibility of the appropriate legislature, not the courts, to amend the law. Most of the judges of our highest court did not wish to become involved in the determination of difficult civil liberties issues — issues they considered as more fittingly resolved by legislatures. As a result, the judges were reluctant to take steps that might weaken the political principle of legislative supremacy. As well as these practical considerations, the judges may also have considered that legislative supremacy was such a basic principle of our constitution that it ought not to be tampered with except through a constitutional amendment.

So faithful was the Supreme Court to the Diceyan view of legislative supremacy that a widely accepted alternative to Dicey's view was never mentioned by the judges. This is the "manner and form" approach to the interpretation of bills of rights. According to proponents of this view such as Ivor Jennings, Geoffrey Marshall and Peter Hogg (1), a bill of rights represents a change in the procedure legislatures follow in creating laws. Such procedures are known as "manner and form" requirements — for example, subjecting proposed legislation to three votes, or "readings," in the legislature. Considered as a change to manner and form requirements, a bill of rights indicates that in addition to voting on a proposal three times, legislators will have to decide whether each statute they enact should be subjected to judicial review under the bill of rights. If they decide that the bill of rights *should* apply to a particular piece of legislation, then they merely enact the legislation. If they decide that the bill of rights *should not* apply, then they indicate this decision by declaring that the new legislation will operate notwithstanding the bill of rights.

If the Court had adopted the manner and form approach, it could have given effect to the Bill without abandoning allegiance to legislative supremacy. And the long-term consequences may well have been significant. A major impetus for a constitutional charter of rights came from those who were disappointed with how the Supreme Court had interpreted the Bill of Rights. For them, the only solution was the replacement of the legislative supremacy of the era of the Bill of Rights with a constitutional supremacy approach under an entrenched charter of rights. Had the Supreme Court given effect to the Bill, the pressure for a constitutional charter of rights would have been considerably less and the 1982 constitutional reforms might have taken on a different form.

In spite of the approaches the judges were taking to the Canadian Bill of Rights, statutory human rights legislation proliferated. This is because bills of rights tend to be popular with the voters, most of whom have little idea of how the bills are interpreted by the courts. In 1971 Peter Lougheed, then leader of the opposition in Alberta, promised voters during the provincial election campaign that if he became premier, the first task of the new Alberta legislature would be the enactment of an Alberta bill of rights. Lougheed won an upset victory, and the Alberta Bill of Rights became law in 1972.

In the early 1970s the image of the government of Quebec Premier Robert Bourassa was tarnished by the human rights violations that occurred during the October Crisis. To counter this image, the government introduced the Quebec Charter of Human Rights and Freedoms into the legislature. The Charter was enacted in 1975. But the strategy of appealing to the electorate with human rights legislation did not succeed for Bourassa, whose government was defeated by the Parti Québécois (PQ) in 1976.

Thus, by 1975, there were four statutory bills of rights in Canada — three provincial bills (in Saskatchewan, Alberta and Quebec) and the Canadian Bill of Rights. However, these bills were generally not taken very seriously by the legal community, and thus little litigation arose from them.

The four bills of rights applied to relations between governments and citizens. What they were intended to do was to protect private citizens from potential human rights violations by a government. They had no effect on human rights abuses in the private sector — for example, discrimination in employment, housing or restaurants. In order to combat such private discrimination, the Ontario legislature had enacted a Human Rights Code in 1962. Unlike the four bills of rights discussed above, the Ontario Human Rights Code was administered by a Human Rights Commission. The commission would investigate complaints of discrimination, and where complaints were well-founded, it would attempt to negotiate a settlement. Because the commission would take a violation of the Human Rights Code to court only as a last resort, very little reliance was placed on the judiciary for enforcement of the code.

All of the other provinces eventually followed Ontario's example, and in 1977 the federal Parliament enacted the Canadian Human Rights Code to control private discrimination within federally regulated workplaces. The human rights commissions have successfully dealt with numerous examples of unjust discrimination, and from this perspective, they have been successful. On the other hand, they can act only if they receive complaints, and consequently a great many cases of private discrimination are left unresolved.

The creation of the Canadian Charter of Rights and Freedoms has not diminished the importance of the human rights codes in combatting private discrimination, because like the four statutory bills of rights, the Charter applies only to violations of civil liberties by governments. The Charter duplicates most of the provisions of the statutory bills of rights. Those parts of the statutory bills that have not been duplicated by the Charter, however, are still in effect. There are two sections in the Canadian Bill of Rights not duplicated by the Charter: the right to the enjoyment of property (section 1[a]) and the right to a fair hearing in accordance with the principles of fundamental justice for the determination of rights and obligations (section 2[e]).

It is ironic that since 1982 the Supreme Court seems to have overcome its reluctance to enforce the statutory bills of rights. In fact, the statutory bills of rights, and also the human rights codes, have been labelled as "quasi-constitutional" by the Supreme Court. In conjunction with the Charter, they have become important mechanisms for promoting human rights in Canada.

Overview

Human rights are about interpersonal respect. How a political system can best protect human rights depends on variables specific to the time and the culture. The liberal democracies have attempted to promote rights through emphasizing individual liberty, procedural safeguards and equality of treatment. Canada's particular approach has been moulded by a somewhat greater stress on the "responsibility" aspect of rights than is the case in countries that put a higher value on the individualistic aspect of rights, and by the heritage of political compromises that created language rights and minority language education rights.

Canada's record of promoting human rights has been mixed. The history of human rights in Canada can be divided into three periods, each reflecting the different sets of mechanisms used to protect rights. During the first period, from Confederation to 1960, legislatures had primary responsibility for safeguarding the human rights principles inherited from the United Kingdom. The judiciary also played a role through its responsibility for upholding the common-law principles that had developed to protect rights. Neither the judiciary nor the legislatures had an unblemished record during this time, but neither did they have an exceptionally bad record compared with other liberal democracies. The second period began with the advent of the Canadian Bill of Rights. Courts were invited by legislatures to take on more responsibility for settling controversial human rights issues, but the invitation was rejected. The third period began in 1982 with the Charter of Rights and Freedoms, the topic of the next chapter.

2

The Charter

The circumstances that led to the adoption of the Charter of Rights and Freedoms help to explain the form the document finally took. These events have also provided the setting for some of the current controversies about the Charter, such as whether the provision allowing legislatures to override parts of the Charter should be removed or whether the Meech Lake Accord weakens women's equality rights.

A visitor to our country who knew little of Canada's most pressing political issues might assume that the Charter came about as a response to human rights abuses or to stave off the threat of such abuses. Although the Supreme Court's narrow interpretation of the Bill of Rights encouraged some pro-civil liberties activists to campaign for an entrenched charter of rights, human rights violations, or the fear of them, did not constitute a major issue in Canada during the ten or fifteen years before 1982. A possible exception was the October Crisis of 1970, when the arbitrary powers provided by the War Measures Act were not always used wisely. Most Canadians, however, supported the government's tough stance against terrorists. Moreover, the man who decided to invoke the War Measures Act, Pierre Trudeau, was the same person who championed the cause of a charter. Public pressure to protect civil liberties can therefore explain only a part of the drive for an entrenched bill of rights.

In fact, Rainer Knopff and F.L. Morton have shown that the goal of entrenching a charter of rights was a key ingredient in the federal government's nation-building strategy from 1967 to 1982. That strategy evolved to contain three elements:

- to create the conditions that would encourage a stronger national identity to counteract the forces of provincialism;
- to patriate the constitution (end the role of the U.K. Parliament in the constitutional amendment process, and provide for an entirely Canadian amending procedure); and
- to extend language rights and to create new "mobility rights" so that Canadians would feel at home in any province and would not be deterred from moving within the country.

It was hoped that the proposed charter would become an instrument of national unity. An entrenched bill of rights that applied across the country would lead, it was expected, to a national discourse about human rights. New national coalitions and identities would be created that would transcend and weaken the forces of regionalism and provincialism.

One problem faced by the government was that Canadians were not very concerned about the patriation issue. As well, the subject of language rights was divisive. Neither the patriation nor the language rights goals were likely to succeed if they were promoted on their own. The federal strategy was to join the proposed charter and patriation in an inseparable package and to include language rights in the broader list of rights and freedoms.

The Road to the Charter

This strategy, however ingenious, could not have worked without the perseverance of someone as determined as Pierre Trudeau. In addition to realizing the strategic value of the proposed charter, Trudeau believed in it for its own sake. This may be because he had first-hand experience with the civil liberties abuses of the Duplessis regime. He had been a vocal critic of the Union Nationale government, and as a result, the government had pressured the universities not to hire him as a law professor. Trudeau became convinced that a constitutional bill of rights would be a more effective means of protecting human rights than the political process and the common law.

As the federal minister of justice, Trudeau had promoted a constitutional charter of rights in a 1968 policy paper, "A Canadian Charter of Human Rights." In the same year, Prime Minister Pearson called the first of what became a series of federal-provincial conferences to consider a constitutional bill of rights and a method of patriating the constitution. The 1968 conference failed to produce an agreement, and in 1970 the federal government established a special committee of Parliament (the "Molgat-MacGuigan Committee") to consider constitutional reform. The committee received 1,700 briefs or representations, many of them recommending that the proposed charter of rights should include protection for groups with special needs, such as the handicapped, women, seniors and the poor. This marked the beginning of a new trend in thinking about human rights in Canada, according to Cynthia Williams. Once the public became formally involved in the charter project, many claims previously thought of as political demands — such as the abolition of compulsory retirement, adequate welfare payments, access to public buildings for the handicapped, and affirmative action programs for women — were presented as human rights. The committee rejected most of the demands of the special needs groups, but the hearings gave these groups experience in using the political process that would prove valuable a decade later.

In 1971 the first ministers reached an agreement, known as the "Victoria Charter," to patriate the constitution and at the same time entrench a charter of rights. The agreement failed to take effect, however, because of objections from Quebec and Alberta. The Quebec cabinet would not endorse the agreement without additional guarantees of cultural sovereignty. In Alberta a provincial election produced a change in government. The new premier, Peter Lougheed, was opposed to the proposed constitutional amending formula in the Victoria Charter because by giving a veto power only to Ontario, Quebec and British Columbia, it made Alberta and the other six provinces "second class."

After this setback, the momentum for constitutional change slowed down considerably. The success of the Parti Québécois in the Quebec election of 1976 became a further obstacle to constitutional reform. Although there were several constitutional reform initiatives during the next few years, it was not until the defeat of the sovereignty-association concept in the 1980 Quebec referendum that there was again a serious opportunity for constitutional reform. In the meantime, Canada's accession to the International Covenant on Civil and Political Rights in 1976 helped supporters of a constitutional bill of rights keep the idea alive.

During the Quebec referendum campaign, Trudeau promised Quebeckers that if they voted "no" to sovereignty-association, they could look forward to a "renewed federalism." After the 60 to 40 per cent victory of the "non" side, he set out to fulfil this promise by reviving his government's nation-building strategy: the patriation of the constitution and the creation of a constitutional charter of rights and freedoms.

A First Ministers' Conference was called for September 1980. The constitutional conference ended with no agreement, and the federal government announced a plan for "unilateral patriation" of the constitution. The plan was that the Canadian Parliament would request the U.K. Parliament to place an amending formula in the constitution (the 1971 Victoria Charter formula would be used), as well as the Charter of Rights, and then abdicate all future responsibilities for changing the Canadian constitution. The federal government claimed that it could accomplish this feat without provincial support because of the conventions that had developed governing the amendment of the constitution. The federal argument was that when a constitutional change had been required in the past, the federal Parliament alone would request the amendment, and the amendment would automatically be enacted by the London Parliament. The BNA Act had been amended twenty-two times since 1867, and no provincial legislature had ever officially participated in the process.

This claim was only part of the truth. Of the twenty-two amendments, only five had affected provincial powers. In each one of these five cases, all the relevant provincial authorities had approved the constitutional amendments. Thus, there was a well-founded claim that a convention of provincial consent existed regarding constitutional amendments that affected the provinces.

Trudeau denied that provincial consent was a convention and determined to push on with unilateral patriation. The patriation resolution, including the proposed charter, was sent to a special committee of Parliament for consideration. The committee held televised public hearings and received almost 1,000 submissions. The hearings, as expected, demonstrated widespread public support for the proposed charter. Prominent among the witnesses before the committee were representatives of many of the special needs groups whose representations had failed to produce the desired results during the Molgat-MacGuigan hearings in 1971. But this time, circumstances favoured the special needs groups.

The government needed all the support it could muster to counteract the eight premiers who opposed unilateral patriation. Early in 1981 the government accepted a series of proposals to expand the provisions of the Charter. The equality rights section (section 15) was broadened according to the recommendations of feminist groups, and a special guarantee of sexual equality (section 28) was added. The equality rights section was also expanded to prohibit discrimination based on mental or physical disability. And two sections were added, one inside the Charter (section 25) and one outside (a provision affirming existing aboriginal rights), to protect native rights. Public response to these proposals was very positive, thus strengthening the government's drive for unilateral patriation.

Meanwhile, the eight provincial governments opposed to unilateral patriation and the Charter — all but Ontario and New Brunswick — launched a counter-offensive. These governments had a variety of reasons for opposing the package, including reservations about the Victoria Charter amending formula, and doubts about the proposed charter of rights. In April 1981 the eight premiers, including René Lévesque, agreed to support an amending formula that was an alternative to the Victoria Charter formula. This so-called Vancouver Consensus formula would require for most future constitutional changes the agreement of Parliament and seven out of ten provincial legislatures representing 50 per cent of the population of the provinces. The premiers also feared that an entrenched charter would not have the positive impact its supporters cheerfully assumed. For example, Saskatchewan's NDP premier, Allan Blakeney, feared that wealthy corporations would pursue litigation under an entrenched charter to limit government social programs and the powers of labour unions. Because judges tend to come from backgrounds sympathetic to business interests, he predicted that such litigation would have a reasonable chance of succeeding.

Three of the eight provinces opposed to the unilateral patriation, Newfoundland, Quebec and Manitoba, launched legal challenges by sending reference questions to their provincial courts of appeal. The courts were asked whether a convention of provincial consent existed and whether such a convention could operate to prevent the Canadian Parliament from proceeding.

The results of the constitutional reference in the three provincial courts of appeal were inconclusive. The courts in Manitoba and Quebec held that provincial consent was not a legal requirement, but the Newfoundland court held that it was. These decisions were appealed to the Supreme Court of Canada, which announced its decision in late September 1981. The decision was so important that, for the first time in Canadian history, television cameras were allowed in the courtroom to record the historic verdict. Unfortunately, one of the judges tripped over a cable and disconnected the main microphone, so that the chief justice's announcement was barely audible. Hearing the announcement, however, would probably not have improved the understanding of the decision for a great many people. The court decided that a convention of "substantial provincial consent" did exist, but that as a convention, it could not be enforced in law. In other words, while no legal rules could stop Parliament from proceeding with the unilateral patriation project, this action would nevertheless break a constitutional convention [5]. Conventions are normally enforced through the political process, not by the courts.

The Supreme Court's decision, which produced no clear winners in the dispute between eight provinces and the federal government, forced the two sides back to the bargaining table. The first ministers met again on November 2, 1981. On the morning of November 4 an agreement was announced to patriate the constitution with the Vancouver Consensus amending formula and with a constitutional charter of rights. All of the first ministers agreed to the package except for René Lévesque. Politically, it would probably have been impossible for a separatist premier to agree to such a renewal of the Canadian constitution. Technically, however, the agreement was close to what Lévesque had already endorsed when he was convinced that Trudeau would never accept the position of the eight provinces that supported the Vancouver Consensus amending formula.

The agreement of November 4 included compromises on both sides. Although Trudeau preferred the Victoria Charter amending formula, he agreed to a modified version of the Vancouver Consensus formula. In return, the eight provinces agreed to a constitutional charter of rights, but only if the Charter contained a clause permitting federal and provincial legislatures to enact specific statutes that would override the Charter. (It was thought that this override procedure would provide a counterbalance to unacceptable or unworkable judicial interpretations about the meaning of the Charter.) Trudeau agreed to the override clause on the condition that every specific use of it would expire automatically after five years and that the clause would not apply to the democratic rights, mobility rights, language rights and minority language education rights. This solution, which enabled legislatures temporarily to exclude judicial review based on sections 2 and 7-15 of the Charter, became section 33 of the Charter.

As noted above, the federal-provincial compromise of November 4 appeared to satisfy most of the points in Lévesque's bargaining position. One of Quebec's demands not met, however, concerned the section of the Charter dealing with minority language education rights (section 23). One of the effects of this provision was that anglophones who had been educated in English anywhere in Canada would have the right to have their children educated in English in Quebec (this was known as the "Canada clause"). Lévesque had wanted the right of an English education in Quebec restricted to children of parents who had been educated in English in Quebec. (This provision was already contained in Quebec's Charter of the French Language [Bill 101] and was known as the "Quebec clause.") Furthermore, the Charter would extend the right to English education in Quebec to children whose parents' mother tongue was English, even if they did not qualify under the Canada clause (this is known as the "mother tongue clause"). Lévesque was opposed to this provision as well. In order to try to weaken Quebec opposition to the patriation/Charter project, a provision was added so that the mother tongue clause would not apply to Quebec until approved by the Quebec National Assembly.

After the November 4 agreement, final preparations were made for the patriation of the Canadian constitution. With the consent of nine provinces, the federal Parliament passed a resolution that requested the U.K. Parliament to amend the Canadian constitution one last time. The Westminster Parliament's Canada Act, 1982, added the Constitution Act, 1982, to Canada's constitution and changed the name of the BNA Act (which remains an integral part of the constitution) to the Constitution Act, 1867. The Constitution Act, 1982, contains the Charter of Rights and Freedoms and the Vancouver Consensus amending formula. The Quebec government sent a reference question to its Court of Appeal asking whether the "substantial provincial consent" the Canadian Supreme Court had declared was part of the old amending convention made the consent of Quebec mandatory. Before the Quebec Court of Appeal could decide the case, the Westminster Parliament had enacted the Canada Act. On April 17, 1982, the Queen signed the Canada Act in a ceremony on Parliament Hill. The era of the Charter of Rights and Freedoms had begun.

Later, both the Quebec Court of Appeal and the Supreme Court of Canada ruled that "substantial provincial consent" did not make Quebec's consent mandatory. Although this interpretation of the convention is questionable, from a political perspective the courts probably had no choice. Legally, the U.K. Parliament had already changed Canada's constitution for the final time. Future changes would have to occur entirely in Canada [7]. Thus, the Charter and the new amending formula applied in law to Quebec, although many

Quebeckers felt that the new constitution lacked moral legitimacy because of Quebec's failure to ratify it.

The election of a federal Conservative government in 1984, and of a Liberal government in Quebec in 1985, opened the door to obtaining, belatedly, the consent of the Quebec legislature to the 1982 constitutional accord. The new prime minister, Brian Mulroney, was anxious to obtain Quebec's official endorsement of the 1982 constitutional changes. He recognized that no constitution, however legally binding it is, can keep a country together unless the people consider it to be legitimate. Premier Bourassa produced a list of five conditions that would have to be met before Quebec would agree to the constitutional accord: recognition of Quebec as a distinct society, more provincial power over immigration, constitutional recognition that three of the nine Supreme Court of Canada judges must be from Quebec, limits to the federal spending power in provincial jurisdiction, and a Quebec veto over future constitutional changes. All of these demands were accommodated in the Meech Lake Accord announced on April 30, 1987. Instead of providing Quebec with a veto over all constitutional changes, however, financial compensation would be provided to provinces that opted out of a constitutional amendment with regard to any matter.

The Substantive Provisions in the Charter

The substantive provisions in the Charter appear in seven parts, which are separated by headings in the text of the Charter: (1) fundamental freedoms, (2) democratic rights, (3) mobility rights, (4) legal rights, (5) equality rights, (6) language rights and (7) minority language educational rights.

Fundamental Freedoms (Section 2)

These are the familiar civil liberties that grew into constitutional conventions in the United Kingdom as a result of the adoption of the ideology of liberalism — the same ones that the Duff Doctrine sought to protect. They include freedom of conscience and religion; freedom of thought, belief, opinion and expression (including freedom of the communications media); freedom of peaceful assembly; and freedom of association. The fundamental freedoms in the Charter are also listed in the Bill of Rights, but the wording of most of them has been slightly changed with the hope of providing greater clarity and comprehensiveness.

Democratic Rights (Sections 3-5)

The Canadian Bill of Rights made no mention of democratic rights, and Trudeau's first proposal for an entrenched charter of rights in 1968 did not suggest entrenching the democratic rights — a shortcoming emphasized in Donald Smiley's 1969 commentary (2) on the Trudeau proposals. This kind of criticism had some effect, because in 1971 the bill of rights in the Victoria Charter included references to the right to vote, universal suffrage and free elections at least every five years. These principles now appear in the Charter.

Section 3 states that "every citizen" has the right to vote in federal and provincial elections, as well as the right to be qualified for membership in the House of Commons and provincial legislatures. Section 4(1) stipulates that no more than five years may elapse between general elections for the House of Commons or provincial legislatures. Section 5 declares that both Parliament and provincial legislatures must have a sitting at least once in every twelve-month period.

Section 4(2) provides that "in time of real or apprehended war, invasion or insurrection," a two-thirds vote in the House of Commons can continue the life of the House beyond five years. There is no limit on how long elections may be delayed; this is left to the development of future conventions. A similar provision is made for provincial legislatures to continue beyond five years in equivalent emergency circumstances.

The guarantee of the rights to vote and to be qualified for elected office in section 3 apply to all citizens. There are no restrictions listed pertaining to age, mental competence or imprisonment, for example. However, legislatures expect to be able to justify some of these restrictions as reasonable limits to the Charter pursuant to section 1, the limitations clause, which is discussed below.

Mobility Rights (Section 6)

One of the federal government's overall policy objectives during the Trudeau era was to promote national unity by making it easier for Canadians to move from province to province to find work. Provincial governments had created a number of restrictions to interprovincial mobility, such as residency requirements for certain provincial benefits and hiring practices favouring current residents of the province. Section 6 was an attempt to limit such restrictions. Section 6(2) declares that "every citizen" and "permanent resident has the right a) to move and take up residence in any province, and b) to pursue the gaining of a livelihood in any province."

It proved impossible to obtain provincial agreement to such an unqualified guarantee of freedom of movement. Newfoundland wanted to be able to give priority in jobs to local residents in the expected off-shore oil fields. Quebec wanted to encourage the use of French by individuals and companies moving to that province. The richer provinces were concerned that persons from poorer provinces might move to the richer provinces simply to take advantage of more-generous social welfare or health benefits. To obtain provincial agreement for the mobility rights, a number of exceptions were specified in sections 6(3) and 6(4). Social service recipients may be subjected to "reasonable" residency requirements. Mobility is also subject to "any [existing] laws or practices of general application in force in a province," except those that blatantly discriminate on the basis of province of residence. Furthermore, provinces with high unemployment can discriminate against residents from other provinces until the unemployment rate reaches the Canadian average. These exceptions have watered down the potential impact of mobility rights considerably.

In addition to the internal mobility rights, section 6(1) also guarantees every "citizen of Canada" "the right to enter, remain in and leave" the country. The right to enter Canada means that citizens travelling abroad cannot be prevented from returning home, for example, for political reasons. The right to remain in Canada means that Canada's extradition laws have been subjected to challenges under the Charter. The right to leave is meant to preclude situations developing in Canada analogous to those faced by Soviet Jews who wish to emigrate but are denied permission. The right to leave may also affect the federal government's ability to place restrictions on the amount of currency Canadian travellers or emigrants may take with them, should the federal authorities ever wish to exercise this power.

The mobility rights in the Charter have had very little impact on the Canadian political system. Until April 1989 there were forty-six section 6 cases reported in all courts in Canada, according to *Charter of Rights Decisions*. In six trial court decisions the Charter claim was upheld, but in only four of these was the claim sustained on appeal. A fifth of all section 6 cases involved litigants who tried to avoid extradition by claiming the right to remain in Canada. None of these attempts were successful. (The Supreme Court has left open the possibility, however, that in compelling situations extradition might be prevented through proceedings under section 7 [12, 24].

In one 1989 case, *Black v. Law Society of Alberta,* the Supreme Court of Canada struck down a Law Society of Alberta rule that prohibited lawyers from entering into a partnership with another member of the Law Society not ordinarily resident in the province. The Court declared that the rule was inconsistent with section 6(2) of the Charter [18]. In a Nova Scotia Court of Appeal case, a Nova Scotia regulation requiring that salesmen be permanent residents in order to receive a licence was struck down [14]. Then there was the British Columbia Supreme Court case in which a medical doctor succeeded in invoking section 6 to obtain a billing number from the province's health insurance agency. The doctor had previously been denied the number simply because she had moved from out of the province [54]. Finally, a probation order that prevented a probationer from entering a particular city in New Brunswick was found to be inconsistent with section 6 by the Court of Queen's Bench [101]. Because there are so few decisions under section 6 and it is not yet clear what impact it will have on government policies, section 6 cases are not discussed in a separate chapter.

It is somewhat ironic that the Supreme Court's first Charter case arose under section 6. This was the case of Joel Skapinker, a South African citizen who had taken a law degree in Canada. The Law Society of Upper Canada, the regulatory body for lawyers in Ontario, had denied Skapinker permission to practise law because he was not a citizen. Skapinker took the Law Society to court under the Charter, claiming that section 6 guaranteed to permanent residents like himself the right "to gain a livelihood in any province." Skapinker lost because the Supreme Court decided that section 6 applied only to persons moving from one province to another or to persons living in one province and working in another [47].

Legal Rights (Sections 7-14)

The legal rights section of the Charter includes a number of procedural safeguards designed to protect those subjected to governmental intervention under the law, such as those accused of federal criminal offences or provincial highway traffic violations and visitors to Canada who are ordered deported by federal immigration authorities. As the legal rights apply to "every person" or "everyone," they apply to any person subjected to federal or provincial authorities — not simply to citizens or permanent residents. According to Supreme

Court decisions, "legal persons," such as corporations, are also covered [42].

The legal rights are a reflection of the second aspect of civil liberties claims mentioned in chapter 1: that when it is acceptable for governments to restrict freedoms, certain procedures must be followed to ensure that freedoms are not unnecessarily restricted.

The legal rights sections of the Charter repeat most of the legal rights listed in the Canadian Bill of Rights, except for the right to a fair hearing in accordance with the principles of fundamental justice to determine rights and obligations (section 2[e] of the Bill) and the right not to be deprived of the enjoyment of property except through the due process of law (section 1[a] of the Bill). These particular rights will continue to be covered by the Bill of Rights rather than the Charter, but they apply only to the central government.

The Charter lists a number of legal rights not covered by the Bill of Rights. For example, the Charter prohibits unreasonable search and seizure, the retroactive criminalization of actions other than war crimes, and double jeopardy, that is, being tried and possibly punished more than once for the same offence [29, 46]. In addition, the Charter provides the right "to be tried within a reasonable time," the right to a jury trial if the offence carries a penalty of five years in jail or more, and the right to the least punishment if the punishment for an offence was varied between the time the offence was committed and the time of sentencing. As well, the Charter goes further than the Bill in protecting the right to counsel by stipulating the right to be informed of the right to counsel upon arrest or detention.

The various legal rights sections of the Charter are arranged in order from the general to the specific, and from the early stages of the criminal process to the later stages. Section 7 is a general guarantee of procedural rights. It states that everyone has the right to "life, liberty and security of the person" unless deprived thereof pursuant to "fundamental justice." Fundamental justice refers to recognized procedural safeguards to ensure fairness of treatment to those who have been detained or put on trial. Many of these procedural safeguards are included in sections 8-14, but section 7 implies even broader protection than the safeguards specifically spelled out in sections 8-14. We will see examples of the scope of section 7 in the *Singh, Therens* and *Morgentaler* decisions in chapter 5. However, the Supreme Court has determined that section 7 may not be interpreted so liberally as to nullify the Criminal Code provision that allows dangerous offenders to be given indeterminate sentences [94, 99] or to preclude the fingerprinting of accused persons [81].

Section 8 prohibits "unreasonable search or seizure." Section 9 forbids arbitrary (meaning unlawful) detention or imprisonment. Section 10 includes a list of rights that apply when a person is arrested or detained, such as the right to counsel and the right to be informed of the reasons for being detained. Section 11 contains rights that come into effect upon being charged with an offence, such as the right to be presumed innocent until proven guilty and the right to a trial within a reasonable time. (The Supreme Court has decided that the issue of unreasonable delay must be raised at a trial and not a preliminary hearing [55]; in one instance, a trial judge's eleven-month delay in reaching a decision after the trial was considered "unreasonable" [103]. Section 12 prohibits cruel and unusual treatment or punishment. The Supreme Court has held that the minimum sentence of seven years imprisonment that the Criminal Code required for illegally importing any narcotic into Canada (including a "joint of grass") violated section 12 [107].

Section 13 stipulates that witnesses in trials be protected from having self-incriminating evidence used against them in future trials. This allows witnesses to concentrate on giving accurate evidence for the trial they are participating in, without having to worry that they might accidentally, or through the urging of the crown, give evidence that could be used against them personally in a future trial. Section 13 also means that accused persons who are tried for particular offences need not worry that their testimony at the trial may be used against them in another trial [33, 95]. Finally, section 14 provides the right to an interpreter for any party in a trial (civil or criminal) or any witness who does not speak the language of the trial, or for any deaf person.

Equality Rights (Section 15)

Section 15(1) states that "every individual" (meaning that only human beings are covered, and not legal persons such as corporations) "is equal before and under the law and has the right to the equal protection and equal benefit of the law without discrimination." Before examining the remainder of this section, it is worthwhile noting that whereas the Bill of Rights protects equality "before the law," the Charter safeguards equality "before *and under*" (emphasis added) the law. The phrase "and under" was added to counteract the narrow interpretation of "equality" the Supreme Court gave to this phrase in the Bill of Rights, especially in cases such as *Lavell* and *Bédard* [4]. In other words, it is not good enough for the courts to ensure that all Indian women are treated equally by judges. It is also necessary for judges to strike down a law that applies unequally without sufficient reason.

Similarly, whereas the Bill mentions the right to the "protection of the law," the equivalent Charter right is to "the equal protection and equal benefit of the law." The reference to "benefit" is there to encourage judges to apply the equality principle not only to laws that protect citizens from unjustified government encroachment, but also to laws that provide a positive benefit, like unemployment insurance. In fact, the addition of the word "benefit" may represent a specific antidote to the *Bliss* decision [19].

Section 15 guarantees equality "without discrimination," which means regardless of the type of discrimination. The section, however, continues by listing a number of specific forms of discrimination that are prohibited: " . . . without discrimination, and in particular, without discrimination based on race, national or ethnic origin, colour, religion, sex, age or mental or physical disability." Apparently, the framers of the Charter (those who participated in drafting it) wished to signal to the judiciary that particular forms of discrimination are especially unacceptable. This list of particularly repugnant forms of discrimination is similar to the list in the Bill of Rights, except that "ethnic origin" has been added to "national origin" to broaden the scope of this category, and "age" and "mental or physical disability" have been added. These latter two additions came about as a result of recommendations from groups representing seniors and the mentally and physically disabled during the parliamentary committee hearings on the proposed charter in 1981. They represented part of the federal government's strategy for increasing the public demand for a charter in the face of provincial opposition to unilateral patriation.

A prominent American Bill of Rights issue in recent years has been to what extent governments can institute affirmative action programs without violating equality rights. An affirmative action program is a government initiative that discriminates in favour of groups that have been the victims of unjustified discrimination in the past so that these groups may achieve equality sooner than otherwise. A specified minimum number of places for blacks in universities and pay equity programs for women are two examples. As Laurence Tribe has noted, while the U.S. Supreme Court is clearly committed to overcoming racial and sexual discrimination, affirmative action programs have not always survived the Court's test for equality [80].

To ensure the constitutionality of affirmative action programs in Canada, section 15(2) of the Charter specifically protects affirmative action programs from being limited by the equality guarantee in section 15(1).

The equality rights in the Charter could potentially have the greatest impact on existing federal and provincial legislation and procedures. This is because almost every law discriminates among individuals or groups in some way. Whenever a law is challenged in court as discriminatory, the crown will have the option of defending the law as a reasonable limit to equality, a defence allowed by section 1 of the Charter, the limitations clause. Because of the potentially enormous impact section 15 could have on government programs, it did not come into force for three years, until April 17, 1985. The delay was meant to allow the federal and provincial governments to review their laws and to change those that discriminated unnecessarily. Although all the governments went through this exercise, the resulting changes were not very far-reaching because the reviewers were unable to guess how section 15 would be applied by the Supreme Court.

Language Rights (Sections 16-22)

Some of the language rights provisions contained in sections 16-22 already existed in section 133 of the BNA Act. For example, sections 17-19, which guarantee that either English or French may be used in parliamentary debates or the proceedings of the courts created by Parliament (the Supreme Court of Canada, the Federal Court and the Tax Court) and require the use of English and French in the Statutes of Canada, Hansard and other official records, duplicate section 133. One purpose of the language rights sections of the Charter is to create the impression that language rights are an important part of the Canadian concept of rights. In addition, sections 17-19 extend the language guarantees of section 133 to New Brunswick.

By 1982 New Brunswick had become an officially bilingual province in all but a constitutional sense. It was the hope of the federal officials that other provinces with a significant francophone minority, such as Ontario, Manitoba and Newfoundland, would also assent to be included in the language rights sections of the Charter, but only New Brunswick agreed. Other provinces, however, may opt in to these sections in the future. Quebec did not opt in because it would have been incongruous for the Parti Québécois government to promote a document that purported to strengthen the bilingual and bicultural nature of Canada. In any case, the language rights contained in section 133 of the Constitution Act, 1867, still apply to Quebec.

Section 16 declares that French and English are the official languages of Canada (meaning the jurisdiction of the central government) and of New Brunswick, and that they have "equal status" and "equal rights and privileges as to their use in all institutions." Although this declaration has a potentially powerful symbolic value, Peter Hogg (1) is doubtful whether it will have much impact on judicial decisions.

Section 20 provides language rights that go well beyond those in section 133. With regard to government services provided by the central government, section 20(1) states that "[a]ny member of the public . . . has the right to communicate with, and to receive available services" in French or English in three circumstances: first, this guarantee applies to the central offices of a government department or other federal institution; second, other federal government offices must provide bilingual services "where there is a significant demand"; and third, bilingual services must be provided where "due to the nature of the office, it is reasonable" to provide such services. These categories are extremely vague, and it will be up to the Canadian judiciary to define them as cases develop. Section 20(2) provides New Brunswickers with the same right to communicate with government and to receive services in the official language of choice, but the right is not limited to any particular set of circumstances.

Section 21 states that the language rights in the Charter should not be interpreted as "abrogating or derogating" from the language rights in section 133. Section 22 directs that other "legal or customary" rights concerning the use of languages other than English or French will continue, unaffected by the Charter.

Minority Language Education Rights (Section 23)

Section 23 is difficult to comprehend at first reading because it is the result of numerous compromises between federal and provincial officials with regard to the contentious language-of-education issue. The first two subsections of section 23 guarantee to Canadian citizens the right to have their children receive "primary and secondary school instruction" in either English or French in any province, if one or more of the following conditions are met:

- the preferred language of education for the children is the mother tongue of one of the parents (the mother tongue clause);
- the preferred language of education for the children is the language in which one of the parents received his or her primary school education somewhere in Canada (the Canada clause); or
- the preferred language of education for one of the children is the language in which one of the child's siblings received, or is receiving, primary school education (the sibling clause).

In 1981 and 1982 Quebec objected both to the Canada clause and the mother tongue clause, as noted above. Although Quebec had no objection to providing an English education to children of anglophone Quebeckers who had received their education in Quebec, the provincial government was determined to educate the children of new immigrants to the province, whether from Canada or from abroad, in French. It feared that with increased immigration into the province and declining birth rates, Quebec might eventually become an anglophone province unless the children of new immigrants became francophones.

Because the Charter was put into effect without the consent of Quebec, a provision was inserted into the final version of the Constitution Act, 1982, that delayed the application of the mother tongue clause to Quebec until such time as the Quebec National Assembly ratified it. However, the Canada clause was imposed on Quebec in spite of Quebec's objections. When the issue eventually went to court after 1982, Quebec attempted to justify the Quebec clause as a reasonable limit to the Canada clause. This important case, known as the *Quebec Protestant School Board* case [8], will be discussed in chapter 7.

The Application Clauses
(Sections 1, 24, 32 and 33)

There are four clauses in the Charter that define its application: section 32, dealing with the laws and activities covered by the Charter; section 1, which suggests the kinds of "reasonable limits" to the Charter that are acceptable; section 33, the legislative override clause; and section 24, which describes how the Charter may be enforced.

What the Charter Covers (Section 32)

The Charter applies only to the relations between governments and persons (including corporations with regard to some clauses). Section 32 states that the Charter applies to Parliament and to provincial legislatures and to the federal and provincial governments (meaning cabinets and the public service, but not the courts; see the *Dolphin Delivery* case [121], chapter 3.) Thus, all statutes created by Parliament and the legislatures are covered by the Charter, as well as all cabinet regulations and the actions of administrative officials who are responsible to a cabinet minister, Parliament or a legislature. The by-laws and administrative actions of municipal authorities are also included, because municipalities are created by provincial legislation. Furthermore, the regulations created by agencies that exercise power on behalf of government fall within the purview of the Charter. Thus, Skapinker was able to sue the Law Society of Upper Canada under the Charter because the regulation of the law profession has been delegated by the Ontario legislature to the Law Society.

The Charter does not cover the private relations between persons. To the extent that human rights are to be enforced in the private sphere, this is accomplished through the eleven human rights codes and the common law. However, the human rights codes, and other legislation regulating private relations, must conform to the Charter. Justine Blainey was able to win the right to play hockey in what was previously a boys-only league because she successfully challenged a provision of the Ontario Human Rights Code that exempted sports associations from provisions that prohibited discrimination based on sex [70]. Similarly, university professors forced to retire at the age of sixty-five are questioning the constitutionality of compulsory retirement by challenging the provisions of the Ontario Human Rights Code that permit discrimination based on age [74].

The Limitations Clause (Section 1)

Section 1 was intended to provide judges with some direction in determining limits to Charter rights. It declares that the Charter "guarantees the rights and freedoms set out in it subject only to such reasonable limits prescribed by law as can be demonstrably justified in a free and democratic society."

To date, three important features of section 1 have emerged from judicial decisions on the Charter. First, the phrase "demonstrably justified" places the onus on the party wanting to limit a right (usually a government) to prove that the limitation is reasonable. In the absence of evidence to the contrary, judges will presume that a limit placed on a right is *not* reasonable [42].

Second, the phrase "prescribed by law" means that a limit must be "expressly provided for by statute or regulation, or results by necessary implication from the terms of a statute or regulation or from its operating requirements. The limit may also result from the application of a common law rule" [109]. In other words, under the principle of the rule of law, government may not take action, including action to limit rights, except through law. For example, the law that created the old Ontario Censorship Board was struck down by the Supreme Court of Ontario because it gave the board an open-ended licence to censor films and videos [75]. The new Ontario censorship law, which created the Ontario Film and Video Review Board, described in rather general terms the kinds of materials that the board could purge. The new law has so far been upheld by the courts. As well, limits may be *implied* by the law [91, 110]. In a recent Supreme Court of Canada decision on the constitutionality of police spot checks, the Court held that the section of the Ontario Highway Traffic Act that allows police officers randomly to stop motor vehicles contains an implied limit to the right not to be arbitrarily detained (section 9 of the Charter).

Third, the Supreme Court of Canada has defined a test for what constitutes a "reasonable limit" that can be "demonstrably justified in a free and democratic society." This test is known as the *"Oakes* test" because it was developed in the case of *The Queen v. Oakes* [129]. (The *Oakes* case itself is an example of the presumption of innocence for a person charged with drug trafficking, and we will consider the case further in chapter 5.) The *Oakes* test has two key components. First, the objective of the government in limiting a right must be of sufficient importance to society to justify encroachment on a right. Second, the limit must be reasonable and demonstrably justified in terms of not being out of proportion to the government objective, and must therefore satisfy three criteria: (a) it must be rationally connected the government objective, and not "arbitrary or capricious"; (b) it should impair the right as little as is necessary to achieve the government objective; and (c) even if all of the points above are satisfied, the effects of the limit cannot be out of proportion to what is accomplished by the government objective — in other words, the cure cannot be allowed to be more harmful than the disease.

Whenever a Charter decision turns on limits to rights in particular situations, legal arguments focus on section 1. It is worth noting that in the United States, where there is a bill of rights with no limitations clause, the Supreme Court created the notion of an "implied" limitations clause. The judges assumed that the framers of the Bill of Rights realized that no right is absolute. The fact that Canada's Charter contains an explicit limitations clause is a reflection of the desire to provide guidance to the judiciary, but it is obvious that the judges are still left with a tremendous amount of discretion in setting limits on rights.

The Legislative Override (Section 33)

Section 33 allows the federal Parliament or a provincial legislature to insert a clause into any specific statute declaring that the statute will operate "notwithstanding" sections 2 and 7-15 of the Charter. Any application of the override will automatically expire at the end of five years, but it may be renewed. This clause does not release legislatures and Parliament from their obligations under the Charter, but it permits them to put off particular cases of judicial review under the Charter so that they themselves can determine their obligations for five-year intervals. The override is a reflection of the skepticism felt by some Canadian politicians about the potential quality of judicial review under the Charter.

A consensus seems to be emerging among our political leaders that the override will only be used in extraordinary circumstances, such as emergency situations or to advance important social policy goals that could be or are being blocked by judicial review. Under most circumstances, however, a government wishing to limit a right would have to justify its action under section 1. Significantly, even the new federal Emergencies Act does not invoke section 33. Although the Emergencies Act, like the old War Measures Act which it replaced, does infringe civil liberties, the government expects to be able to justify such restrictions under section 1 of the Charter.

Section 33 has been used only in three circumstances to date. The Quebec National Assembly, when controlled by the Parti Québécois, amended all pre-1982 Quebec statutes to include an override clause, and also included an override clause in all new legislation as a form of protest over being left out of the constitutional accord. Second, the government of Saskatchewan used the override clause in legislation that settled a public service strike in 1986. The government feared that if the Supreme Court found a right to strike in section 2 of the Charter, the back-to-work legislation would be ineffective. As it turned out, since the Supreme Court has denied that a right to strike exists in the Charter (see chapter 3), Saskatchewan's use of the override was unnecessary. The third instance was the Quebec government's decision to use the override to protect the commercial signs provisions of the province's Charter of the French Language following a Supreme Court decision of December 1988 that struck down some of these provisions (see chapter 3).

Enforcement (Section 24)

Section 24(1) gives "anyone" the right to apply to a court for a "remedy" if that person thinks that his or her rights under the Charter have been "infringed or denied." This section gives the judiciary very broad scope to enforce the provisions of the Charter and to invent creative "remedies" for violations. Although section 24 does not empower persons whose rights have not been directly affected to apply to a court, and although it does not allow for applications from persons concerned about possible *future* violations of rights, Peter Hogg (1) maintains that these kinds of applications may often be made in any case pursuant to other statutory or common-law provisions.

Probably the most interesting attempt by a litigant to take advantage of section 24(1) occurred in 1982. An RCMP inspector, Claude Vermette, was being tried for his alleged involvement in the raiding of the offices of the Parti Québécois. During the trial, Premier René Lévesque "attacked in colourful and abusive language" the credibility of witnesses at the trial. The trial judge discontinued the trial because Lévesque's remarks might prejudice the outcome, and a new trial was ordered. Vermette objected to the new trial because he felt that no trial could be fair after Lévesque's remarks. He obtained an order for a stay of proceedings, but the order was overruled by the Supreme Court in 1988 [114]. Mr. Justice Gérard La Forest wrote that "the reckless remarks of politicians [cannot be allowed to] frustrate the whole judicial process."

Section 24(2) gives judges the option to exclude evidence from trials if in the collecting of the evidence a Charter right was violated. Judges may exclude evidence if its admission "would bring the administration of justice into disrepute." Chapter 5 will review the *Therens* decision [109], in which evidence from a breathalyzer test was excluded pursuant to section 24(2).

The Interpretive Clauses of the Charter (Sections 25-31)

The interpretive clauses are intended to provide guidance to judges in their attempts to interpret the Charter.

Aboriginal Rights (Section 25)

Section 25 directs judges not to interpret the Charter "so as to abrogate or derogate from any aboriginal, treaty or other rights or freedoms that pertain to the aboriginal peoples of Canada." This clause specifically mentions the Royal Proclamation of 1763 and current and future land-claims agreements. Therefore, to the extent that the Indian Act is seen by judges as promoting treaty rights or land claims, it will be upheld. This is in spite of the fact that the Indian Act singles out a particular racial group, and therefore might be considered "discriminatory" contrary to section 15 were it not for section 25.

The Royal Proclamation of 1763, during the British era, was the first constitution of what is now Canada. In this document, the British authorities agreed to protect the aboriginal peoples of British North America from unfair treatment at the hands of the British settlers. Many native leaders therefore regard the Royal Proclamation as a guarantee of their sovereignty. It is unlikely, however, that the courts will often interpret the Royal Proclamation according to the native understanding of it. The British and Canadian courts have almost always interpreted the Royal Proclamation and the treaties from the perspective of British and Canadian law; the view the natives had of these documents has not been considered relevant. This is partly because of the principle of legislative supremacy, which has allowed more-recent federal and provincial legislation to take precedence over the treaties and the Royal Proclamation. Therefore, the declaration in section 25 that the Charter cannot erode rights "that have been recognized" by the Royal Proclamation, or rights "that now exist" in the land-claims agreements, could mean only that the Charter cannot be interpreted so as to *further* erode the rights that the native peoples of Canada thought they had in the Royal Proclamation and the treaties. In fact, the courts do seem to be adopting a narrow approach to the interpretation of section 25. According to F.L. Morton and M.J. Withey, natives brought nineteen claims to court under section 25 between 1982 and 1985 and lost all nineteen.

The native peoples had wanted a declaration in the Constitution Act, 1982, that their original rights under the treaties and the Royal Proclamation would be reinstated and protected. Such a declaration could have resulted in very significant costs to the federal and provincial governments, and the first ministers were not willing to yield on this point. As a result, there was strong opposition by native groups to the 1982 constitutional amendment.

All that the native spokespersons were able to win, in addition to section 25 of the Charter, was a declaration in section 35 of the Constitution Act, 1982, that the "existing [rather than the original] aboriginal and treaty rights of the aboriginal peoples of Canada are hereby recognized and affirmed" and a promise of a future constitutional conference that would include the first ministers and the leaders of native organizations. The constitutional conference was held in March 1983 and led to a constitutional amendment (section 35.1) that established that before future constitutional amendments could be completed affecting section 25 of the Charter or other constitutional provisions referring to the native peoples, a constitutional conference would be held involving the first ministers and native leaders. At the 1983 conference, it was also agreed that at least two more such conferences would be held.

At the last of these conferences, which was held in 1987, native leaders suggested a constitutional amendment that would give the bands the right to negotiate self-government agreements with Ottawa and provincial governments. Such agreements would have constitutional status. This proposal was not accepted by several of the provincial premiers on the grounds that it was too vague. Within two months, however, all the first ministers agreed to the Meech Lake Accord, which contained a similarly "vague" provision. The accord would allow the provinces to negotiate immigration agreements with Ottawa that could assume constitutional status. (There is an important difference between the proposed native self-government amendment and the immigration procedure in Meech Lake, however. With regard to the latter, the federal government would have no responsibility to negotiate, whereas the aboriginal peoples wanted the right to negotiate agreements.) The failure of the Canadian political system to give priority to the resolution of native rights issues represents a major gap in the human rights apparatus in Canada. The issue is bound to remain a prominent one.

Multiculturalism (Section 27)

Section 27 instructs judges to interpret the Charter "in a manner consistent with the preservation and enhancement of the multicultural heritage of Canadians." There is mixed opinion as to whether this clause will serve a merely symbolic function or whether it might actually have an important impact on the interpretation of the Charter.

In the 1985 case in which the Supreme Court struck down the federal Lord's Day Act [82], the multiculturalism clause was mentioned as one reason why a law favouring the Christian religion could not stand against the Charter's equality guarantee. The multiculturalism clause, however, was not critical to the outcome of the case.

Sexual Equality (Section 28)

Section 28 declares that "[n]otwithstanding anything in this Charter, the rights and freedoms referred to in it are guaranteed equally to male and female persons." This section came about as a result of the urging of several women's organizations, whose members were concerned that equality rights for women might be overridden through section 33 and that judges, who are predominantly male, might consider limits to sexual equality as "reasonable" under section 1.

Although section 28 in many respects duplicates the prohibition of discrimination based on sex in section 15, section 28 cannot be overridden under section 33. Furthermore, the very forceful opening words of section 28 might encourage judges not to subject sexual equality to reasonable limits, or at least to demand higher standards for limits to sexual equality.

It is ironic that, according to Morton and Withey, of fourteen sexual discrimination cases in all levels of court in Canada that were raised under section 15 or 28 or both, twelve were brought by men. Nine litigants were successful in their actions to protect sexual equality, eight of them men.

Denominational School Rights (Section 29)

There is no doubt that the special rights granted to denominational schools under section 93 of the Constitution Act, 1867, violate in principle the equality rights provisions in section 15, since they result in special privileges to some, but not all, religious denominations. However, in creating the Charter, Canadian legislators had no intention of abolishing denominational school rights; after all, these rights had been considered an essential part of the Confederation bargain for the original four provinces. (As well, denominational school rights were created in each of the provinces that joined Canada after 1867.)

Section 29 states the clear intention of the framers of the Charter that the denominational school rights in Canada's original constitution be continued: "Nothing in this Charter abrogates or derogates from any rights or privileges guaranteed by or under the Constitution of Canada in respect of denominational, separate or dissentient schools." Chapter 6 will consider the Supreme Court decision that resulted from the extension of funding to Roman Catholic high schools in Ontario in 1985.

Miscellaneous (Sections 26, 30-31)

There are three remaining interpretive clauses. Section 26 instructs judges not to interpret the Charter so as to deny "the existence of any other rights or freedoms that exist in Canada." This means that the Charter does not take precedence over rights that may be found in other constitutional documents (such as the original language rights). Further, section 26 seems to suggest that judges should not hesitate to apply the statutory bills of rights and the human rights codes merely because of the existence of the Charter.

Section 30 states that whenever the word "province" appears in the Charter, it is understood to include the Yukon and Northwest Territories. Section 31 indicates that the purpose of the Charter is to limit the powers of government and that therefore the Charter may not be interpreted so as to extend existing powers.

The Charter and Its Critics

There are three major reasons why the Canadian Charter of Rights and Freedoms became reality: Pierre Trudeau, the nation-building strategy of the federal government, and the legacy of the Supreme Court's interpretation of the Bill of Rights. Had any one of these ingredients been missing, it is unlikely that the Charter would have materialized during the 1980s.

Certainly, public concern about protecting and promoting rights and liberties played a role in generating popular support for the concept of a charter of rights, but as already noted, public pressure was not the primary reason for the Charter's creation by the political elite. Trudeau was determined to succeed in his charter project, and his overriding goal was to give Canadians a national code of values to promote national unity. He hoped that the Charter would promote a continuing national dialogue about Charter questions that would cut across the preoccupation with provincial issues. From the perspective of this nation-building strategy, the language rights were a central feature of the document. To entrench the Charter in the constitution seemed to be the only way of getting the judiciary to take it seriously, based on experience with the Bill of Rights. As Allan Blakeney has remarked, "They convulsed the nation to convince the judges."

A great deal has been written about the potential of the Charter as a nation-building tool by authors like Russell (8), Williams, Knopff and Morton. Further, while the Charter was not created primarily to promote human rights, its supporters are optimistic that it will be a valuable tool in that cause.

Charter skeptics base their reasoning on several premises: the Charter undermines legislative supremacy; the Charter will work in the interests of the powerful in society who can afford the cost of litigation; the Charter diverts attention from the most serious threats to social well-being; and courts are inappropriate institutions for policy-making regarding human rights.

Contemporary political commentators who are concerned about the erosion of legislative supremacy are not worried, as A.V. Dicey was, about the *theory* of legislative supremacy. Instead, they are worried about the erosion of democratic skills in society. As Carole Pateman has shown, democracy means far more than holding elections. A democratic society will lose its ability to promote human excellence if its citizens have not learned to participate intelligently in making decisions about important public policy issues, such as human rights. The Charter may transfer an important part of this responsibility from the democratic process to the (unelected) judiciary. In the United States, where the judiciary has played the predominant role in human rights policy-making for two centuries, some political theorists are concerned, according to Leonard Levy, that the ability of average citizens to think carefully about civil rights issues has atrophied to some extent.

The second argument is that because litigation is expensive, the determination of human rights issues through the courts will tend to work in favour of those who can afford the costs. For example, during the last few years the National Citizens' Coalition, a well-financed right-wing lobby group, has spent an estimated $500,000 to support Merv Lavigne's attempt to curtail union contributions to political parties through a Charter challenge (*Globe and Mail*, January 31, 1989). More will be spent before the case is heard by the Supreme

Court of Canada. Charter litigation also forces less-advantaged groups to spend large sums on law firms in order to defend themselves. Ontario unions have allegedly already spent $400,000 defending themselves in the *Lavigne* case [72].

The third argument is that the Charter diverts attention from the more serious threats to social well-being. According to Charter critics like Patrick Monahan and Michael Mandel, the Charter is likely to result in a significant reduction in the ability of governments in Canada to assist and protect the disadvantaged in society. This is because the Charter focuses on preventing state infringements on individual liberty, but such infringements are often necessary in order for the state to intervene on behalf of those in need. For example, in the B.C. Motor Vehicle Act case [69], the Supreme Court interpreted the "right to liberty" broadly so that it would be more difficult for provincial governments to enforce the suspension of licences of poor drivers. The result is that while poor drivers will enjoy fewer restrictions on their liberty, more innocent people may be injured in traffic accidents.

The fourth argument — that courts are inappropriate institutions for policy-making regarding human rights — is the most complex. It is claimed that there are three factors that make courts poorly suited to resolve human rights policy issues: (1) the doctrine of *stare decisis*, (2) the adversary system and (3) the backgrounds of the judges.

Stare Decisis

In common-law jurisdictions, precedents are applied to current cases according to a set of principles known as *stare decisis*. According to *stare decisis*, every court must follow the precedents established by a higher court in the same court system, and the precedents of the highest court "trump" those of any lower courts. In the absence of conflicting precedents established by a higher court, a court usually follows its own precedents. The precedents of higher or equal-status courts in another common-law jurisdiction are influential but not binding. (Therefore, American Bill of Rights precedents are often cited in Charter cases, but they are only sometimes followed.) Precedents must be followed only when the facts in the current case and the precedent case are substantially the same. If a judge considers the facts in a current case to be significantly different, the judge may "distinguish" the precedent and depart from it.

Thus, all courts in Canada must follow precedents established by the Supreme Court. The Supreme Court itself almost always follows its own precedents. In the mid-1970s the Court announced that it might occasionally overrule its own precedents (or those established by the Judicial Committee of the Privy Council) if it considered those precedents to be clearly wrong or inappropriate. Since that time, the Supreme Court has overruled fewer than ten precedents. Such over-ruling will not occur frequently because it would destroy the predictability of the decision-making process in courts.

Stare decisis makes the decision-making process in courts fundamentally different from the policy-making process that takes place in the policy development sections of government departments and in cabinets and legislatures. In courts, established principles must stand, errors can very rarely be admitted, and changes in approach are few. In the executive and legislative branches, established principles can more easily evolve, errors can more easily be admitted, and changes in policy are to be expected as values and priorities change and as more is learned from research.

The decision-making process in courts, which is called adjudication, works best when judges can apply relatively clear rules (statutes or the common law) to factual situations. The training of judges and lawyers is fitted to that process. With regard to policy development, the policy branches of government departments, cabinets and legislatures have different resources that have been honed to that particular process. These include skilled policy research staff, facilities for conducting pilot studies and evaluations, links with other social science research institutions, access to experts connected with various interest groups, and the ability to conduct public hearings. None of these resources are available to courts.

When judges are asked to give meaning to unclear laws or to speculate on the meaning of law in the absence of a factual situation, they move from the adjudicative into the policy-making realm. Policy-making means the development of programs that will meet specific goals effectively and at the least cost. Of course, it is impossible to establish a precise dividing line between adjudication and policy development so that judges would only adjudicate and policy developers never make decisions that could be considered adjudicative ones, but an example will illustrate the difference between the two processes.

In 1985 the Supreme Court had to decide whether refugee claimants from India, who were about to be deported without having had an oral hearing, were entitled to a hearing either under the Charter or the Bill of Rights. The question was basically a legal one: did the guarantees of "fundamental justice" in section 7 of the Charter and section 2(e) of the Bill require an oral hearing? From a legal perspective, the answer was relatively clear. The common-law principle of natural justice, implied both by section 7 of the Charter and section 2(e) of the Bill, indicated that an oral hearing was required. (See the *Singh* case [125] in chapter 5.)

In the same case, the Court had to consider another question: does the denial of an oral hearing constitute a reasonable limit (under section 1) to the right to fundamental justice? This question is related more to policy development than to adjudication. From a policy development perspective, this question cannot be answered effectively without research to indicate whether the determination of refugee status can be undertaken accurately through a process that does not involve an oral hearing or whether an oral hearing is the most effective of various approaches. Policy-makers would be likely to undertake scientific evaluations of various methods to answer the question and to recommend the approach that is best in terms of both accuracy and cost. Lacking these resources — which are inappropriate for adjudication in any case — the Court could consider only the arguments presented by counsel for the government (the party on which the onus of proof rested). Counsel for the government, unaccustomed to making policy-related submissions, tried to justify the denial of an oral hearing by invoking "administrative convenience." Quite understandably, this reasoning did not seem convincing, and the Court decided that the denial of an oral hearing did not constitute a reasonable limit. Although the Court may well have stumbled into making the right decision, the way in which the decision was made leaves something to be desired. This illustrates how the courts, as institutions, are ill-prepared for making policy decisions. (See L.A. Pal and F.L. Morton for other examples.)

The Adversary System

The adversary system is an approach to adjudication utilized in common-law systems. According to this system, it is the responsibility of the litigants to present the judges with all the facts and theory that they need to make their decisions. Judges may not carry out an independent investigation of the facts. Although they may research legal theory and precedents on their own, they are not usually provided with many resources to do this, and they are expected to rely primarily on the information presented by counsel for the litigants. It has only been in recent years that Supreme Court of

Canada judges and provincial appeal court judges have been assigned law clerks to assist them with their legal research. Trial court judges rarely have such assistance. Thus, if decisions about the meaning of the Charter seem to take into account only a narrow range of possibilities, this is usually because the lawyers presenting the case have, through lack of knowledge or through design, narrowed the possibilities in advance.

Counsel on both sides tend naturally to argue as forcefully as they can on behalf of their clients. With regard to Charter litigation, it is usually the case that a private person or corporation is challenging a federal or provincial law or the actions of a federal or provincial official. Therefore, in almost every Charter case, lawyers for the "crown" (the name given to the state as a legal person) will tend to argue for the most restrictive and narrow interpretation of the Charter in order to uphold what they perceive to be the interests of their client. This is ironic when one remembers that the Charter's supporters in the federal and some provincial cabinets claimed in 1981 that the Charter would protect our rights forever in the broadest possible way.

The Backgrounds of Judges

The principle of judicial impartiality is critical to successful adjudication. There is no doubt in the author's opinion, based on extensive interviews with judges in Ontario, Alberta and Manitoba, that judges generally do their best to be as impartial as possible. However, when they are faced with having to give meaning to general phrases that could have a number of plausible meanings (such as many of those in the Charter) and there are few if any guiding precedents, the principle of impartiality may be of little assistance. In these cases, judges may apply what they perceive to be the standard of the "average reasonable person," but that perception may be influenced by the judges' personal experiences and backgrounds. The following summarizes how judges' backgrounds differ from those of the average Canadian. The information was obtained from studies by Peter Russell (6), Guy Bouthillier, Dennis Olsen and John Hogarth and from research conducted by Peter McCormick and the author.

Canadian judges tend to overrepresent the British and French ethnicities and to underrepresent the minority ethnicities. Non-Caucasians are especially underrepresented. The underrepresentation of the minority ethnicities, and particularly of the non-Caucasians, may be problematic. Some members of the minority ethnicities might be skeptical about the ability of the judiciary fully to comprehend issues in cases involving culture-specific factual situations. It also means that the Canadian judiciary lacks the insights that could be provided in judicial decisions about equality rights if they were written by judges who had personal experiences with discrimination.

Only about 5 per cent of the two thousand Canadian judges are women, although three out of the nine Supreme Court of Canada judges are women. The gross underrepresentation of women in the judiciary is a result of the fact that the legal profession was (as a result of social values and prejudice) dominated by men until recent years. As Russell has put it, the underrepresentation of women means that "insights and knowledge needed for intelligent adjudication are often lacking." Moreover, the stereotypic views that some male judges still occasionally exhibit about the "proper role of women" may influence some judicial decisions, as Mary Eberts has demonstrated.

Because judges are generally appointed from among the ranks of lawyers with many years of experience in private practice, judges are older than the average adult Canadian. The average age of superior court judges in Canada varies from about fifty-five to about sixty-five, depending on the province. Most provincial court judges appear to be, on average, one to three years younger. The average age of Supreme Court of Canada judges, as of February 1989, was sixty-three. Their average age at appointment was fifty-eight. As long as it is considered important for judges to be recruited from the ranks of experienced lawyers, it is inevitable that they will be older. This may mean that judges, as policy-makers, find it more difficult to consider the policy implications of changing social values than do the relatively younger policy-makers in the executive and legislative branches.

Judges are disproportionately married. In 1984, for example, 93 per cent of Alberta judges were married compared with about 80 per cent of the general population in the same age bracket. Only 3 per cent of Alberta judges were single or divorced — a much smaller proportion than the general population. Of the thirteen judges who served on the Supreme Court of Canada in 1988 and 1989 (there were four retirements), ten were married, one was single and two were widowed. Those who had been married had an average of three children. As a result, judges may have some difficulty in understanding the problems of Canadians who are single (whether heterosexual or gay) or divorced.

Judges tend to adhere disproportionately to the main-line religions in Canada: Roman Catholic, Anglican, United Church and Jewish, for example. Non-Christians and those from the minor Protestant religions tend to be underrepresented on the bench. This factor may make it somewhat more difficult for the judiciary as a whole to understand the differential impact some laws (such as Sunday-closing laws) have on non-Christians.

As might be expected, judges come disproportionately from upper social class backgrounds. In Alberta, for example, 46 per cent of the fathers of federally appointed judges and 52 per cent of the fathers of provincial court judges were businessmen or professionals, a group that comprised only 9 per cent of Alberta males in 1931 (around the time most of these judges were born). Conversely, 42 per cent of Alberta judges had fathers who were labourers or farmers, who made up 87 per cent of the province's male population when the judges were children. Only two of the first fifty Supreme Court of Canada judges were born into working-class families. The income of judges is also significantly higher than that of the average Canadian. As of April 1, 1988, Supreme Court of Canada judges earned $136,200 per year, and Federal Court judges earned $127,700. Provincial superior court judges earned $127,700 per year, while provincial court judges earned up to about $105,000 annually. (Most judges earned significantly more than their judicial salaries before their appointment.)

The question of whether the judiciary should be more representative of the social class backgrounds of Canadians is a difficult one. There are some like Dennis Olsen who think that the upper-class nature of the judiciary indicates the failure of our governing system to implement the liberal-democratic value of equality. Others think that because being born in a middle- or upper-class family does provide advantages to children who aspire to a judicial career, a non-partisan appointment process that is structured to recruit the very best judges will always recruit judges disproportionately from the middle and upper classes. Moreover, judges from a working-class background may not necessarily be more sympathetic to the claims of workers when decision-making concerns issues that are more policy-oriented than legal. Russell (6) has observed that "some very tough attitudes may be engendered in the person who has had to struggle and 'make it the hard way.' "

During Canada's first century, almost all judges appointed to every level of court in Canada were supporters of the party that controlled the government that appointed them. Before the First World War, many if not most of these had been candidates for office (successful or unsuccessful); since that time, the proportion of judges who were candidates has fallen to a level of perhaps 10 to 20 per cent of judges.

This change is particularly evident with regard to the Supreme Court. Only two judges appointed since 1949 have been candidates for elected office.

Some progress has been made in establishing less partisan methods for making judicial appointments during the past two decades, particularly with regard to provincial court appointments in some provinces. The current Canadian judiciary is composed partly of judges appointed under the old partisan systems and partly of judges selected according to the newer approaches.

Supreme Court decisions about the Charter are critical to the political impact of this document, and therefore it is particularly important to consider the backgrounds of Supreme Court judges. The nine judges serving on the Supreme Court in February 1989 had on average fifteen years experience in the practice of law and ten years experience as a judge before appointment to the Supreme Court. They had served on the Supreme Court an average of four years. Most had two degrees, a bachelor's degree and a law degree. Only one judge, La Forest, had been a full-time law professor, although three had part-time teaching experience. Thus, most of the judges had a solid grounding in legal practice and the art of adjudication, but most had only the standard training of lawyers in legal theory. Most had little or no training in policy analysis.

Was It Worth It?

In summary, the opponents of the Charter claim that the adjudicative process in the courts is not the most conducive environment for the development of effective policies for promoting human rights. Courts have little in the way of research facilities, litigation is dominated by the wealthy, and civil liberties issues come to court in a haphazard manner. In addition, judges are not the most likely candidates to champion civil liberties. Few judges have much training in theories of human rights, and because of their work, they tend to be both business-oriented and cautious.

As judges interpret the Charter, Canadians will ask themselves whether the Charter was worth all the trouble it took to create it or whether the skeptics were right after all. The next five chapters summarize a number of key Charter decisions — decisions that will be pivotal in the ultimate judgment Canadians form about the Charter.

3

The Fundamental Freedoms

Section 2 of the Charter declares that "everyone" has freedom of (a) conscience and religion, (b) thought, belief, opinion and expression, (c) peaceful assembly and (d) association. Obviously, these are general words that could be interpreted in a wide variety of ways with regard to specific situations. For example, section 2 provides no guidance as to whether freedom of religion rules out Sunday-closing laws, or whether freedom of association means that workers have a constitutionally protected right to strike. It is silent about whether Canadians may always express themselves in the language of their own choice or whether the Quebec government may prohibit languages other than French on commercial signs. These are the kinds of policy issues that judges are called on to decide.

The Supreme Court of Canada has handed down six major decisions that indicate how it has begun to approach section 2. The *Big M* and the *Edwards* decisions concern the constitutionality of Sunday-closing laws, and two others — *Dolphin Delivery* and the *Alberta Labour Reference* — consider whether the Charter implies the right of workers to picket and to strike. Finally, the *Ford* and *Devine* decisions deal with the relation between freedom of expression and Quebec's restrictions on the use of English on commercial signs.

The Sunday-Closing Issue

The Big M Case [82]

The first section 2 case to reach the Supreme Court was *Regina v. Big M Drug Mart Ltd.*, which was decided in April 1985. About six weeks after the Charter came into effect in 1982, Big M Drug Mart of Calgary was charged with contravening the federal Lord's Day Act by selling goods on a Sunday. Big M claimed that the Lord's Day Act violated the Charter's guarantee of freedom of religion and that therefore the act should be declared inoperative. (It is interesting that although a corporation cannot have a religion, corporations can challenge statutes as violations of freedom of religion because the references to "everyone" in section 2 and "anyone" in section 24 of the Charter include corporations.)

This argument was accepted by the Alberta Court of Appeal, but the crown appealed to the Supreme Court. Big M won again in our highest court, much to the surprise of those who thought that the Court might take the same tack as in the parallel case under the Canadian Bill of Rights — the *Robertson and Rosetanni* case [117], which was reviewed in chapter 1.

Chief Justice Brian Dickson wrote the main opinion in *Big M*. There are four important features of his decision: (1) the Bill of Rights precedent, (2) the purpose of the Charter, (3) freedom of religion and (4) whether the Lord's Day Act might be a reasonable limit to freedom of religion pursuant to section 1 of the Charter.

The Bill of Rights Precedent

Chief Justice Dickson handled the *Robertson and Rosetanni* precedent by pointing to one of the differences between the Charter and the Bill. He reminded his readers of the troublesome declaration in section 1 of the Bill that "in Canada . . . there have existed and shall continue to exist . . . the following human rights and fundamental freedoms . . . . "

> [T]he Canadian Charter of Rights and Freedoms does not simply "recognize and declare" existing rights as they were circumscribed by legislation current at the time of the Charter's entrenchment. The language of the Charter is imperative . . . . [T]he Charter is intended to set a standard upon which *present as well as future* legislation is to be tested.

Dickson's comments about the *Robertson and Rosetanni* case constitute an early indication that the Supreme Court intended to take a far more activist approach when interpreting the Charter than it had taken when interpreting the Bill.

The Court concluded that the Lord's Day Act violated the Charter's guarantee of freedom of religion because the act had a clearly religious purpose: to force all Canadians, under the threat of criminal sanction, to observe the Christian sabbath. To demonstrate the religious purpose of the act, Dickson traced the wording of the legislation to a 1677 English statute, An Act for the Better Observation of the Lord's Day Commonly Called Sunday.

Dickson's judgment in *Big M* implies that in *Robertson and Rosetanni* the Court had been forced to conclude that the Lord's Day Act did not violate freedom of religion because of the strait-jacket created by the unfortunate wording of section 1 of the Bill. Thus, Dickson did not find the reasoning in *Robertson and Rosetanni* very convincing. In *Robertson and Rossetani*, the Supreme Court had reasoned that although the purpose of the Lord's Day Act was originally to apply the criminal law to religious observance (thus making it valid federal legislation), over the years the effects of the law had evolved so as make it purely secular in purpose (so that it did not infringe freedom of religion).

Understandably, Dickson was not impressed with this "shifting purpose" approach to the Lord's Day Act, even though the U.S. Supreme Court had adopted the same kind of rationale to avoid striking down state Sunday observance laws as violations of the American Bill of Rights. He noted that it would be improper for the courts to second-guess the original legislature about the legislation's purpose. Furthermore, the shifting-purpose approach would create uncertainty in the law. At any point, a litigant could claim that a law had become unconstitutional because its purpose had changed.

Dickson asserted that a law could be considered an infringement of the Charter either because of its purpose or its effect. Both the purpose and the effect of statutes would have to conform to the Charter. This declaration is one of several significant features of the *Big M* decision that will have an impact on interpretation of the Charter for years to come.

The Purpose of the Charter

The chief justice used this early Charter case to comment on the Charter's purpose. His approach is clearly in the philosophic tradition of liberalism:

A truly free society is one which can accommodate a wide variety of beliefs, diversity of tastes and pursuits, customs and codes of conduct. A free society is one which aims at equality with respect to the enjoyment of fundamental freedoms and I say this without any reliance on s.15 of the Charter. Freedom must surely be founded in respect for the inherent dignity and the inviolable rights of the human person.

He also reiterated what had been said about the purpose of the Charter in a 1984 case, *Hunter v. Southam:* "[T]he purpose of the Charter [is] . . . the unremitting protection of individual rights and liberties." He added that the central feature of the fundamental freedoms section of the Charter (section 2) is "the notion of the centrality of individual conscience and the inappropriateness of governmental intervention to compel or to constrain its manifestation."

In its 1984 Charter decisions, the Supreme Court had decided to adopt a "purposive" approach to Charter interpretation [42]. In other words, the Court would attempt to ascertain from historical, political or philosophic sources the purpose of each of the rights guarantees in the Charter, and it would apply the guarantees accordingly. This purposive approach is reflected in Dickson's comments about the purpose of the Charter, the purpose of section 2 as a whole and the purpose of the guarantee of freedom of religion in section 2.

Freedom of Religion

It follows from the Court's general discussion of the Charter that the guarantee of freedom of religion is not an isolated right, but part of the overall goal in a liberal society to emphasize the "centrality of individual conscience." Dickson's judgment in *Big M* also alluded to some of the practical reasons for respecting freedom of religion as learned from the lessons of history. He noted how in post-Reformation Europe, both Roman Catholic and Protestant monarchs had attempted to impose their beliefs on all their subjects, not often with great success but always at the cost of many lives. According to Dickson, during the seventeenth century in England people eventually realized that "belief itself was not amenable to compulsion." Therefore, the position that the minority must conform to the traditions of the religious majority, either for the sake of convenience or to promote "the truth," was no longer acceptable. It follows that one of the purposes of the Charter's guarantee of freedom of religion is to protect "religious minorities from the threat of 'the tyranny of the majority.' "

In his discussion of freedom of religion, Dickson made an interesting comment that stands out because it would seem to have more in common with a theological treatise than with legal reasoning: "Attempts to compel belief or practice denied the reality of individual conscience and dishonoured the God that had planted it in His creatures." While this comment is not necessary to Dickson's analysis, a judge of his talent usually does not make such a statement without reason. One possible explanation for his observation is that it could be intended to provide future courts with a guideline for interpreting the religious connotation of the preamble to the Charter: "Whereas Canada is founded upon principles that recognize the supremacy of God and the rule of law."

As indicated in chapter 1, many of the civil liberties in the Charter can be thought of as logical derivatives from the principle of the rule of law. But the connection between the concept of "the supremacy of God" and the Charter is not clear. In fact, by recognizing a deity, the phrase would seem to contradict the guarantee of freedom of conscience in section 2. As it happens, the reference to the supremacy of God in the preamble to the Charter is copied from the Canadian Bill of Rights. It was included at the insistence of some members of Parliament who were anxious to please their constituents. Little thought was given to the apparent contradiction between this phrase and section 2(a). That was left for the courts to work out.

Dickson's brief foray into theology in the *Big M* may provide a way out of the dilemma for future courts. If the supremacy of God can be interpreted to mean that freedom of conscience must be respected, there is no necessary contradiction between the preamble to the Charter and the affirmation of freedom of conscience in section 2(a). Such an interpretation could have a significant impact on the outcome of the school prayer challenges, for example.

The Section 1 Analysis

Even though the Court decided that the Lord's Day Act infringes freedom of religion, it is possible that the legislation could nevertheless be sustained as a reasonable limit to rights, pursuant to section 1 of the Charter. In fact, counsel for the federal government argued that the Lord's Day Act should be considered a reasonable limit for two reasons. First, most religions advocate a day of rest, and because Christians are in the majority in Canada, the Christian day is the most practical. Second, it is important for there to be a common weekly day of rest in society so that families can spend time together. (Keep in mind that this decision occurred prior to the Court's development of the *Oakes* test for section 1.)

Dickson dismissed the first argument because the purpose of the guarantee of freedom of religion is to protect religious *minorities,* not the majority. He accepted that the second argument had some merit but pointed out that legislation creating a weekly holiday from work for secular rather than religious purposes would fall under provincial jurisdiction pursuant to section 92(13) of the Constitution Act, 1867: that is, under the provincial powers over "property and civil rights," rather than the federal criminal law power. (In 1903 the Judicial Committee struck down the provincial Sunday observance laws because they were worded more as federal criminal law than as provincial labour legislation. The phrase "civil rights" in section 92[13] has been interpreted by the Judicial Committee to mean essentially private law, as opposed to civil liberties or human rights. Labour legislation, such as the stipulation of hours of work and holidays, falls within the scope of private law.)

The Supreme Court's decision in *Big M* had the effect of transferring primary responsibility for Sunday-closing legislation from the federal government to the provinces. In 1903 the Judicial Committee awarded the federal government jurisdiction over legislation like the Lord's Day Act because it constituted a criminal prohibition based on a religious purpose. With the Charter, that kind of criminal legislation became unconstitutional. It remained possible, however, for the provinces to enact weekly-day-of-rest legislation that had a purely secular purpose. Dickson's judgment in *Big M* constituted a fairly broad hint that such legislation might be found constitutional by the Court.

In fact, Ontario's secular-Sunday closing legislation, the Retail Business Holidays Act, was declared to be constitutional by the Supreme Court at the height of the Christmas shopping rush in 1986. The legislation had been challenged by four retailers who had been convicted of operating on Sundays contrary to the provincial legislation. This decision is considered below.

The Edwards Books and Art Decision [88]

Ontario's Sunday-closing legislation, in contrast to the federal Lord's Day Act, is phrased in purely secular terms. It creates a weekly secular holiday — Sunday — and forbids retail establishments to do business on that day. There are many exemptions — for example, corner grocery stores, drug stores, service stations and recreational services.

The legislation permits retail businesses with fewer than eight employees and with less than 5,000 square feet to remain open on Sundays if they close on Saturdays. In 1983 four Ontario retailers were charged with violating the Sunday-closing laws. Three, including Edwards Books and Art Ltd., had remained open on Sundays without being closed on Saturdays, and they were convicted. The fourth, a kosher grocery store that was closed on Saturdays but opened on Sunday with more than seven employees, was acquitted by the Ontario Court of Appeal.

The majority on the Supreme Court, led by Chief Justice Dickson, decided that the Sunday-closing legislation did not constitute a direct violation of the guarantee of freedom of religion in the Charter. They did find, however, that the legislation represented an "indirect and unintentional" breach of freedom of religion. It was indirect because it resulted in placing a disproportionate burden on those who did not recognize Sunday as a day of rest. It was unintentional because the purpose of the legislation was not to discriminate against non-Sunday observers, but rather to create a weekly holiday.

The Court decided that even if a violation of freedom of religion was indirect and unintentional, it nevertheless constituted a violation of the Charter. But this particular violation was found to be a reasonable limit pursuant to section 1. Thus, it was the Court's section 1 analysis that was the critical feature of the Sunday-closing decision.

The Section 1 Analysis

The Court's majority had no difficulty in giving the legislation a passing grade concerning the first part of the *Oakes* test for the application of section 1 (see chapter 2) — whether the government objective that violated the Charter right was of "substantial" importance:

> A family visit to an uncle or a grandmother, the attendance
> of a parent at a child's sports tournament, a picnic, a swim,

or a hike in the park on a summer day, or a family expedition to a zoo, circus, or Exhibition — these, and hundreds of other leisure activities with family and friends are amongst the simplest but most profound joys that any of us can know. The aim of protecting workers, families and communities from a diminution of opportunity to experience the fulfillment offered by these activities, and from the alienation of the individual from his or her closest social bonds, is . . . a pressing and substantial concern.

The second part of the *Oakes* test — the three-pronged proportionality test — presented the Court with more difficulties. The first prong, whether the legislation is logically connected with the government objective, raised the questions of why the legislation dealt only with retail businesses and why it created so many exemptions if the object of creating a common pause day was of such pressing concern.

The chief justice referred to a 1970 study by the Ontario Law Reform Commission on Sunday closing. The report showed that, outside the retail trade, most employees who object to Sunday work are able to avoid Sunday work even if their employers are open on Sundays. A variety of factors make this possible, for example, the high rate of unionization and the ability of well-trained persons to find other jobs that do not require Sunday shifts. In the retail industry, however, it would be more difficult for workers to avoid Sunday work were the law to permit it. There is a low rate of unionization, and unskilled retail workers cannot so easily find other employment. Moreover, once some retail businesses in an area open on Sundays, others may feel forced to open in order to meet the competition.

The Law Reform Commission recognized that there is a tension between the goal of creating a common pause day and that of ensuring that there are quality leisure activities available to families for Sunday outings. This is because some people in the leisure industry must work on Sundays if quality leisure activities are to be available. Legislation must strike a balance between these goals, and the chief justice was satisfied that Ontario's Sunday-closing law had succeeded. Even though there was some overlap of the goods and services offered by establishments that could and those that could not open on Sundays, the chief justice attributed this inconsistency to "simplicity and administrative convenience," which he said "are legitimate concerns for the drafters of such legislation."

The Minimal Interference Issue

The second prong of part two of the *Oakes* test — whether the legis-lation interferes with freedom of religion as little as reasonably pos-sible — presented the Court with its most difficult problem in this case. According to Dickson, what the Court must decide "is whether there is some reasonable alternative scheme which would allow the province to achieve its objective with fewer detrimental effects on religious freedom." It is in answering this kind of question that the new policy-making role the Charter has created for the courts be-comes most evident.

The Court considered three alternative approaches to the creation of a common pause day: (1) providing employees with a right to refuse to work on Sundays, (2) allowing employers who could demonstrate a sincere religious conviction to open Sundays, provided that they close on the day prescribed by their religion and (3) remov-ing the restriction on Saturday-closing retailers that prevents them from employing more than seven staff on Sundays or from operating with more than 5,000 square feet.

The first alternative was found inadequate because employees who wanted promotions would feel pressured to work on Sundays without complaint. The second alternative was criticized because it would require employers to submit to the indignity of having to prove the sincerity of their religious beliefs. The third alternative, however, caused a split in the Court's decision. The majority, led by Chief Justice Dickson, found the third alternative lacking because the larger an enterprise that opened on a Sunday, the greater the likelihood that it would employ persons who objected to Sunday work, and these persons would feel pressured to work on Sundays to advance their careers. From this perspective, the employee and square-foot restric-tions seemed reasonable.

Madame Justice Bertha Wilson dissented from the majority on this point. She favoured the third alternative, both from practical and philosophic perspectives. From a practical standpoint, she claimed that the crown had not produced enough evidence to show that large enterprises that closed on Saturdays but opened on Sundays tended to employ Sunday observers who would feel pressured to relinquish their right not to work on Sundays. She reminded her readers that the Supreme Court had found that the Ontario Human Rights Code placed on employers a "duty to accommodate" the religious beliefs of employees [60]. In other words, the code gives employees the right not to work on their religion's holy day without loss of seniority or career advancement opportunities, so long as this does not cause "undue hardship" to the employer. From her perspective, the majority's rejection of the third alternative was based on speculation rather than on hard evidence.

Wilson claimed that unless the third alternative was adopted, the result would be a "compromised scheme of justice." This is a term invented by the American legal philosopher Ronald Dworkin (2). According to Dworkin, legislatures should apply a set of policy principles equally to all cases, without internal exceptions that subtract certain groups from the benefits or burdens of legislation. The failure to give Saturday-closing retailers the same benefits as Sunday-closing retailers was therefore unacceptable to Wilson.

Justices La Forest and Beetz also broke with the majority on this issue, but for reasons very different from those of Wilson. Whereas all the other judges thought that the legislature had a duty to accommodate those who observe Saturday as a holy day, Beetz saw no need to cater to a person's "deliberate choice" to give priority to religious beliefs over economic considerations. La Forest considered that if the courts prescribed a duty to accommodate non-Sunday observers, a new set of problems would arise that would be too complex for the adjudicative process to handle effectively. He noted that the creation of exemptions always leads to additional policy problems about how to treat fairly those who are detrimentally affected by the exemptions. He pointed out that in five provinces Sunday-closing legislation did not provide exemptions for Saturday observers, and he doubted whether the courts were capable of effectively judging the policy implications of each of these laws. It was his view that decisions about exemptions are apt to be more solid if made by executive and legislative branch policy-makers who have the tools of policy research and analysis at their disposal. "These choices require an in-depth knowledge of all the circumstances. They are choices a court is not in a position to make." In effect, La Forest urged the Court not to accept a policy-making role under the Charter in cases where this role could reasonably be avoided.

Having dealt with the first and second prongs of the second part of the *Oakes* test in great detail, the majority had no difficulty in finding that the Sunday-closing legislation passed muster regarding the third prong of the test. Dickson concluded that "the infringement is not disproportionate to the legislative objectives. A serious effort has been made to accommodate the freedom of religion of Saturday-observers."

The Impact of the Decision

The Ontario Sunday-closing case was one of the most difficult faced by the Supreme Court. Not only are the issues raised by the case extremely complex, but the Court was under pressure to render its judgment more quickly than it otherwise might have. Most observers expected the Court to issue its decision late in the fall of 1986. In early December the Court had not been heard from, and several large retail outlets, notably The Bay and Simpsons, announced that they would remain open on Sundays to accommodate the Christmas shopping season. The stores evidently anticipated that the Court would strike down the Sunday-closing legislation. The Ontario attorney general interpreted the stores' actions as a flagrant disregard of the principle of the rule of law, and announced that all violators would be prosecuted. As more and more stores chose to remain open on Sundays to compete with the stores that had already so decided, it became questionable whether the Sunday-closing law could be adequately enforced.

It was against this background that the Court announced its decision on December 19. Some weaknesses in the decision are therefore to be expected. For example, the decision does little to clarify the principle from *Oakes* that legislation that is to be upheld under section 1 cannot infringe a Charter right more than is reasonably possible. It is not clear whether the Sunday-closing laws in the five provinces that do not accommodate Saturday observers will be ruled unconstitutional because they do not go far enough to minimize their infringement on freedom of religion. Has the Ontario approach become the "minimum standard" other provinces must now follow? Moreover, the Court did not tackle the question of whether the legislature must attempt to accommodate those whose holy day is other than Saturday or Sunday. The majority stated that this was because no evidence was presented concerning the issue.

Another freedom of religion issue that the Supreme Court has considered concerns whether freedom of religion means that religious schools can operate without the necessity of obtaining a government permit. The Court decided in *Jones* that religious schools should not be exempt from meeting provincial education requiremnts as long as these do not "unduly encroach" on religious convictions [93]. The

Jones and *Edwards* decisions both illustrate that while the Court considers freedom of religion to be important, like other human rights, it cannot be considered absolute.

It is ironic that after winning the court battle, the Ontario government has decided to repeal its Sunday-closing legislation and replace it with legislation that will give municipalities the responsibility to set Sunday-closing regulations. Given the Supreme Court's emphasis on the need for a legislature to minimize indirect and unintentional violations of freedom of religion, it is open to question whether the new legislation will be found constitutional. All that is certain is that the Sunday-closing issue is in its early innings in the courts.

The Right to Picket and to Strike

Since December 1986, the Supreme Court has made two major decisions concerning the right to strike. The first of these was *Retail, Wholesale and Department Store Union, Local 580 v. Dolphin Delivery* [112].

The Dolphin Delivery Case

Dolphin Delivery is a Vancouver courier company that had been receiving about a fifth of its business from another courier company, Purolator, for whom it was doing deliveries. In June 1981 Purolator locked out its employees in a labour dispute, and Dolphin Delivery continued to make deliveries indirectly for Purolator, which was handling business through a third company, Supercourier. In November 1982 the union representing the Purolator employees gave notice to Dolphin Delivery that the union would picket Dolphin Delivery unless it ceased doing business with Supercourier. Dolphin Delivery, opposed to the threatened picketing, applied for a court order that such picketing would be illegal.

Although most labour relations matters fall under the jurisdiction of provincial governments, this particular dispute fell under federal jurisdiction because it dealt with an industry engaged in interprovincial transportation and communications. The Canada Labour Code, however, did not specify whether the union should be allowed to picket in a case like this. Therefore, the legality of the picketing would have to be determined according to common law. Pending this determination, Dolphin Delivery obtained a B.C. Supreme Court injunction ordering the union not to picket until the legal issue could be resolved. The union appealed the decision to grant the injunction on the grounds that it violated the freedom of expression protected by section 2(b) of the Charter. After losing in the B.C. Court of Appeal, the union appealed again to the Supreme Court of Canada.

In addition to considering whether the injunction represented a violation of the Charter, the Court had to deal with two more basic issues. First, because the determination of the issue depended on the common law, the Court had to decide whether the Charter can apply to the common law. Second, because the dispute was between private parties, the Court had to decide whether the Charter applies to private litigation.

Application of the Charter to the Common Law

Justice William McIntyre, who wrote the majority opinion, had no difficulty in finding that the Charter can override the common law when the two conflict. Section 52 of the Constitution Act, 1982, which defines the formal constitution of Canada, declares that the constitution, which includes the Charter, is the "supreme law of Canada, and any law that is inconsistent with . . . the Constitution is . . . of no force or effect." The Court considered that the phrase "any law" is clearly broad enough to include the common law. What remained to be considered was whether the Charter applied to *all* common law or just to common law in the public rather than the private sphere.

Application of the Charter to Private Law

The question about the application of the Charter to private litigation governed by the common law rather than by statutes was more difficult to answer. Section 32 of the Charter states that the Charter applies to Parliament, legislatures and governments in Canada. At the time of the Charter's adoption, the majority of legal scholars thought that section 32 meant that the Charter applied to public law litigation — that is, disputes in which a government was a party — but not usually to private law litigation — that is, disputes between private individuals or corporations. It was generally accepted, however, that some private law cases would have Charter implications, such as cases that relied on statutes dealing with private law that might infringe the Charter. The Court had confirmed this application of the Charter to the private law in the *Skapinker* case [47](discussed in chapter 2).

Moreover, some, like Peter Hogg (1), thought the Charter would also apply to private law cases determined solely according to common law if the common law authorized a court to make an order that violated the Charter. According to this view, the word "government" in section 32 of the Charter should be interpreted as meaning the institutions that govern a country, including the courts. Since the time of Montesquieu, political scientists have thought of government as containing three branches — the legislature, the executive and the judiciary. From this perspective, the law created by the courts — the common law — would have to conform to the Charter to the extent that the courts take governmental action — that is, make orders. Mr. Justice William McIntyre rejected this interpretation of section 32. The word "government" is sometimes used narrowly to mean only the executive branch of government, and he concluded that this is how the word should be interpreted in section 32. Thus, he claimed, court orders in the private law field made solely pursuant to the common law are not subject to the Charter, unless the action of government is involved.

McIntyre reasoned that to expand the definition of "government" in section 32 to include the courts would result in the Charter applying to practically all private litigation, since all private law cases end with court orders unless they are settled out of court. None of the Supreme Court judges who heard the *Dolphin Delivery* case were willing to countenance so broad an application of the Charter. Nevertheless, McIntyre stated that the "judiciary ought to apply and develop the principles of common law in a manner consistent with the fundamental values enshrined in the Constitution." This statement raises the question of why the judges would be so insistent on excluding common-law Charter claims dealing with private law if they intend to interpret the common law consistently with the Charter anyway. The answer may be that formal Charter litigation with regard to private matters regulated by the common law would present the courts in Canada with countless issues that would not only take them further into the policy-making realm, but could increase the backlogs of cases.

Although the Court's approach to private litigation is understandable given that from the beginning it was generally accepted that the Charter would not apply to most private litigation, the decision is problematic. In the *Dolphin Delivery* case the Court affirmed that the regulations created by "creatures of Parliament and the Legislatures," such as municipal councils, marketing boards, and regulatory agencies such as the CRTC (Canadian Radio-television and Telecommunications Commission), are subject to the Charter. The courts, however, are also creations of either Parliament or legislatures, and yet the regulations they create, known as the common law, are *not* subject to the Charter. It seems incongruous to exempt the courts from the Charter in this way.

The Freedom of Expression Issue

It was clear to Mr. Justice McIntyre that picketing is a form of expression and is therefore protected by section 2(b) of the Charter in all public law cases and in private law cases where the constitutionality of a statute or regulation is an issue. McIntryre wrote, "The union is making a statement to the general public that it is involved in a dispute, that it is seeking to impose its will on the object of the picketing, and that it solicits the assistance of the public in honouring the picket line." The only judge who disagreed with this reasoning was Mr. Justice Beetz, who maintained an approach consistent with the one he had developed in the *Dupond* case [1] (see chapter 1). In that case, Beetz, writing for the majority, could find no element of expression in a political demonstration.

Because of the Court's reasoning that private law cases decided under common law were not covered by the Charter, the union lost the case. Because the Court found no Charter violation, there was no need for the Court to consider whether an injunction that violated freedom of expression could be upheld under section 1. However, the Court decided to comment on this issue anyway in an attempt to clarify the law. Without applying the two-part, three-pronged test in *Oakes,* McIntyre simply concluded that because Supercourier was a third party not directly involved in the labour dispute, it would be reasonable to limit freedom of expression in order to prevent harm to the third party: "It is reasonable to restrain picketing so that the conflict will not escalate beyond the actual parties. While picketing is, no doubt, a legislative weapon to be employed in a labour dispute by the employees against their employer, it should not be permitted to harm others."

Although Madame Justice Wilson agreed with McIntyre's conclusion on this issue, she was critical of the way in which he reached it, and so wrote a separate opinion in which she dissented in part. She would have preferred the careful application of the *Oakes* test to the facts of the case, rather than McIntyre's quick assumption that preventing harm to a third party obviously constitutes a reasonable limit. Wilson's point is sound. At the very least, a carefully reasoned argument on this point would help to insulate the courts from the often-heard criticism that judges tend to be more sympathetic to business interests than to union claims.

In a later case, the Supreme Court found that picketing is protected by section 2(b) but that to prohibit the picketing of courthouses is a reasonable limit under section 1. In this decision, known as the *BCGEU* case [21], the issue was whether the British Columbia Government Employees Union could be prohibited from picketing at the entrances to courthouses. The union went on strike on November 1, 1983, as part of a general labour protest against the government's new restrictive labour legislation. When the chief justice of the B.C. Supreme Court arrived at the Vancouver Courthouse at 8:00 a.m. on November 1, he immediately issued an injunction prohibiting picketing at courthouses. He issued the injunction on his own motion and acting *ex parte* (meaning that the union's side was not presented). The order made provision for the union to apply for an order to set aside the injunction. The union applied for such an order, but the application was dismissed. The union appealed all the way to the Supreme Court of Canada, primarily on the grounds that the injunction violated the right to freedom of expression in section 2(b) of the Charter.

The main decision of the Supreme Court, written by Chief Justice Dickson, relied on the *Dolphin Delivery* decision to the effect that picketing is a form of expression protected by section 2(b). However, Dickson concluded that the injunction was a reasonable limit under section 1. The objective of the injunction — "assuring unimpeded access to the courts" — was of sufficient importance to pass the first part of the *Oakes* test. This is because access to the courts is necessary to preserve the rule of law and also to protect the rights in the Charter itself. The injunction also met all three requirements in the second part of the *Oakes* test. In particular, the injunction restricted the right of union members as little as possible by leaving "the Union and its members free to express themselves in other places" and by providing for a method whereby the injunction could be challenged. Moreover, the chief justice refrained from using a more restrictive procedure — charging picketers with contempt of court for blocking access to the courts.

> Finally, there was a proportionality between the effects of the injunction on the protected right and the objective of

maintaining access to the court . . . . A significant element
. . . of the objective of the injunction order was to protect
Charter rights [by allowing litigants to continue to bring
Charter claims to court]. The Charter surely does not self-
destruct in a dynamic of conflicting rights.

Thus, although the Supreme Court has recognized that union picketing is protected by section 2(b) of the Charter, in two decisions the
Charter was interpreted in a way that in the end was of no assistance
to the union cause.

The Alberta Labour Reference [76]

During the 1970s and early 1980s, there were several strikes in
Alberta involving nurses and public servants. In 1983 the legislature
amended its labour legislation to prohibit strikes and lockouts involving public servants, hospital employees, firefighters and nurses. (The
police were already prohibited from striking.) The legislation
provided for compulsory arbitration to settle disputes involving these
employees, limited the matters the arbitration boards could consider,
and required the boards to consider the government's fiscal goals.

As Leo Panitch and Donald Swartz have recounted, labour leaders
in the province strongly opposed the 1983 amendments. They claimed
that these amendments violated section 2(d) of the Charter —
freedom of association. In order to settle the issue, the government
referred the question of the constitutionality of the legislation to the
Alberta Court of Appeal. This court could find no protection of a right
to strike in section 2(d). The unions appealed this decision to the
Supreme Court of Canada. In the meantime, Premier Peter Lougheed
announced that if the Supreme Court found a right to strike in the
Charter, the legislation would be re-enacted with a section 33 override
attached to it. It became unnecessary for the government to use
section 33 when the Supreme Court upheld the Alberta Court of
Appeal decision.

The Majority Decision

The opinion of the majority on why freedom of association does not
imply the right to strike was written by Mr. Justice McIntyre. He
described six approaches to defining the meaning of freedom of
association. Beginning with the most conservative, they are as follows:

- Freedom of association means simply "the right to associate with others in common pursuits." However, the government may limit the "objects" or "actions" of groups.
- Freedom of association means "the freedom [of groups] to engage collectively in those activities which are constitutionally protected for each individual."
- Freedom of association means that whatever persons may lawfully do as individuals, they "are entitled to do in concert with others."
- Freedom of association means that groups have a right to engage in "collective activities which may be said to be fundamental to our culture and traditions."
- Freedom of association means that groups have a right to engage in those activities "which are essential to the lawful goals" of the group.
- Freedom of association means that groups have a right to engage in any activity, subject to reasonable limits pursuant to section 1 of the Charter.

Having established these six choices, McIntyre described the last three as "unacceptable." From his perspective, the Charter is a document designed primarily to protect *individual* rights. Denominational school rights, continued by section 29, and aboriginal rights, protected by section 25 of the Charter, are listed as the only two exceptions to this general rule.

The purpose of freedom of association, according to McIntyre, is to protect the individual's right of association, not to establish a third category of group rights. To illustrate the problems that might arise when groups may do what individuals cannot, he cited the example of a gun club claiming the right of its members to bear arms, although individuals not belonging to the club could not claim such a right. For McIntyre, only the first three approaches to freedom of association are acceptable, as they do not create special group rights. Lest some might think this approach would trivialize the concept of freedom of association, McIntyre quoted from de Tocqueville to the effect that the individual right to associate with others is "inalienable" and one of the "foundations of society."

The Minority Decision

Chief Justice Dickson, in a decision concurred in by Madame Justice Wilson, attacked the majority's definition of freedom of association as being "legalistic, ungenerous, indeed vapid." If freedom of association merely allows individuals to do in concert with others what they are free to do alone, then the "express conferral of a freedom of association [in section 2(d)] is unnecessary." Dickson described how individual workers are powerless if they bargain individually with management. Unless unions have the power to strike, unions and management cannot bargain as relative equals. He related how the collective-bargaining process, including the right of unions to strike, had led to a general atmosphere of labour peace. In addition, collective bargaining, with the strike as the ultimate weapon, had resulted in workers having a say in the conditions of their employment and thus in promoting their "sense of identity, self worth and emotional well-being." He noted that there is no individual equivalent of the right to strike and that section 2(d) was intended to prevent legislatures from "precluding associational conduct because of its concerted or associational nature." In other words, the freedom to belong to a labour union is of little value if the union cannot engage in the one activity that makes it viable — the strike.

If we consider these formal, legal arguments, the Dickson-Wilson approach seems more convincing. However, almost as an aside, the majority gave another reason for not finding a right to strike in section 2(d): the inappropriateness of courts as policy-makers in the labour relations field. McIntyre pointed out that the history of labour relations in Canada had proven that "specialized labour tribunals are better suited than courts for resolving labour problems."

> Judges do not have the expert knowledge always helpful and sometimes necessary in the resolution of labour problems . . . . If the right to strike is constitutionalized, then [labour disputes] become matters of law. This would inevitably throw the courts back into the field of labour relations and much of the value of specialized labour tribunals would be lost.

Mr. Justice Le Dain, with Beetz and La Forest concurring, made the same point: "It is surprising that in an area in which this Court has affirmed a principle of judicial restraint in the review of administrative action we should be considering the substitution of our judgment for that of the legislature." If the right to strike is constitutionalized, then every piece of back-to-work legislation and every statute limiting the right to strike of essential employees will likely be the subject of a court challenge.

Although this argument has nothing to do with the attempt to give a legal definition to section 2(d), it is more convincing than the main reasons of the majority. For several decades, progressive labour lawyers have been imploring judges to exercise restraint and stay out of labour disputes as much as possible. Since not many judges are from labour backgrounds or have experience in industrial relations, they have shown a remarkable ability to make unenlightened decisions in this field. The labour relations boards that exist in all jurisdictions in Canada were established as an alternative to courts, and the consensus of legal scholars is that these boards have shown much more wisdom in dealing with labour disputes than have the courts. From this perspective, the majority decision in the *Alberta Labour Reference* shows good sense. The Court has bowed to legislative supremacy not because legislative supremacy is sacrosanct, but because the legislative-administrative wing of government is more likely to produce effective policies regarding the right to strike than are the courts.

The weakness of this approach is that it does not recognize that denying a constitutional protection for the right to strike is quite different from judicial restraint in the face of ordinary legislation. The denial of a constitutional right to strike is apt to be interpreted by many as a judicial stamp of approval for an anti-labour government's program of severely restricting the right to strike. Armed with this weapon, such a government might be tempted to go very far in trying to reduce the power of organized labour, resulting in an increasingly hostile labour climate in Canada.

For example, not long after the Supreme Court decision, the United Nurses of Alberta, which had been denied the right to strike, decided to stage an illegal strike. The government's strategy was to deal harshly with the strikers, who could now be accused not only of breaking the law, but also of ignoring the constitution. Tension between the strikers and the government was far greater than during any of the previous legal nurses' strikes in the province, and the dispute continued well into a third week. One of the demands of the nurses was the repeal of the anti-strike legislation. In the end, the nurses were able to attract a fair amount of public sympathy because of their surprisingly low wages. A negotiated settlement was reached, and the government agreed to reconsider its anti-strike legislation. It is quite likely that had the Supreme Court found a right to strike in section 2(d) of the Charter, the nurses' strike would have been settled considerably sooner.

Chief Justice Dickson explained how he would have decided the section 1 issue (whether limiting the right to strike is a reasonable limit) if the majority had found a right to strike in section 2(d). He stated that "the protection of services which are truly essential . . . is a legislative objective of sufficient importance" to pass the first part of the *Oakes* test. Dickson concluded, however, that the legislation would not pass the second part of the test. Although it was clear that the police and firefighters provide essential services — that is, services "whose interruption would endanger" the life, personal safety, health, security or the rule of law regarding all or part of the population — Dickson said that the crown had failed to show why public servants and hospital employees other than nurses or doctors should be considered essential. Thus, part of the legislation failed the "rational connection" prong of the second part of the *Oakes* test. Moreover, the legislation, in Dickson's opinion, did not encroach on the right to freedom of association as little as possible. For example, the legislation left it to the discretion of a government board whether an arbitration board should be established during a labour dispute or whether bargaining or mediation should continue indefinitely. Furthermore, the legislation totally excluded certain matters from being referred to arbitration, and the crown could not justify these exclusions.

The kind of reasoning the chief justice pursued with regard to section 1 is indicative of the kind of approach that, if section 2(d) were considered to include a right to strike, the courts would have to adopt in every case in which a legislature limited the right to strike. The question Canadians need to consider is whether the majority was correct in concluding that the courts are not the appropriate body to make these kinds of decisions. It may well be that the majority's decision will become accepted as the best course of action. On the other hand, if the majority is considered to have erred, it would be possible for section 2(d) to be amended to include an explicit right to strike.

Other Right-to-Strike Cases

The Court decided two other right-to-strike cases concurrently with the *Alberta Labour Reference*. These cases concerned the federal "6 and 5" wage restraint legislation of 1982 and the back-to-work legislation enacted by the Saskatchewan government in 1984 to resolve the dairy workers' strike. In both cases, the majority decided that the impugned legislation was constitutional for the same reasons as were given in the *Alberta Labour Reference*. Justices Dickson and Wilson dissented in both cases, concluding that violations of section 2(d) had occurred. Their reasoning about the application of section 1 provides a further example of the kinds of issues judges would have to consider if the Charter is ever amended to include an explicit right to strike.

The Public Service Alliance Case [66]

The federal 6-and-5 wage restraint legislation extended all collective agreements or arbitration awards for two years for federal public sector employees and railway workers. In addition, public servants and railway workers had their compensation increases limited to 6 per cent in the first year and 5 per cent in the second year. Other employers in areas falling under federal jurisdiction were urged, but not required, to adopt a similar program to fight inflation.

Chief Justice Dickson concluded that, with one exception, the federal legislation passed the section 1 test. The exception was that part of the legislation that prohibited collective bargaining regarding non-compensatory matters such as employee safety, management rights, grievance procedures, seniority, and employee participation in partisan political activity. Dickson could find no rational connection between these prohibitions and the government's objective — the control of inflation. Dickson had been urged by the union to conclude that the entire 6-and-5 program was not rationally connected with the objective of fighting inflation — some economists had testified that the strategy was not working. Dickson, however, rejected the broader argument because

> it would be highly undesirable for the courts to attempt to pronounce on the relative importance of various suggested causes of inflation, such as the expansion of the money supply, fiscal deficits, foreign inflation, or the built-in inflationary expectations of individual economic actors. A high degree of deference ought properly to be accorded to

the government's choice of economic strategy in combatting this complex problem.

This is a good example of how judges may avoid a policy-making role by deferring to the policy decisions of the legislative and executive branches.

Madame Justice Wilson would have rejected the entirety of the 6-and-5 legislation according to the section 1 test. She considered that the singling out of public sector employees and railway workers for harsher treatment than other employees under federal jurisdiction was arbitrary and not rationally connected with the goal of fighting inflation. She also concluded that the 6-and-5 legislation, by treating public sector employees more strictly, violated the guarantee in the Canadian Bill of Rights to "equality before the law and the protection of the law." (The union had raised the equality question under the Bill because the Charter's equality clause, section 15, had not yet come into effect.)

The fact that the judges were called upon to make policy decisions about the causes and cures of inflation — something that is definitely not an adjudicative function — indicates that the majority of the Court may have been wise in avoiding this kind of issue entirely by interpreting section 2(d) as not including a right to strike.

The Saskatchewan Dairy Workers Case [122]

In the case involving Saskatchewan's back-to-work legislation for the dairy workers, the chief justice concluded that the legislation passed the section 1 test. From his perspective, the reason why the banning of strikes in essential services should be considered a reasonable limit to the right to strike is to prevent third parties from being "unduly harmed." In the case of the dairy workers' strike, the strike, if continued, would result in undue harm to milk producers because of "three unusual features: (i) the producer in this case was the sole outlet for the suppliers' only product; (ii) the produce in question was highly perishable; and (iii) because of the biological imperatives of the cow, the supplier could not mitigate losses by ceasing production."

Madame Justice Wilson, however, was not convinced by the evidence submitted to the Court that the dairy workers' strike would cause undue hardship to milk producers. She pointed out that the crown had presented no evidence at all about the effects of the strike on the producers. The only evidence came from newspaper articles submitted, but by the union, not the crown. Wilson considered the published interviews with union officials, dairy managers and farmers to be "completely self-serving," and therefore unreliable. Although she seemed prepared to consider the back-to-work legislation as a reasonable limit if appropriate evidence was produced, she concluded that "the government has simply failed to discharge its onus under s. 1." It is possible that Dickson's greater willingness to accept the evidence might be related to his familiarity with farm issues on account of his western Canadian, rural roots.

The Language of Commercial Signs in Quebec

The Canadian political system can be regarded as a complex experiment around the issue of whether the members of two linguistic groups, anglophones and francophones, can each fulfil their aspirations in a federal liberal democracy in which the most numerous group is dominant in nine out of ten provinces. There are many complicating factors in this experiment. Because the language of the majority is also the dominant language of North America and the language of commerce and science in most of the world, the members of the majority group have never known what it is like to have a mother tongue that is in danger of extinction. Thus, they have difficulty in appreciating the concerns of the francophone minority, which regards the preservation of the endangered French language and culture in North America as a goal of overriding concern.

Since they form a majority in Quebec, francophones have used the provincial government as a vehicle for preserving and promoting their language within Quebec by requiring the use of French in the workplace and limiting the use of English. However, Quebec is also a liberal society that values human rights, such as freedom of expression. Thus, the collective desire of the francophone community to preserve and promote its language has come into direct collision with the liberal ideal of individual freedom of expression.

Another dimension to the issue is the lingering resentment among some in the francophone community against previous generations of anglophone Quebeckers, some of whom regarded themselves as the superior class in Quebec society. Such a "social hangover" is apt to lead to emotional overreactions on both sides. The public tensions emanating from this situation cannot help but be taken into account by the government when drafting language policy and by judges when engaging in policy-making pursuant to the Charter.

Bill 101 and Civil Liberties Legislation

In 1977 the Parti Québécois government enacted Bill 101, the Charter of the French Language. Among many other provisions, the bill prohibited the use of English on most commercial signs, although in some cases (such as for stores with not more than four employees) English or another language could be used alongside French. These provisions were designed primarily to tackle the language issue in Montreal, where the great majority of anglophones resided. From the perspective of the Parti Québécois, the problem was not the use of English by anglophones, but the image of anglophone dominance that English signs presented to immigrants (whom the Quebec government wanted to assimilate into the francophone community) and to the francophones themselves.

It should be pointed out that Bill 101 guaranteed to anglophones and other linguistic minorities the untrammelled right to use their language for political, social, cultural and educational purposes. Newspapers, television stations, radio stations and educational institutions were exempted from the bill's signs and advertising provisions. The commercial signs provisions of Bill 101 were designed to give the streets of Quebec a "French look," with the hope that everyone would absorb the message that the French language is a permanent fixture in Quebec, not the quaint relic of an ethnic minority on the road to assimilation.

There was some question as to whether these provisions violated the Quebec Charter of Human Rights and Freedoms, which had been enacted by the Liberal government in 1975. Section 3 of the Quebec Charter of Rights states that "[e]very person is the possessor of . . . freedom of expression," and section 10 declares that "[e]very person has a right to full and equal recognition and exercise of his human rights and freedoms, without distinction . . . based on [among other categories] language." However, section 9.1 of the Quebec Charter of Rights is a limitations clause that the PQ claimed would save Bill 101 against a challenge from the Quebec Charter of Rights. Section 9.1 reads as follows:

> In exercising his fundamental freedoms and rights, a person shall maintain a proper regard for democratic values,

public order and the general well-being of the citizens of Quebec.

In this respect, the scope of the freedoms and rights, and limits to their exercise, may be fixed by law.

When the Canadian Charter of Rights and Freedoms came into effect in 1982, the PQ provincial government enacted a blanket override of the Charter as a protest against being excluded from the 1982 constitutional accord. The override legislation amended all Quebec statutes enacted prior to 1982, including Bill 101, so that each statute would contain a clause stating that it would operate notwithstanding sections 2 and 7-15 of the Charter. As well, the government routinely included a Charter override clause in each piece of legislation passed after the blanket override, including an amendment to Bill 101 enacted in 1983 but which came into force in 1984. This practice of overriding the Canadian Charter was discontinued by the Quebec Liberal government elected in 1985, but the previous overrides remained in effect for their natural five-year life spans.

The Challenges to Bill 101

In 1978 Allan Singer, a stationer in the predominantly anglophone Montreal suburb of Pointe Claire, was charged with continuing to display his store sign (as he had for thirty years) in English only in contravention of Bill 101. He was convicted. Then, in conjunction with several other merchants, he sought a declaration from the Quebec Superior Court that the guarantees of equality and freedom of expression in the Quebec Charter of Rights nullified the commercial signs provisions of Bill 101, including those allowing English signs on smaller stores as long as French was also used. The case became known as *Devine v. Quebec* [28] after one of the other merchants. Singer lost in the Quebec Superior Court and the Quebec Court of Appeal, but went on to appeal to the Supreme Court of Canada. In the Supreme Court, the Canadian Charter became an issue because one of the override clauses that protected Bill 101 from Charter scrutiny had expired. In addition, lawyers for Devine and Singer argued that the override procedures used by the Quebec legislature were procedurally incorrect and therefore not effective.

Meanwhile, another somewhat different challenge to Bill 101 was developing. In 1984 several merchants, including Brown's Shoe Store, brought a motion before the Quebec Superior Court requesting a declaration that the provisions of Bill 101 that prohibited English contravened both the Quebec Charter of Rights and the Canadian Charter of Rights. (Unlike Singer and Devine, these merchants did not object to using bilingual signs, but only to the provisions making French the exclusive language of signs.) As in the *Devine* case, lawyers for these merchants argued that the procedures used by the Quebec legislature to override of the Canadian Charter were ineffective. This case became known as *Ford v. Quebec* [33]. Ford and the other merchants were successful in obtaining the declaratory judgment striking down parts of Bill 101. The Quebec government unsuccessfully appealed to the Quebec Court of Appeal in 1986. Quebec then appealed to the Supreme Court of Canada.

The Supreme Court released its judgment for both the *Ford* and *Devine* cases on December 15, 1988. In both decisions, only one opinion was presented, and it was attributed to the entire panel consisting of Dickson, Beetz, McIntyre, Lamer and Wilson. (Estey and Le Dain had participated in the hearing but resigned from the Court after the hearing and took no part in preparing the judgment.) The *Ford* case, in which the major issue was whether the Quebec government could prohibit French-only signs without violating either the Quebec Charter of Rights or the Canadian Charter, will be considered first below. The judgment in *Ford* will then be compared to that in *Devine,* in which the chief issue was whether the Quebec government could require bilingual signs.

The Ford Case and the Issue of French-Only Signs [37]

The *Ford* case dealt with four major issues:

- the effectiveness of Quebec's blanket override of the Canadian Charter of Rights and Freedoms;
- whether the prohibition of English on signs violates freedom of expression as protected by section 2(b) of the Canadian Charter and section 3 of the Quebec Charter of Rights;
- if freedom of expression has been violated, whether it can be justified pursuant to the limitations clauses in the Canadian Charter (section 1) or the Quebec Charter of Rights (section 9.1); and
- whether the prohibition of English on signs violates the guarantee of equality in section 10 of the Quebec Charter of Rights.

The Effectiveness of Quebec's Blanket Override

The merchants succeeded in the Quebec Court of Appeal. They had argued that the words "expressly" and "provision" in section 33 of the Canadian Charter (see the Appendix) imply that when a legislature wishes to override the Charter, it must state precisely which provisions of an act are to take precedence over the Charter. As well, the merchants claimed that the legislature must declare which particular rights contained in section 2 or sections 7-15 are to be overridden. To this submission was added the argument that the democratic process requires legislators to deliberate about the specific implications of the overrides being contemplated. It was suggested that these required procedures are defeated both by the blanket override and by the routine override used after 1982.

The Supreme Court was not persuaded by these arguments. The Court claimed that the position of the merchants amounted to a claim that section 33 was a directive to legislatures to deliberate about the use of the override in a particular way. The Court held that, on the contrary, section 33 is a merely procedural set of instructions. All that is required to meet the requirements of section 33 is for a legislature to state which section numbers in the Charter are to be overridden. Thus, both the blanket override applying to pre-1982 statutes and the routine overrides used since that time are effective. (The Court also decided that a legislature could not enact a retroactive override of the Charter. In other words, the earliest that an override could become effective would be the date of proclamation of the override legislation.)

As a result of the Court's view of section 33, section 58 of Bill 101 — which prohibits "public signs and posters and commercial advertising" unless they are in French — was still protected from the Canadian Charter at the time of the hearing thanks to an amendment to Bill 101 proclaimed in 1984. Of course, section 58 was still subject to the Quebec Charter of Rights. However, section 69 of Bill 101, which allows only "the French version of a firm name" to be used on signs in Quebec, was subject to the Canadian Charter because the section 33 override that applied to section 69 had expired, having been enacted in 1982. (It will be remembered that section 33 overrides automatically expire after five years.)

The argument of the merchants about the need for careful deliberation about the use of section 33 constitutes an example of a good point raised in the wrong forum. From a legal standpoint, the Supreme

Court's conclusion that section 33 is merely procedural is sound. From the perspective of democratic theory, the merchants' argument that section 33 requires more than routine consideration by legislatures is compelling. It is the kind of issue that should be considered not in a court, but by the politically aware Canadian public with a view to pressing for reforms either in section 33 or in legislative procedure in general that would force legislators to consider more carefully the invocation of section 33. For example, section 33 could be amended to require public hearings before its application in normal circumstances or afterwards during emergencies.

Freedom of Expression

As noted in chapter 2, the Supreme Court has declared that it will interpret similar phrases similarly in the Canadian Charter and the various statutory bills of rights, such as the Quebec Charter of Rights. Therefore, the Court will give "freedom of expression" in section 2(b) of the Canadian Charter the same meaning as "freedom of expression" in section 3 of the Quebec Charter of Rights.

The Court broke the question of the meaning of "freedom of expression" into two sub-issues: (1) whether "freedom of expression" includes the language in which ideas are expressed or merely the ideas themselves, and (2) whether "freedom of expression" includes commercial expression.

Counsel for the Quebec government had argued that the purpose of freedom of expression in a liberal democracy is to protect the expression of ideas themselves, not the medium (language) in which the ideas are expressed. Counsel suggested that the ability to present ideas is a "freedom" in the traditional liberal sense, whereas the ability to use a particular language to express these ideas is a privilege that can be regulated by government within the confines of the language rights sections of the constitution. Because the language rights sections of the constitution (sections 16-23 of the Canadian Charter and section 133 of the Constitution Act, 1867) provide specific but limited guarantees of language privileges, such privileges were not intended by the constitution to be broadened by being considered as included in section 2(b).

The Court rejected this suggested approach. Of the language rights sections of the constitution, the Court said that they are intended to impose obligations on government . . . [to provide] specific opportunities [for Canadians] to use English or French, or to receive services in English or French, in concrete, readily ascertainable and limited circumstances. In contrast, what the respondents seek in this case is a freedom as that term was explained by Dickson . . . [in the *Big M* decision]: "Freedom can primarily be characterized by the absence of coercion or restraint. If a person is compelled by the state . . . to a course of action or inaction which he would not otherwise have chosen, he is not acting of his own volition and he cannot be said to be truly free."

Because merchants are compelled not to use English, their freedom of expression is constrained. Moreover, the Court quoted from sociological evidence to the effect that "[l]anguage itself is content, a reference for . . . the societal goals and the large-scale value-laden arenas of interaction that typify every speech community." This respect for language, the Court claimed, had been adopted by the Charter of the French Language itself, which stated in its preamble that "the French language [is] the distinctive language of a people . . . [and] the instrument by which that people has articulated its identity." The Court concluded that language is

a means by which a people may express its cultural identity. It is also the means by which the individual expresses his or her personal identity and sense of individuality . . . . That suggests that "freedom of expression" is intended to extend to more than the content of expression in its narrow sense.

Therefore, freedom of expression includes the freedom to express ideas in the language of choice, and not merely the freedom to express ideas in the language specified by the government.

On the question of whether freedom of expression includes commercial expression, the Court referred to U.S. case law on this question for possible guidance. The U.S. Supreme Court had decided that the First Amendment guarantee of freedom of speech included commercial speech. It pointed out that freedom of commercial speech protects audiences (listeners) as well as advertisers and that audiences may have a "keener by far" interest in obtaining information about commercial products than "in the day's most urgent political debate" [133]. However, the American judges had also decided that commercial speech deserved a lesser degree of protection than political speech.

The Court noted that the U.S. judges had been subjected to much criticism for their approach to commercial speech because of the difficulty in drawing the line between "commercial speech" and "political speech." As a result, the Canadian judges rejected the American approach of dividing expression into two types — commercial and non-commercial — and then providing less protection to non-commercial speech. However, they accepted the argument that commercial speech is important because it protects audiences as well as advertisers:

> Given the earlier pronouncements of this Court to the effect that the rights and freedoms guaranteed in the Canadian Charter should be given a large and liberal interpretation, there is no sound basis on which commercial expression can be excluded from the protection of s.2(b) .... Over and above its intrinsic value as expression, commercial expression which, as has been pointed out, protects listeners as well as speakers, plays a significant role in enabling individuals to make informed economic choices, an important aspect of individual self-fulfillment and personal autonomy.

This conclusion demonstrates how judges, because of their social backgrounds and practice experience, may be sympathetic to the claims of commercial interests. (In contrast, they may be uncomfortable with the claims of labour, as the right-to-strike cases discussed earlier demonstrated.) Although the Court's reasoning about the value of commercial speech does have some merit, to suggest that the sign on Brown's Shoe Store — "Bravo Bravo. Brown's quality, Bravo's price" — is as important to human freedom as the ability to debate publicly the ideals of Christ, Locke and Marx, for example, seems to be stretching the point. One of the implications of this decision is that all statutes that regulate advertising, such as those restricting tobacco advertising or advertising directed towards children, will now be subject to Charter challenges. Just as the Court found a way out of adjudicating the right-to-strike cases under the Charter, it could also have avoided the commercial advertising cases by declaring that commercial advertising is not protected by freedom of expression.

Whether the Commercial Signs Provisions Are a "Reasonable Limit"

The attorney general of Quebec submitted as evidence a number of studies in sociolinguistics concerning the dangers faced by the French language in Quebec. These studies indicated that the French language in Canada is threatened with extinction because of the declining proportion of the francophone population, the tendency of francophones outside Quebec to assimilate, the usual practice of immigrants to Quebec of assimilating with the anglophone population, and the anglophone domination of the upper echelons of the business community. The studies showed that prior to Bill 101, the heavy use of English on commercial signs in Montreal suggested to new immigrants that to learn English was as acceptable, or perhaps more acceptable, than learning French; to francophones that English was the language of the future; and to anglophones that there was no need to learn French. The purpose of the commercial signs provisions of Bill 101 was to change this *visage linguistique,* or linguistic impression, of Quebec (and particularly Montreal) and to promote the use of French among all language groups.

The Court concluded that the studies demonstrated the importance of the government's objective in enacting the commercial signs provisions of Bill 101. Thus, the first part of the *Oakes* test for the acceptance of reasonable limits to rights — that the government's objective must be of substantial importance — was met. Moving to the second part of *Oakes,* the Court concluded that there was a rational connection between the signs provisions of Bill 101 and the goal of preserving and promoting the French language. However, the judges reasoned that the commercial signs provisions failed to limit freedom of expression as little as necessary to achieve the goal of preserving and promoting the French language. In other words, the sociolinguistic studies did not

> demonstrate that the requirement of the use of French only is either necessary for the achievement of the legislative objective or proportionate to it. That specific question is simply not addressed by the materials. Indeed, in his factum and oral argument the Attorney General of Quebec

did not attempt to justify the requirement of the exclusive use of French . . . . Thus, whereas requiring the predominant display of the French language, even its marked predominance, would be proportional to the goal of promoting and maintaining a French "visage linguistique" in Quebec and therefore justified under s.9.1 of the Quebec Charter and s.1 of the Canadian Charter, requiring the exclusive use of French has not been so justified.

Through this reasoning, the Court provided the Bourassa government with a broad hint that if Bill 101 were amended so as to provide for the predominant but not exclusive use of French on commercial signs, such a provision would be found by the Court to be in conformity both with the Canadian Charter and the Quebec Charter of Rights. As we shall see, the Bourassa government did not take the bait. If the "French predominance" solution had been accepted by the provincial government, however, the Court would have been drawn even more deeply into policy-making by having to decide what ratio of French lettering to English lettering constitutes an acceptable level of French predominance.

Equality and the Quebec Charter of Rights

The Court had no difficulty in finding that section 58 of Bill 101, the section prohibiting the use of any language other than French on commercial signs, is discriminating. In other words, this provision has a harsher effect on non-francophones than on francophones. It has "the effect of nullifying the right to full and equal recognition and exercise of this freedom [to express oneself in the language of one's choice]." Thus, the challenged commercial signs provisions violate the guarantee of equality in the Quebec Charter of Rights, as well as the guarantee of freedom of expression.

The Ford Decision and the Charter

The Ford decision [37] tackled a number of complex Charter issues. According to it, legislatures may invoke the section 33 override simply by following the correct technical procedure of declaring which numerical sections of the Charter shall not apply to a piece of legislation. Even if this procedure is put into place by a "blanket" override of previous legislation, it is nevertheless effective.

The *Ford* decision also determined that freedom of expression includes the freedom to express oneself in the language of choice and that commercial advertising is protected by the Charter. As well, it decided that the freedom to express oneself in commercial advertising in the language of choice can be limited by a requirement that the official language, if its existence is endangered, must be included on all signs and given prominence.

These pronouncements carry with them profound implications for the future development of policies in Canada concerning freedom of expression, language and human rights in general. For example, should legislators be forced to consider more carefully the imposition of the section 33 override? Does commercial advertising really merit Charter protection? Is the forced use of French in addition to the language of choice truly a reasonable limit to freedom of expression? These are important questions that are the proper subject of public debate as well as judicial consideration. The judicial reasoning about these issues, however, might help to inform such public debates, if they occur.

The Devine Case and Bilingual Signs [31]

The major issue in *Devine* was whether the Quebec government could require the use of French in commercial advertising, such as signs and commercial forms (like invoices and applications for employment), in addition to the merchant's language of choice. That question was really answered in *obiter dicta* in the *Ford* decision: the requirement that French be used in addition to the language of choice does violate the guarantee of freedom of expression in both the Canadian Charter and the Quebec Charter of Rights, but this requirement constitutes a reasonable limit pursuant to the limitations clauses in both documents. (*Obiter dicta,* or "words in passing," are the parts of a judicial decision that are not essential to the outcome.) Thus, much of the *Devine* decision simply reiterates the reasoning contained in the more comprehensive *Ford* decision.

There were two unique aspects of the *Devine* decision. The first was whether some certain types of language legislation might be *ultra vires* a provincial legislature because only the federal Parliament, acting under its criminal jurisdiction, is empowered to enact such legislation. The second was whether a government regulation requiring the mandatory use of French alone (as opposed to the mandatory use of French in addition to another language) violates the equality clauses in the Canadian Charter and the Quebec Charter of Rights.

The Jurisdictional Issue

Allan Singer argued that legislation that prohibits signs unless they are in French (with or without another language) is really criminal legislation because it creates a prohibition backed by a threat of punishment in the form of a stiff fine. (Corporations violating the commercial signs provisions of Bill 101 were liable to a fine of up to $5,750 for a second offence, plus a fine of up to $2,300 per day for carrying on a business without a certificate from the Office de la langue française.) Because only the federal Parliament may enact criminal legislation pursuant to section 91(27) of the Constitution Act, 1867, such legislation, it was submitted, is outside of the competence of the provincial legislature. The Supreme Court did not accept this interpretation of the criminal law. A criminal law, the Court declared, is one that deals with "some traditional criminal law concern such as morality or public order." The Court described the commercial signs provisions of Bill 101 as dealing with the regulation of business within the province, a subject matter falling within provincial jurisdiction.

The Equality Issue

The question of the possible impact of the equality clauses in the Canadian Charter (section 15) and the Quebec Charter of Rights (section 10) was also raised in the *Ford* case. However, this issue was ultimately of little importance, because the French-only provisions in Bill 101 were struck down primarily as violations of freedom of expression. In *Devine,* however, since the bilingual signs provisions of Bill 101 were upheld as reasonable limits to freedom of expression, the equality issue became critical to the outcome of that case.

The Court skilfully sidestepped the opportunity to provide a substantive interpretation of section 15 of the Canadian Charter. It noted that because section 1 applied to section 15 as well as to section 2(b) — freedom of expression — it would first tackle the question of whether section 1 might apply differently to section 15 than to section 2(b). (It will be remembered that the Court had already decided that the requirement of bilingual signs and business forms was a reasonable limit to freedom of expression.) The Court decided that the section 1 limitation would apply to section 15 in the same way. Therefore, there was no need for the Court to decide whether the bilingual signs provisions violated section 15, and it did not offer an opinion on this question.

The Court could not quite so easily sidestep the equality clause in the Quebec Charter of Rights. This is because the limitations clause in the Quebec Charter of Rights, section 9.1, does not apply to the equality clause (section 10). Nevertheless, the Court interpreted the guarantee of equality in section 10 of the Quebec Charter of Rights narrowly so as to allow the bilingual signs provisions to stand. Their reasoning was that section 10 guarantees the "equal recognition and exercise of [a person's] human rights and freedoms" and that it had already been decided that the bilingual signs provisions did not violate freedom of expression, as limited by section 9.1. Therefore, because freedom of expression as acceptably limited was not violated, the equal recognition of freedom of expression could not be considered as infringed.

The Court's handling of the equality issue demonstrates that very often judges will try to decide a complex issue by applying a narrow legal point, rather than having to consider the broader policy implications of a case. This is not meant as a criticism of the judges; it is simply one of the characteristics of adjudication that makes it a rough tool for policy-making.

The result of the *Devine* decision is that the Court upheld the power of the Quebec National Assembly to require the use of French, alongside the merchant's preferred language, in commercial signs and commercial documents. Such a requirement could be enforced without violating either "freedom of expression" in the Canadian Charter of Rights or the Quebec Charter of Rights, or "equality" in the Quebec Charter of Rights.

Political Jurisprudence and the Ford and Devine Decisions

The question of the constitutionality of the commercial signs provisions of Bill 101 presented the Court with its most difficult political predicament since the constitutional reference in 1981. The judges were obviously aware that their twin Bill 101 decisions would become a political football and that they would have to bear some responsibility for the political fallout which was bound to come from the decisions — *whatever* conclusions were reached.

The commercial signs provisions of Bill 101 are extremely popular among francophone Quebeckers. These provisions had markedly changed the *visage linguistique* in Quebec. With the exception of the signs belonging to businesses like those of Singer and Devine, unilingual English signs had virtually disappeared from the streets of

Quebec after the passage of Bill 101. Even bilingual signs had become rare. The commercial signs provisions seemed visibly and dramatically to have reversed the decline of French in Quebec — hence their popularity among the francophone population. The success of Bill 101 also indicated to some Quebec nationalists that Quebec could possibly maintain its culture and language while remaining part of Canada.

Aware of this situation, the Supreme Court found a way to allow the Quebec government to preserve the central core of the commercial signs provisions — requiring the predominance of French on every sign — without violating the essential spirit of freedom of expression in the Canadian Charter or the Quebec Charter of Rights. The evidence presented by the Quebec government, however, did not justify the *exclusive* use of French on signs as a reasonable limit on freedom of expression designed to preserve the French language.

What the Court could not elegantly consider in the legal context was that Bill 101 represented a mixture of a rational and an emotional response to the language issue in Quebec. The rational response, according to the evidence before the Court, was to require the predominance of French on all commercial signs. The continued existence of English on commercial signs, however, tended to rekindle the image of the *maudit anglais* among francophones who remembered the days of the condescending anglophones. The Supreme Court's suggested compromise was greeted by huge protests among Quebec nationalists, and so the Bourassa government concluded that the Supreme Court's "French predominant" solution was politically unacceptable. Four days after the Supreme Court decision, Premier Bourassa announced that his government would invoke the override provisions of both the Canadian Charter and the Quebec Charter of Rights to prohibit the use of any language but French on outdoor signs. English and other languages would be allowed only indoors, and only if the indoor signs could not be easily read from the outside. But with regard to chain stores and franchise outlets, only French would be allowed even inside. Violators would face stiff fines and even jail sentences.

The Bourassa response was denounced by civil libertarians outside Quebec and by anglophones inside Quebec. Amnesty International announced that it would defend anyone who went to jail as a result of contravening the new language legislation, Bill 178. Many castigated the framers of the Charter of Rights for including section 33, the override provision, and they redoubled their efforts to have it removed. Bourassa claimed that if the Meech Lake Accord had been in effect, he would not have needed to resort to section 33, because the Supreme Court would have upheld all of Bill 101. However, according to Peter Hogg's analysis of the accord (2), Bourassa's claim seems unconvincing. The "distinct society" clause, being merely interpretive in nature, would not have provided the Court with any means of applying the sociolinguistic evidence differently.

If the reaction of the extreme Quebec nationalists, as well as the prohibition of any non-French language at all on outdoor signs, can be considered as unnecessarily overzealous attempts to protect the French language, the reaction of the anti-section 33 forces can be considered naive. Section 33 gives judges a certain amount of freedom to "call it like it is." This is because judges are aware that section 33 offers governments a quick antidote to Supreme Court decisions on the Charter that cause political crises. Section 33 takes the pressure off the judges to solve political crises with their decisions. Instead, they can concentrate on developing more lasting interpretations of the Charter, leaving the short-term crises to the politicians. Without section 33, it is conceivable that the Supreme Court might have interpreted freedom of expression more narrowly in an attempt to smooth over current linguistic tensions in Quebec. Judges are aware that it is difficult to impose human rights on an unwilling population. Rights can only flourish when reason triumphs over petty hatreds and jealousies.

Given the emotional climate of Quebec, Bourassa's "inside-outside" solution to the commercial signs issue was predictable. A greater respect for the rights of anglophones and others will likely not be politically feasible until the old class tensions between anglophones and francophones are reduced — and unless it becomes clear that French will survive even when some English is allowed on outdoor commercial signs. Because section 33 override clauses expire after five years unless renewed, the issue of whether freedom of expression should yield to the needs of the *visage linguistique* will not go away.

There is a positive side to this issue. The dialogue and debate section 33 encourages may help to promote greater public respect for human rights in the long run because public debate may encourage private reflection. Moreover, because section 33 allows governments temporarily to side-step the effects of some Charter decisions, it may encourage judges to interpret the Charter more liberally than they otherwise might, so that narrow interpretations of fundamental rights are less likely to be frozen into the constitution.

The Supreme Court and the Fundamental Freedoms

The Supreme Court has given the fundamental freedoms much greater protection under the Charter than it did under the Bill of Rights. At the same time, the Court is obviously struggling to create an appropriate balance between giving broad protection to individual rights, on the one hand, and respecting the policy decisions of the legislative and executive branches of government, on the other. Although the Court has defined the freedoms of religion and expression broadly, it has managed to uphold provincial Sunday closing and some of the commercial signs provisions in Quebec's Bill 101. (Another example of this search for a balance is the Supreme Court's decision in the *Canadian Newspapers* case [83]. The Court found that the Criminal Code provision that requires judges to prohibit the publication of the names of the victims of sexual assault if the victims so request, violates section 2(b). However, the Court held that this infringement of freedom of the media is a reasonalbe limit under section 1.)

The Supreme Court is interpreting the fundamental freedoms in the Charter from the perspective of the ideology of liberalism. Although this approach is useful in giving meaning to "freedom of religion," it is less helpful in unravelling the concept of "freedom of association." This is because freedom of association is closely connected with the growth of the labour movement that occurred after the development of classical liberal theory. But aside from the theoretical issue, the majority on the Court may have chosen not to find a right to strike in section 2(d) for a very practical reason — the fear of entangling the courts more deeply in labour litigation.

The ideology of liberalism guided the Court's interpretation of "freedom of expression" in relation to the commercial signs provisions of Quebec's Bill 101. But here we witnessed a direct collision between the liberal, and therefore individualistic, bent of the Charter and the collective desire of the majority of francophones in Quebec to take the steps they considered necessary to preserve their language. The issue is how to balance the right of individuals to advertise in their own language against the right of francophones to preserve their culture and language. To put this in more basic terms, all Quebeckers, both francophones and anglophones, as members of a rights-conscious society deserve to be respected and owe respect to each other. What language policies will best promote this interpersonal respect?

There are no easy answers to such a question because it is a question about promoting human values. An answer cannot be deduced from "correct" legal reasoning any more than a computer stuffed full of all the relevant facts could settle the issue. Likewise, there are sensible arguments on both sides of the Sunday-shopping debate, and there are good reasons either for extending the meaning of freedom of association to include the right to strike, or for not doing so. The most workable answers are likely to emerge after a thoughtful public airing of these questions during which the basic goal of optimizing interpersonal respect is kept front and centre. It is important for Canadians to consider these issues further, and the Supreme Court's reasoning about them at least provides a useful point of departure.

4

Democratic Rights

Democratic rights are protected by sections 3-5 of the Charter. Section 3 states that every citizen has the right to vote in provincial and federal elections and to run for office in these assemblies; section 4 provides that there must be federal and provincial elections at least every five years (with exceptions possible during war or civil strife); and section 5 mandates Parliament and provincial legislatures to sit at least once a year. To date, all of the reported Charter challenges raised pertaining to democratic rights have occurred under section 3. None of these cases have yet been decided by the Supreme Court of Canada.

There have been fewer than one hundred reported cases to September 1988 concerning democratic rights. The cases considered below will be presented according to the following categories:

- whether certain classes of persons, such as prisoners or the mentally handicapped, can be barred from voting;
- whether particular restrictions on voting or registering to vote are constitutional;
- whether specific qualifications for candidacy are acceptable;
- whether regulations restricting the political activity of public servants are permissible; and
- miscellaneous issues, such as election spending limits and whether large discrepancies between the number of voters in urban and rural constituencies infringe the right to vote.

Until the 1988 federal election, the majority of cases related to the first issue, especially the question of whether prisoners could vote.

However, the second kind of issue has now become the most common; during the election campaign at least a dozen persons initiated court cases because their names had not been included on the voters' list. Very few cases of the last three types have arisen.

Classes of Persons Denied the Vote

Many groups in addition to prisoners and the mentally handicapped have been denied the vote at various times in our history. For example, women were excluded from voting until 1916, when Manitoba gave them the right to vote in provincial elections. All the provinces eventually followed Manitoba's lead; Quebec was the last in 1940. Women won the right to vote in federal elections in 1918. Some provinces prevented Canadians of Asian origin from voting until the early part of this century (see chapter 1). Native Canadians living on reserves could not vote until 1960. There are five groups, however, that are still sometimes disenfranchised by the federal and provincial elections acts: prisoners, those in institutions for the mentally handicapped or the mentally ill, judges, minors and non-citizens. A broad interpretation of section 3 may extend the right to vote to some in the first four of these groups. Although non-citizens do not have rights under section 3, they could still press for broader voting rights under the equality rights of the Charter.

One reason for denying prisoners the vote is because voting is one of a number of liberties denied to them as part of the punishment. (The U.S. constitution allows the state legislatures to deny the vote indefinitely to persons convicted of criminal offences.) Some legislators have considered that the mentally handicapped, the mentally ill and minors are incapable of voting intelligently. The purpose of the denial of the vote to judges was to promote judicial independence and impartiality. If judges cannot vote, there is no incentive for politicians to try to influence them, and possibly infringe their independence in so doing. As well, there is no need for judges who cannot vote to make up their minds about election issues, a process that might affect their impartiality.

Prisoners and the mentally handicapped have been active in claiming the right to vote through Charter challenges in the courts.

Prisoners

Only the province of Quebec allows prisoners to vote in provincial elections. The elections acts in the other nine provinces and for

Canada exclude prisoners from the voters' lists. Prisoners have so far been only partly successful in winning the right to vote through Charter litigation.

Shortly after the Charter came into effect in 1982, inmates in remand centres in Saskatchewan successfully applied for a court order to allow them to vote [71]. Remand inmates are prisoners waiting for trial; they have not been convicted. The crown was unable to demonstrate that the failure to provide the remand inmates with facilities for voting constituted a reasonable limit.

Also in 1982, persons on probation in British Columbia won the right to vote through Charter litigation [116]. Prior to the case, B.C. was the only province that denied probationers the right to vote. The crown claimed that the purpose of denying the right to vote to probationers was to prevent "unfit persons" from voting. However, the crown was unable to establish to the satisfaction of the court why probationers were unfit to vote in B.C. but fit to vote in the rest of Canada. This decision indicates how the Charter can promote national standards with regard to matters within the jurisdiction of the provinces.

Attempts to persuade judges that convicted prisoners serving sentences should be allowed to vote have been somewhat less successful. In 1983 prisoners in B.C. unsuccessfully challenged the federal Elections Act. A judge in the B.C. Supreme Court concluded that although the denial of voting rights to prisoners could not be justified on the grounds of protecting society, it could be justified for practical reasons. For example, it is well known that prisoners convicted of sexual offences or child abuse are liable to be beaten or killed by other prisoners. Therefore, the real names of such persons are usually not made available to the other prisoners. The publication of a voters' list, however, might destroy such anonymity. As well, the judge felt that electioneering activities in prisons could endanger some prisoners or party workers [44].

A week before the 1984 federal election, a prisoner in a federal penitentiary in Ontario applied to the Federal Court of Canada for an interlocutory injunction to allow him to vote in the election. (An interlocutory injunction is a court order prohibiting a potentially harmful action until the fundamental issue of a court case can be decided.) The injunction was granted in the trial decision, but this decision was reversed two days later in the Federal Court of Appeal. The Appeal Court concluded that to grant the injunction would be to decide the issue without giving the crown the right to respond in a full trial [3]. On the day of the election, the Supreme Court of Canada rejected without reasons an application for leave (or permission) to appeal.

In 1985 prisoners in a federal penitentiary in Quebec applied for a court order to allow them to vote in the provincial election. As noted above, Quebec permits prisoners to vote in provincial elections, but officials in the federal penitentiaries would not allow facilities for the prisoners to vote. The federal crown argued that the denial of the vote to the prisoners was justified because of security reasons and administrative difficulties. This reasoning failed to persuade the judge, and prison officials were ordered to make provisions for the prisoners to vote [48]. This case did not consider the substantive issue of whether a government can deny the right to vote to prisoners through legislation, but only the issue of whether administrative inconvenience is a reason for preventing prisoners from voting when provincial legislation otherwise allows them to vote.

The Manitoba courts have also considered the issue of prisoners' voting rights. In March 1986, a week before the provincial election, prisoners in a federal penitentiary applied to the Queen's Bench for an order to have their names placed on the voters' list. The prisoners failed to achieve their main objective, although they achieved some success in their attack on the provincial Elections Act [13].

The judge decided that the total denial of the vote to all prisoners in the provincial Elections Act was an infringement of section 3 of the Charter that cannot be justified under section 1, the limitations clause. The Supreme Court of Canada had recently developed a test for the application of section 1 in the *Oakes* decision, and the Manitoba judge applied the newly established standards.

The judge concluded that the government's objective — denying the vote to persons not fit to have it — passed the first part of the *Oakes* test (the government's objective must be sufficiently important). However, the means chosen to limit the right — denying the vote to every prisoner, whether serving a one-day sentence or a life sentence — did not meet the first two components of the second part of the test. First, the judge failed to see a rational connection between preventing unfit persons from voting, and denying the vote to someone serving a one-day sentence. Second, he claimed that a blanket disqualification did not represent the least obtrusive means of achieving the objective. The section of the Elections Act that denied the vote to prisoners was declared of no force or effect.

Nevertheless, the judge refused to order that the prisoners' names be added to the voters' list. He felt that the legislature must be given the opportunity to consider the issue and to amend the Elections Act so that it would meet the proportionality requirements of the *Oakes* test. In other words, the denial of the vote to the most serious offenders might meet the proportionality requirements. In the meantime, "it is neither just nor appropriate that the votes of the qualified and registered electors should now be diluted."

The day before the election, other Manitoba prisoners applied to the Manitoba Court of Appeal for an order to allow them to vote the next day. The court decided that even if the Charter guaranteed prisoners the right to vote, it was inappropriate for the court to order that the prisoners could vote. This was because of the lack of time to make appropriate arrangements, together with the fact that the prisoners had failed to suggest what kind of arrangements could reasonably be made [50].

The approach at the Manitoba courts contrasts with an Ontario Supreme Court decision in July 1988. Mr. Justice John Bowlby struck down the section of the Ontario Election Act that denies the vote to prisoners. According to Thomas Claridge, Judge Bowlby was of the opinion that "the rehabilitation of convicts would be assisted by enabling them to participate in the electoral process. The judge said that 'even with the most flagrant crime there must exist hope of reform. This is the philosophy of our penal system.'"

The contrasting decisions in several provinces about prisoners' voting rights illustrate how judges can differ about what kinds of policies best conform to the Charter.

Other Groups

Prior to the 1988 federal election, legislation was introduced into the House of Commons that would have given the vote to judges, citizens living overseas and mentally handicapped and mentally ill patients. The bill also dealt with limits to candidates' election expenses. When weaknesses in the election expenses section surfaced, the bill was shelved until after the election.

Some institutionalized mentally handicapped and mentally ill patients, not content to wait until the next election to vote, applied to the Federal Court for an order that would allow them to vote. They won. Because the government had just taken the first steps to enfranchise them, the crown could not convincingly argue that these persons should be denied the vote. As a result, federal enumerators called on institutions for the mentally handicapped and mentally ill before the election. Patients who could state their name, age, citizenship and residence were placed on the voters' list. (According to D. Lipovenko, only about 50 of 800 residents at the Huronia Regional Centre in Orillia, Ontario, were able to meet these requirements.) Some provinces, including Ontario, have already enfranchised the mentally handicapped and the mentally ill for provincial elections.

The National Anti-Poverty Association considered initiating a Charter challenge to the requirement that voters must have a place of residence. The association noted that this requirement had the effect of disenfranchising the homeless. However, the association did not find a suitable case for a Charter challenge before the election, as Susan Delacourt has reported. (The reason that voters must have an address is to discourage the multiple enumeration of individuals.)

A group representing persons under eighteen also considered applying to a court for an order requiring the enfranchisement of some minors. They decided, however, to wait until they had done more research before going to court.

Restrictions on Voting

Sometimes, otherwise eligible voters find themselves disenfranchised because they have been missed by enumerators, are unable to be in their home riding at election time, or have not fulfilled local residency requirements in time for the election. About twenty persons have challenged these kinds of restrictions as violations of the section 3 right to vote. During the six weeks prior to the 1988 federal election, at least a dozen citizens raised these kinds of issues in court. Most were unsuccessful, either because the challengers had failed to give adequate notice to the crown — various statutes require that if a constitutional issue is to be raised, adequate notice must be given — or because the judges decided that such important matters could not be decided within the short time period before the election.

In most Canadian provinces and territories, there are residency requirements ranging from six months to a year for voting in provincial or territorial elections. In 1982 a Saskatchewan resident who had not resided in the province for the required six-month period applied to the Court of Queen's Bench for an order that would allow his name to be entered on the provincial voters' list. The court decided against the claim on the grounds that residency requirements are common in "free and democratic" societies and that it is a legislative task, not a judicial one, to decide what specific period ought to apply [127].

In a similar case in the Yukon Territory, the Territorial Supreme Court decided in 1985 that a twelve-month residency requirement was unconstitutional. The crown had argued that a residency requirement was necessary to prevent election results from being distorted by a last-minute influx of non-residents or by persons merely passing through, and that residency requirements allow voters to develop a commitment to the community. The judge was not persuaded by any of these arguments, and concluded that a residency requirement was simply another relic of past anti-democratic restrictions on voting, such as property or educational qualifications, or being male. However, this decision was overturned on appeal. The Territorial Court of Appeal decided that the residency requirement passed all of the elements of the *Oakes* test. In particular, the requirement was rationally connected with the objective of ensuring that voters "show some connection with the province or territory before deciding upon local matters" [40].

In 1983 two B.C. residents who were registered voters, but who were attending law school in Ontario, telephoned the deputy registrar of voters in British Columbia to find out how they could cast absentee votes in the provincial election. They were told that no mechanism existed for them to vote unless they returned to B.C. They applied to the Supreme Court of B.C. for an order that the provincial government must provide a mechanism for absentee voting to comply with section 3 of the Charter. The judge rejected the petition, claiming that it was the students' fault that they could not vote, not the government's. In 1985, however, this decision was overturned on appeal. The B.C. Court of Appeal noted that provisions for absentee voting existed in seven of ten Canadian provinces, for some federal voters and in all U.S. jurisdictions. Therefore, "the right to vote as guaranteed by s.3 of the Charter is denied to B.C. registered voters where the sole reason they are unable to exercise their right to vote is that no procedural mechanism exists which would reasonably enable them to do so" [41].

In two other B.C. cases, voting regulations were unsuccessfully challenged. If a registered voter moves to another constituency in Canada and fails to re-register before twenty days prior to the federal election, that person's vote will apply to the old constituency. The B.C. Supreme Court considered the twenty-day rule to be a reasonable limit to section 3 [124]. In the second case, a voter challenged the stipulation in the provincial Elections Act that the voter's choice must be marked with an "X" and not a tick mark. The B.C.

Court of Appeal decided that section 3 of the Charter merely guarantees the right to vote; the legislature has the authority to determine, within reason, how that right is to be exercised [135].

The Canada Elections Act provides that rural voters whose names have been missed by the enumerators can have their names added to the voters' list on election day. Urban voters, however, cannot be sworn in on election day; they have until two weeks prior to the election to ensure that their names are on the list. In Edmonton, representatives of several thousand voters missed by the enumerators attempted to obtain a court order to have their names added to the voters' list. They not only claimed that their section 3 rights had been infringed, but also that the Elections Act unfairly discriminated against urban voters contrary to section 15 of the Charter (the equality rights section). Four days prior to the election, a Queen's Bench judge refused to hear the argument because the required fourteen days notice of a Charter challenge had not been given to the attorney general of Canada (*Globe and Mail,* November 18, 1988, A10).

These cases indicate that, by and large, judges tend to accept the current rules and regulations governing how Canadians may cast their ballots unless these rules are clearly out of line with the rules in other Canadian jurisdictions — like the absentee voting requirements in British Columbia. In this way, the Charter is promoting more uniformity concerning provincial voting procedures.

Candidacy

Some of the various elections acts in Canada prevent certain persons from running as candidates in elections. For example, persons convicted of criminal offences could not run in provincial elections in Nova Scotia for the five years following their conviction until this provision was struck down in the *MacLean* case, discussed below. Other statutes or regulations preclude some classes of employees from seeking or accepting elected office unless they resign their position. These provisions have been challenged in several cases.

The most famous of the challenges involved Billy Joe MacLean, the former Nova Scotia cabinet minister who was convicted of fraud for submitting false expense claims in 1986. Not only was MacLean forced to resign from the cabinet, but the Nova Scotia legislature declared his seat vacant. The Nova Scotia Elections Act prohibited him from running for office for five years. MacLean challenged this provision as a violation of section 3 of the Charter. He won his case in the Nova Scotia Supreme Court [53]. The judge concluded that the

Elections Act failed to meet the rational connection test prescribed by the *Oakes* case because it was a sweeping prohibition that applied to all offenders, no matter how minor the offence. MacLean was therefore able to contest the by-election for his vacated seat. In the campaign, he claimed that he had been guilty only of poor bookkeeping, and he was re-elected to the legislature. However, he went down to defeat in the provincial general election of 1988.

The B.C. Municipal Act prohibits persons convicted of an indictable offence from running for municipal office until five years after the completion of their punishment. A British Columbia man convicted of breach of trust in 1980 was sentenced to three years imprisonment. He was paroled after one year. In 1987 he wanted to run for the office of alderman, but the local returning officer refused his nomination because five years had not elapsed since the completion of his parole. The man appealed this decision as a violation of section 3 as well as of section 15 (equality rights) of the Charter. A provincial court judge rejected the Charter arguments. He concluded that section 3 applies only to provincial and federal elections, not to municipalities. As well, he reasoned that section 15 of the Charter (which does apply to municipalities) was intended to outlaw discrimination based on categories people cannot do anything about, such as sex, age, colour or mental disability, or categories related to a person's basic beliefs, such as religion. Because the appellant could have avoided his criminal activities, the judge concluded that section 15 was not intended to preclude discrimination based on a person's criminal record [97].

In the 1982 Alberta provincial election, H. Jonson, a high school principal in the town of Ponoka, won a seat in the legislature. The County of Ponoka School Board gave the principal a leave of absence without pay so that he could complete his term as MLA. A provincial election was called in 1986, and during the election campaign, the board passed a new policy that would continue Jonson's leave of absence for only one year, should he win the election. Jonson won the election and challenged the board's new policy in court. He claimed that the new policy violated sections 3 and 15 of the Charter, as well as similar provisions in the Alberta Bill of Rights. The board defended its position by claiming that the Charter did not apply to its policies. The Queen's Bench judge held that the Charter did, in fact, apply to the decisions of school boards, because such boards exercise powers they have been delegated by the provincial legislature. While the judge could find no violation of a Charter right in the board's new policy, he concluded that the new policy was "unreasonable" from the standpoint of administrative law because it was implemented in the midst of an election campaign. The judge ordered that the MLA was entitled to retain his designation as principal and to be granted a leave of absence without pay for the duration of his current term as MLA [45].

Although there have been very few cases concerning candidacy, these cases illustrate that those seeking to have candidacy restrictions removed seem to have a reasonable chance of succeeding.

Political Activities of Public Servants

All jurisdictions in Canada have to some extent limited the freedom of public servants to participate in political activities. The four western provinces and Quebec have the fewest restrictions. Most public servants in these provinces may participate in political activities as long as these activities do not interfere with their work and are not carried out during their hours of employment. The restrictions are more strict in Nova Scotia, in the federal public service and in Ontario, although the latter two jurisdictions have recently proposed changes that would ease the constraints.

In 1986 provincial public servants in Nova Scotia and federal public servants challenged the restrictions on their political activities as violations of section 2 (freedom of expression, assembly and association) and section 3 of the Charter. Regarding section 3, it was argued that the constraints on the political activities of public servants confined the campaign resources available to some candidates, thereby limiting their right under section 3 to be a candidate.

The outcomes of the two cases were quite different. In Nova Scotia, the Civil Service Act prohibited public servants from engaging in any partisan political activity and from contributing funds to a political party. A Nova Scotia Supreme Court judge accepted that the purpose of this restriction — to promote an impartial public service — met the requirements of the first part of the *Oakes* test (an objective of substantial importance). However, the legislation failed the second part of the test, the proportionality requirements. The restrictions amounted to a blanket prohibition of political activities; they did not limit rights as little as was necessary to achieve the purpose of the legislation [39].

Federally, the Public Service Employment Act prohibits public servants from working for or against candidates for Parliament or a provincial legislature, or for or against a political party. Public servants, however, are allowed to attend political meetings and to contribute funds to political parties. The public servants who challenged these provisions wished to engage in some "low-level" political activities, such as attending a party convention as a delegate and canvassing on behalf of a candidate. The Federal Court interpreted the provisions of the act broadly so as to permit many of the activities the public servants wished to participate in. Thus, the judge concluded that there had been no violation of section 3. He also concluded that while in some respects the act did violate section 2, these breaches were reasonable limits under section 1. In the opinion of the judge, the act limited Charter rights as little as possible in order to promote impartiality in the public service [63].

A Supreme Court decision about the political rights of public servants deserves mention: *OPSEU v. Attorney-General for Ontario* [62]. Although it was not a Charter case, it has implications for the Charter. Before the Charter came into effect in 1982, the Ontario Public Service Employees Union (OPSEU) initiated a court challenge to the provisions of the Ontario Public Service Act that prevented provincial public servants from participating in federal political activities. OPSEU claimed that under the Duff Doctrine a provincial law could not interfere with federal political activity nor with freedom of expression. When the case reached the Supreme Court of Canada in 1986, the union hoped that the Court would also consider the implications of sections 2, 3 and 15 of the Charter. The Court, however, decided not to consider the Charter issues because the facts of the case dated from pre-Charter times.

OPSEU lost the case essentially because the provincial law was considered to have only an incidental effect on federal elections, its basic purpose being to promote the impartiality of the provincial public service. The Court's decision may indicate how it will consider Charter challenges to laws that restrict the political activities of public servants. It is also important because, for the first time in Canadian history, a majority on the Supreme Court adopted the Duff Doctrine. The majority decision was written by Mr. Justice Beetz. Given his abrupt dismissal of the Duff Doctrine in the *Dupond* decision (see chapter 1), the following words of Beetz are remarkable:

> There is no doubt in my mind that the basic structure of
> our Constitution as established by the *Constitution Act,
> 1867* contemplates the existence of certain political in-
> stitutions, including freely elected legislative bodies at the

federal and provincial levels. In the words of Duff C.J.C. in *Re Alberta Statutes* at p. 133, "such institutions derive their efficacy from the free public discussions of affairs . . ." and, in those of Abbott J. in *Switzman v. Elbling* at p. 328, neither a provincial legislature nor Parliament itself can "abrogate this right of discussion and debate." Speaking more generally, I hold that neither Parliament nor the provincial legislatures may enact legislation the effect of which would be to substantially interfere with the operation of this basic constitutional structure. On the whole, though, I am inclined to the view that the . . . legislation [in question] . . . affects federal and provincial elections only in an incidental way.

It is significant that Beetz made it part of his holding that the preamble to the Constitution Act, 1867, prohibits both Parliament and provincial legislatures from interfering with free elections, including free public discussion. Beetz has not only revived the Duff Doctrine, he has adopted the most far-reaching version of it proclaimed thus far, holding that neither the federal Parliament nor the provincial legislatures can limit free expression in relation to the democratic process. The significance of this revival of the Duff Doctrine lies in the fact that the preamble to the Constitution Act, 1867, cannot be overridden by section 33 of the Charter.

It also appears, however, that in future when the Court is faced with a Charter case relating to the political activities of public servants, it may be somewhat sympathetic to what will no doubt be the position of the crown — that the restrictions are a reasonable limit designed to promote public service impartiality.

Other Cases

Of all the cases involving political activities, the 1984 *National Citizens' Coalition* case has had the greatest impact on the political process [57]. The National Citizens' Coalition (NCC) is a right-wing interest group that has on several occasions launched Charter cases to try to restrict government or union constraints on business activities.

In 1974, legislation was enacted that limited campaign expenditures by parties and candidates, but it contained a loophole that made it fairly easy for individuals and interest groups to advertise for or against parties or candidates without reference to the spending limits.

According to Canada's chief electoral officer, "a number of persons who were not acting ... with the knowledge and consent of candidates or registered agents of political parties have ... spent unlimited sums of money to promote or oppose a particular candidate or registered party, sums which they do not have to account for in terms of sources or amount." The result was that the election spending limits were becoming meaningless, and some low-income candidates were worried about being squeezed out of the political process. To remedy that deficiency, and to provide for greater equality of access to the democratic process, Parliament enacted provisions that would plug the loophole by prohibiting individuals and interest groups from advertising for or against political parties during election campaigns unless they did so under the auspices of a political party and within the campaign expense limits. This 1983 legislation had the support of all three political parties. Individuals and groups were still free to advertise their views with regard to specific issues as long as parties were not mentioned.

In the Alberta Court of Queen's Bench, the NCC challenged these provisions as violations both of section 2(b) (freedom of expression) and section 3 of the Charter. Mr. Justice Donald Medhurst, however, based his decision on section 2. In defence of the Elections Act, the crown argued that the legislation is simply a

> logical step in the formulation of a legislative scheme which would protect the integrity of the election of members of political parties to Parliament within the philosophy which started with the abolition of bribery and coercion of voters, and has proceeded to the point where members seeking election must be represented by responsible agents; are limited in the amount of money they can spend; and are precluded from engaging in a last-minute spate of publicity in order to sway public opinion.

The NCC, on the other hand, maintained that the impugned provisions clearly infringed the Charter and that there was no evidence that the breach of the Charter was necessary to promote fair elections. The judge accepted this argument. In the absence of clear guidelines for the operation of section 1 — the *Oakes* test for the application of section 1 had not yet been formulated by the Supreme Court of Canada — the judge concluded that violations of sections 2 and 3 could not be justified unless the crown could produce specific examples of how excessive advertising by non-party groups had actually resulted in harm. Lawyers for the crown had presented several examples of how various groups had taken advantage of the loophole in the 1974 legislation, but the judge was not convinced that merely taking advantage of the loophole resulted in harm.

The government decided not to appeal this decision. According to Janet Hiebert, since an election was approaching, a decision to appeal might have been politically damaging. As well, because the *NCC* decision came just three months before the 1984 federal election, the chief electoral officer decided not to enforce the provisions affecting interest-group advertising so that the same rules would apply both inside and outside Alberta.

This result meant that, subsequently, interest groups and businesses were free to spend unlimited funds during election campaigns advertising for or against political parties. This had little impact on the 1984 election campaign, but the 1988 election was a different story. Businesses and other interest groups were free to spend as much as they wished to advertise for or against political parties. As it turned out, the Conservative party was clearly the primary beneficiary. Most Canadian and U.S. businesses supported free trade, and they spent large sums to promote a Conservative victory.

The final kind of challenge to election laws under section 3 of the Charter concerns the distribution of voters in constituencies. Section 3 declares that "every citizen of Canada has the right to vote." This declaration seems to carry with it the implication that every citizen has the *equal* right to vote. Voting rights would not mean much if, for example, a legislature decreed that university professors or property owners or men would be entitled to ten votes each. If section 3 alone does not guarantee equality in the right to vote, section 15, the equality section, likely has that effect.

In most provinces and at the federal level, there are more voters in urban constituencies than in rural ones. There is an extreme example of this situation in British Columbia. The most populous riding in the province has about 36,000 voters, while the least populous has only 2,500. This means that a vote in the rural constituency is worth more than fourteen times as much as a vote in the urban constituency. In 1986 the B.C. Civil Liberties Association initiated a case in the B.C. Supreme Court in which it was alleged that the gross underrepresentation of voters in the large urban ridings violated the implied equal right to vote in section 3. This kind of argument has impressed U.S. judges faced with similar challenges based on the U.S. Bill of Rights, according to Walter Tarnopolsky and Gerald Beaudoin. Legislatures are generally not allowed to create more than a 20 per cent discrepancy between the populations of large and small ridings south of the border.

Before the main issue concerning section 3 could be heard, the B.C. Supreme Court was asked to determine the procedural question of whether the provincial electoral law was open to Charter challenges. To avoid a section 3 challenge to the electoral law of British Columbia, the crown argued that because the electoral law was part of the province's constitution, it should be considered equal in status to the Charter and therefore exempt from Charter review. The B.C. Supreme Court rejected this argument in October 1986, and the Civil Liberties Association proceeded with its litigation [32]. In April 1989 Chief Justice Beverley McLachlin decided in favour of the B.C. Civil Liberties Association. In her decision, which was her last before taking up her duties in the Supreme Court of Canada, she said that although allowances could be made for geographic and regional factors, the electoral boundaries must be drawn so as to promote equality of population in the electoral districts.

The Charter and Democratic Rights

Patrick Monahan, a professor of law at Osgoode Hall Law School, has argued that if Canadian courts attempt to interpret the Charter so as to maximize democratic values, the dissonance between the democratic process and the fact that unelected officials (judges) are called on to make fundamental policy decisions about the Charter can be reduced. To date, have Canadian courts, through their interpretation of democratic rights, advanced the ideals of democratic participation in government?

This question can certainly not be answered unequivocally. The decision that has had the greatest impact on electoral activity, the *National Citizens' Coalition* case, has certainly not advanced the ideal that all Canadians, rich and poor, should have equal access to the political process. The decisions that have extended the vote to the mentally ill and the mentally handicapped in institutions, and to some prisoners, could be considered as promoting democracy if one considers democracy to consist primarily of the right to vote. But democracy implies much more than simply voting; as Carole Pateman has shown, it also implies meaningful citizen participation. The designing of strategies that promote democracy in the broad sense is a policy-making function that will probably be taken up, if at all, more by legislatures than by courts.

When policy decisions are made in a court, the issues considered by the judges are usually limited to those raised by counsel. In the cases discussed above, judges were asked to condone the denial of the vote to prisoners because of administrative convenience or safety considerations, or as an element of punishment. Issues such as the potential rehabilitative value of voting in prisons, or the broader implications of democracy, were not often raised by counsel. This is understandable; lawyers have little expertise in the field of public policy development or political philosophy.

One contribution the judiciary can make to policy development with regard to democracy is to point out what kinds of restrictions on voting or candidacy seem to be arbitrary or not carefully considered by the policy-makers, and thus may be unfair. For example, the failure of the B.C. legislature to provide a mechanism for absentee voting in the 1980s may have been an oversight of the drafters of the legislation rather than a carefully reasoned policy.

The Charter has raised numerous questions about the appropriateness of the rules governing voting and candidacy in Canada. Without the Charter, some of these issues might not have received much attention from legislators and policy-makers in the public service. Therefore, although the courts lack the policy-making tools of the legislative and executive branches, they can contribute positively in some ways to the policy-making role.

5

Legal Rights

About 90 per cent of all Charter arguments raised in reported cases across all Canadian courts, according to F.L. Morton and M.J. Withey, deal with one of the legal rights sections — sections 7-14. The heavy use of the legal rights sections by litigants is partly a result of the familiarity lawyers have with legal rights in that most of these rights are simply codifications of common-law principles. As well, the legal rights sections give lawyers the opportunity to raise additional arguments regarding cases that would have gone to court anyway because of the criminal process. In contrast, many of the cases litigated under sections of the Charter dealing with the fundamental freedoms, democratic rights, mobility rights, equality rights and language rights are cases mounted specifically to raise a Charter challenge.

When the Charter was in its infancy, observers like Peter Russell (5) predicted that cases based on the legal rights sections were likely to produce the least controversial decisions because judges would simply continue to apply the same principles with which they were familiar under the common law. However, some legal rights decisions have had a surprising impact either on the criminal justice system or on government policies. This is mainly because of two factors: (a) the inclusion of some "new" legal rights in the Charter as well as a broader description of some older ones (see chapter 1), and (b) the fact that the Charter, as part of the constitution, invites judges to expand the traditional common-law protections. This chapter will consider eight of the Supreme Court's most prominent legal rights decisions. The cases will be reviewed in chronological order.

Unreasonable Search and Seizure: Hunter v. Southam [42]

On April 19, 1982, two days after the Charter became law, officers from the Combines Investigation Branch appeared at the *Edmonton Journal*. They demanded to search the newspaper's offices, and they had with them a search certificate granted by the Restrictive Trade Practices Commission, the body responsible for enforcing the federal Combines Investigation Act. The certificate read as follows:

> You are hereby authorized to enter upon the premises hereinafter mentioned, on which I believe there may be evidence relevant to this inquiry, and examine thereon and copy . . . any other book, paper, record or other document that in your opinion may afford such evidence. The premises referred to herein are those occupied by or on behalf of Southam Inc., 10006-101 Street, Edmonton, Alberta, and elsewhere in Canada.

The search went ahead. Southam Inc., owner of the *Journal,* decided to test the Charter by requesting a court order to strike down the section of the Combines Investigation Act that authorizes such searches. Southam claimed that the act violated section 8 of the Charter, which declares that everyone has a right to be secure against unreasonable search or seizure. The Supreme Court of Canada decision was handed down in September 1984.

In order to appreciate the significance of the decision, it is useful to keep in mind that in the decade immediately prior to this case there was an enormous expansion of newspaper chains like Southam and Thomson, as Frederick Fletcher and Daphne Gottlieb relate. This change began to generate public concern, which came to a head in August 1980. Both Thomson and Southam had owned a newspaper each in Ottawa and Winnipeg. One newspaper from each chain closed in each city, leaving Southam with a virtual monopoly in Ottawa, and Thomson in a similar position in Winnipeg. The public outcry which resulted led to the creation of the Kent Royal Commission on Newspapers, which reported in 1981. The commission hinted that the two newspaper chains may have breached the Combines Investigation Act in closing the two newspapers. The subsequent investigation by the Combines Branch led to the search of the *Edmonton Journal* offices.

Chief Justice Dickson wrote the unanimous opinion for the full Court. He pointed out that in order for the Court to give legal definitions to terms like "unreasonable search or seizure," it could not rely either on a dictionary or on the rules of construction that had been developed for non-Charter cases. Neither approach would lead to conclusive results. Dickson declared that the Court would take a "purposive" approach towards resolving such issues, meaning that the Court would define the various provisions of the Charter according to their historical and political purposes. Dickson quoted Viscount Sankey's decision in the 1930 "persons" cases (see chapter 1), in which Sankey described the Canadian constitution as "a living tree capable of growth and expansion within its natural limits." Dickson claimed that the Court needed to give the Charter a broad interpretation, rather than to "read provisions of the Constitution like a last will and testament lest it become one."

Dickson said that the purpose of section 8 was to protect a right to privacy. He pointed out how common-law judges had for centuries protected individual privacy from illegal encroachment by the state, and he mentioned specifically the judgment of Lord Camden in *Entick v. Carrington* [36] (see chapter 1). He said that a reasonable search would be one in which "the interests of the state in [intruding] come to prevail over the interests of the individual in resisting [state intrusions]." Building on the common law relating to trespass, Dickson defined a "reasonable search" as one which is (a) authorized by a statute (this principle protects the rule of law) and (b) conducted after a search warrant is issued, unless the need for a search is so pressing that it would be unrealistic to obtain a warrant. The search warrant can be issued only by an impartial party (someone capable of "acting judicially," though not necessarily a judge), and that party must be satisfied that there are probable grounds to believe that an offence has been committed and that the evidence is located in the specific place to be searched.

For several reasons, the search procedures utilized by the Restrictive Trade Practices Commission did not pass this test. First, the search warrant was not issued by an independent party. The members of the commission, who could issue search warrants, also had investigative powers. Therefore, they could not be considered impartial, since they had an interest in the conduct of the investigation. Second, the Combines Investigation Act did not require that a search warrant be issued only after evidence had been presented to show probable cause; rather, the act required only the possibility of finding evidence.

Dickson claimed that to accept such a low standard would be to "authorize fishing expeditions of considerable latitude." Third, the warrant did not indicate a particular place but would allow all Southam offices in Canada to be searched. Dickson described such a warrant as "tantamount to a license to roam at large on the premises of Southam Inc" — an unreasonable invasion of privacy.

One naturally wonders whether the Supreme Court's standard for protecting individual privacy might prevent public officials like those in the Combines Investigation Branch from effectively carrying out their duties. Peter Russell (5) discovered that by the time of the Supreme Court decision in *Hunter v. Southam,* the Combines Investigation Branch had already modified its procedures for obtaining warrants so that they would comply with the higher standards. It appears that the lower standards were more convenient for the branch, but the new standards do not present any serious difficulties. The ability of the Charter to promote higher standards of procedural fairness in public administration is one of its positive effects.

Since the *Hunter v. Southam* decision, the Supreme Court has indicated some of the characteristics of what it will consider a "reasonable" invasion of privacy. In the *Hufsky* decision [91] in 1988, the Court decided that a police officer's demand to see a person's driver's licence and insurance card during a spot check is *not* "an intrusion on a reasonable expectation of privacy . . . . There is no such intrusion where a person is required to [comply] with some legal requirement that is a lawful condition of the exercise of a right or privilege." The Court has also held that "writs of assistance" (blanket search warrants sometimes issued to the police for as long as they hold office) are unconstitutional [90, 105], that taking a blood sample without legal authorization contravenes section 8 [87] and that, at Canada's ports of entry, persons whom the authorities wish to strip-search must be given the opportunity to contact counsel before the search can take place [106].

Fundamental Justice and Refugee Determination Procedures

Canada's Immigration Act defines three kinds of immigrants who may apply to become permanent residents of Canada: persons who qualify according to a points system that takes into account employability and likelihood of adapting successfully to Canadian life; persons sponsored by relatives in Canada who are citizens or permanent residents; and persons who are refugees according to the Geneva Convention, that is, persons in need of protection because they have a well-founded fear of persecution in the country they are fleeing, owing to such factors as their beliefs or race.

Some refugees who wish to apply to Canada for protection do so at Canadian government offices abroad. Others come directly to Canada and make a refugee claim upon entry. According to the refugee determination process in place up to the *Singh* decision [125] in 1985, those in the latter group were eventually examined under oath by an immigration officer, and the transcript of the examination was sent to the Refugee Status Advisory Committee. The committee would then advise the minister or his or her delegate about whether the applicant met the definition of a Convention refugee, and the minister would make a final determination. If the minister decided against the applicant, the applicant could appeal the decision to the Immigration Appeal Board within fifteen days. The Appeal Board would review the applicant's transcript and evidence submitted by the minister, but the applicant was allowed neither to examine the minister's evidence nor to have an oral hearing.

The events leading to the *Singh* decision involved Satnam Singh and several other Sikhs from India who had fled their home country because, they claimed, of the persecution they had suffered at the hands of Indian government authorities. The Refugee Status Advisory Committee kept a list of refugee-producing countries, and India was apparently not on the list. The troubles between the Sikhs and the central government had only recently begun, and at the time it had not been established by Canadian immigration officials whether Indian government officials sometimes persecuted innocent Sikhs who were not participating in terrorist activities. (Later, the Refugee Status Advisory Committee recognized that there were some cases of unjustified persecution of Sikhs in India.) Thus, Singh's application for refugee status was rejected, his appeal was dismissed by the Immigration Appeal Board, and he was ordered to be deported to India. Singh then appealed to the courts for a declaration that the refugee claimant procedures violated section 7 of the Charter, which guarantees "everyone" the right to "life, liberty and security of the person" unless "deprived thereof . . . in accordance with the principles of fundamental justice." It should be noted that section 7 refers to "everyone," which means every human being, whether a citizen of Canada, a permanent resident or a visitor (whether visiting legally or illegally).

When the case was first heard by the Supreme Court, some judges were disappointed that no arguments were presented about the possible relevance of section 2(e) of the Canadian Bill of Rights, which provides a right to a "fair hearing in accordance with the principles of fundamental justice for the determination of [a person's] rights and obligations." The Court reserved its decision and requested written submissions from both sides about this section of the Bill. These submissions were considered before the Court handed down its decision.

The panel assigned to the case consisted originally of seven judges, but Mr. Justice Julien Chouinard became ill and was unable to participate in the decision. Thus, the *Singh* decision is one of the few in which an even number of judges rendered a judgment. The six judges decided unanimously in favour of Singh, but three based their decision on the Bill of Rights, while the other three grounded their reasoning on the Charter. The Court handed down its decision in April 1985.

The Charter Decision

Madame Justice Bertha Wilson wrote the decision based on the Charter, with Dickson and Lamer concurring. Wilson was faced with two major questions. First, was Singh deprived of the right to life, liberty and security of the person? And if so, were the procedures followed in accordance with the principles of fundamental justice?

The phrase "life, liberty and security of the person" can reasonably be interpreted in a number of different ways. For example, "life," "liberty" and "security of the person" could be considered as separate concepts, the deprivation of any of which could be enough to trigger a potential violation of section 7. On the other hand, the phrase could be considered as a single concept. Wilson left open the question whether one or the other of these views should prevail, but she specified that even if the "single right" approach were eventually to be adopted, each of the three elements of the right would have to be defined by the Court. Because the "security of the person" element was the one that most directly applied to Singh's situation, Wilson discussed possible meanings of the term.

A broad interpretation of "security of the person" might contain one of the rights included in the *Universal Declaration of Human Rights*: "a standard of living adequate for . . . health and well-being . . . including food, clothing, housing and medical care and necessary social services, and the right to security in the event of . . . circumstances beyond [a person's] control." Wilson said that it was not necessary for the Court to decide whether such a broad definition should be adopted, because "even if one adopts the narrow approach advocated by the counsel for the Minister, 'security of the person' must encompass freedom from the threat of physical punishment or suffering as well as freedom from such punishment itself." Thus, she concluded that the refugee determination procedures infringe the right to security of the person if they permit the authorities to deport someone to a country where his or her life would be endangered.

In approaching the second question concerning the meaning of fundamental justice, Wilson concluded that fundamental justice must at least include the factors that the Supreme Court had already determined [34] were implied by the phrase "fundamental justice" in section 2(e) of the Canadian Bill of Rights. For example, a "tribunal which adjudicates upon ... rights must act fairly, in good faith, without bias and in a judicial temper, and must give to [litigants] the opportunity adequately to state [their] case." Wilson allowed that procedural fairness "may demand different things in different contexts," but she nevertheless was "of the view that where a serious issue of credibility is involved, fundamental justice requires that credibility be determined on the basis of an oral hearing." This is because without an oral hearing a refugee applicant would not have the opportunity of learning about all the minister's evidence and therefore would not be able to respond thoroughly to the case against him or her. As a result, Wilson decided that the breach of security of the person was not in accord with the principles of fundamental justice.

Counsel for the government had "devoted relatively little time in the course of argument" to the question of whether a violation of section 7 could be upheld as a reasonable limit pursuant to section 1. In the absence of such evidence, Wilson determined that the violation of section 7 could not be justified under section 1.

The Bill of Rights Decision

Mr. Justice Beetz wrote the decision for the three judges who based their reasoning on the Bill of Rights; Estey and McIntyre concurred. Although Wilson in her decision agreed that the Bill "continues in full force and effect," those judges who based their decision on the Bill expressed no opinion about the applicability of the Charter. Thus, it is reasonable to conclude that the Bill of Rights was more central to the *Singh* decision than was the Charter. The *Singh* decision could therefore be considered as the first case since *Drybones* in which the Supreme Court had struck down a part of a statute based on the authority of the Canadian Bill of Rights. (In his decision, Mr. Justice Beetz declared part of section 71[1] of the Immigration Act inoperative.)

This resurrection of the Bill is a puzzling phenomenon. According to the *Therens* decision, discussed below, fear about abandoning legislative supremacy was the major reason why the Court gave a narrow interpretation to the Bill prior to 1982. Perhaps the judges have assumed that the advent of the Charter in 1982 signalled a softening of the importance of legislative supremacy in Canada, and that they were thus now free to give effect to the Bill. Beetz even referred to the statutory bills of rights as "constitutional or quasi-constitutional documents." Beetz interpreted the words "fundamental justice" in section 2(e) of the Bill in a similar fashion to the way Wilson had interpreted the same phrase in section 7 of the Charter. But Beetz pointed out that section 2(e) of the Bill has a broader application than section 7 of the Charter. Section 2(e) of the Bill provides "persons" — human or corporate — with the right to fundamental justice in any case that affects their rights or obligations (which includes a wide range of situations). On the other hand, section 7 of the Charter provides only human persons with the right to fundamental justice, and then only if they are faced with the loss of their life, liberty or security of the person. Although Beetz was convinced that section 2(e) of the Bill applied to a person seeking refugee status, he was unwilling to express an opinion as to whether the scope of section 7 of the Charter was broad enough to cover such persons.

The Impact of the Singh Decision

The *Singh* decision sent shock waves through Canada's Department of Employment and Immigration that are likely to continue to be felt for a number of years. The department had been totally unprepared for the Supreme Court ruling that refugee claimants should receive oral hearings. For two years after the *Singh* decision, the department was unable to develop a new refugee determination process that would incorporate the elements of fundamental justice specified by the Supreme Court. Instead, the old system continued, except that refugee claimants whose applications were dismissed by the Refugee Status Advisory Committee were granted oral hearings on appeal. As a result, the backlog in the determination of refugee cases increased from one year to more than three years. Some who appealed were bona fide refugees who would have been deported to their home country to face persecution or death had it not been for the *Singh* decision. Others, however, were not true refugees, but persons who wanted to immigrate to Canada for economic or family reasons and were unable to meet the regular criteria for immigration or family sponsorship.

Some self-styled "immigration consultants" and a few un-scrupulous lawyers began to advise their overseas clients that if they could not qualify to enter Canada under the immigration points system or the relative sponsorship program, they should come to Canada and claim refugee status even though they were not true refugees. The strategy was that because the refugee determination process was so backlogged, by the time they had exhausted their final appeal, they would have demonstrated that they could live as good Canadian citizens and perhaps the government would allow them to stay for "humanitarian" reasons. The result of the government's failure to act quickly to resolve the backlog of refugee cases was that thousands of refugee claimants arrived in Canada from countries like Portugal, Turkey and Brazil, which produce few, if any, refugees.

In February 1987 the government responded to the crisis by refusing to accept refugee claimants at the Canada-U.S. border without an appointment. This reduced considerably the chances of bona fide Central American refugees finding asylum in Canada. Most were not granted asylum in the United States, because the U.S. government backed most of the regimes the refugees were fleeing from. For the United States to accept refugees from El Salvador, Guatemala or Honduras would be to admit that the U.S. was supporting repressive regimes. The new procedure at the Canadian border had the effect of turning back many bona fide refugees from Central America, while false refugee claimants could still fly directly into Canada from countries such as Portugal and Brazil. Finally, in May 1987 the government introduced Bill C-55, the new refugee determination bill.

The strategy behind Bill C-55 was to force the processing of most refugee cases to Canadian government offices abroad so that the procedures would not be constrained by the Charter. Persons claiming refugee status at a border or airport would have seventy-two hours to establish a "credible basis" for their claim or face deportation. Persons arriving from a "safe third country" could not even apply for refugee status in Canada. The government refused to provide a list of "safe third countries," but refugee support groups in Canada feared that it would include friendly countries such as the United States and many European countries that are known to deport bona fide refugees.

Bill C-55 was vehemently denounced by the Canadian Bar Association, refugee support groups, all of the major churches, the Canadian Jewish Congress and many other religious and secular groups because of its potential violations of human rights. The government began to back away from the legislation. Then, in the summer of 1987, the arrival by ship on the coast of Nova Scotia of 174 East Asians, most of whom were Sikhs and all of whom claimed refugee status, created the kind of publicity the government needed to pursue the passage of Bill C-55. (It is ironic that the Sikhs came as they did partly because of the realization that once Bill C-55 became law, it would be difficult for many bona fide refugees to apply to come to Canada.) Not only was Bill C-55 pushed through the House of Commons, but a companion bill, C-84, was introduced which would empower Canadian authorities to apprehend ships suspected of carrying refugee claimants on the high seas and force them to sail away from Canada, whether or not the claimants were bona fide refugees, and whether or not the ship was seaworthy. Moreover, Bill C-84 would empower the government to prosecute persons assisting false or bona fide refugees if the refugees had not applied for refugee status under the very restrictive procedures contained in Bill C-55. The maximum penalty for such assistance was ten years in prison.

Bills C-55 and C-84 were stalled in the Senate until the summer of 1988. The Senate forced several amendments that softened some of the provisions in both bills, although the central thrust remained unchanged. The Senate received hundreds of submissions on the bills, almost all of them critical of the legislation because of its disregard for basic human rights. Every one of the dozens of submissions received from persons with legal training claimed that the bills violated the Charter.

The *Singh* case and the fallout from it illustrate how the Charter can have a positive influence on the protection of human rights in the courts but at the same time give rise to the development of compensatory constraints by policy-makers in the executive branch. Rather than devising a system that would provide refugee claimants with procedural safeguards which the Court said were guaranteed by the Charter and the Bill of Rights, the government decided to create a system that would make it difficult for refugee claimants to invoke Charter rights in the first place.

Clearly, Canada and the other liberal democracies will be faced with the problem of balancing a fair refugee-determination system against the need to prevent abuse, and against the pressures of local prejudices and misinformation, for years to come. Judicial policy-making under the Charter of Rights and the Bill of Rights will play an important part in shaping how Canadians respond to this issue.

The Right to Life and Security vs. the Cruise Missile: The Operation Dismantle Case [61]

In 1983 a number of organizations that were opposed to the testing of the U.S. cruise missile in Canada joined forces to mount a constitutional challenge to stop the tests. The organizations included some peace groups, labour unions, women's groups, church organizations and medical doctors. The cruise missile is a small, low-flying, computer-guided weapon that can evade radar detection until eight minutes before it reaches its target.

The anti-cruise groups feared that once the cruise became operational, the danger of nuclear war would be greatly increased. This is because Soviet officials would have only seconds to decide whether to launch a retaliatory attack after their radar screens had picked up what *might* be a U.S. cruise missile attack. Moreover, because satellite detection of cruise missiles is impossible, agreements to limit nuclear weapons would become unlikely, thus leading to an escalation of nuclear weapons capabilities. Cruise tests were planned in northern Canada because the geography is similar to that in the Soviet Union. The anti-cruise groups reasoned that since the testing was an integral part of the development of the cruise, the testing contributed to the likelihood of a nuclear war. The increased risk of war deprived all Canadians of their security of the person, and a war itself would deprive many Canadians of their lives, contrary to the guarantees of life and security of the person in section 7 of the Charter.

When Operation Dismantle brought its case to the Federal Court of Appeal, lawyers for the government argued that the claim should not proceed to trial because there was no reasonable cause of action. The Federal Court upheld the government's position, and the anti-cruise groups appealed to the Supreme Court of Canada. Meanwhile, the cruise tests took place in March 1984. The Supreme Court released its decision in May 1985. The Court unanimously upheld the decision of the Federal Court.

The Court had three important questions to answer. First, are cabinet decisions subject to the Charter, even though no statutes are involved? Second, are issues like the government's defence policy "justiciable," that is, do they raise true legal questions? And third, if the first two questions are answered in the affirmative, should this particular case proceed to trial?

In Canada, federal and provincial cabinets derive their authority from two sources: legislation and the prerogative power. The prerogative power is inherited from pre-democratic English times when the monarch was the supreme power. Prerogative powers may be limited or abolished through legislation, but Parliament has not chosen to abolish the prerogative powers of the cabinet over foreign affairs and national defence. Counsel for the government had argued that the Charter should not apply to the prerogative powers of the cabinet. However, the judges all agreed that the wording of section 32(1)(a) of the Charter, which declares that the Charter applies, among other things, to the "government" of Canada, is broad enough to include all cabinet decisions. In chapter 2 it was noted that because of the adversary system, government lawyers will tend to argue for the narrowest possible interpretation of the Charter, even though the government that spearheaded the Charter boasted that it would protect the rights of Canadians in the broadest possible way. This particular issue is a good illustration of that tendency.

Government lawyers also claimed that matters such as defence policy are not justiciable. The justiciability issue was suggested to them by a reading of U.S. Supreme Court cases dealing with the U.S. Bill of Rights, which have drawn a line between cases that raise "legal" issues and those that raise "political" issues. The former are justiciable, or proper for a court to hear, while the latter are not. The justiciability doctrine is based on the U.S. theory of the separation of powers. One branch of government is not supposed to encroach on the duties of another branch. "Legal" issues belong to the judiciary, while "political" issues belong to the legislature or executive.

The Canadian Supreme Court decided that to apply the U.S. justiciability test to Charter issues was inappropriate. Instead of asking whether a particular issue is legal or political, the Canadian Court decided to ask whether a particular government action violated the Charter. Madame Justice Wilson described this approach as follows:

> The question before us is not whether the government's defence policy is sound but whether or not it violates the

> [anti-cruise groups'] rights under s.7 .... [I]f we are to
> look at the Constitution for the answer to the question
> whether it is appropriate for the courts to "second guess"
> the executive on matters of defence, we would conclude
> that it is not appropriate. However, if what we are being
> asked to do is to decide whether any particular act of the
> executive violated the rights of the citizens, then it is not
> only appropriate that we answer the question; it is our
> obligation under the Charter to do so.

Thus, the Supreme Court of Canada has provided a wider scope for
issues capable of being litigated under the Charter than the U.S.
Supreme Court has for issues that may be litigated under the
American Bill of Rights.

The majority decision, which was written by Chief Justice Dickson, concluded that there was no basis for Operation Dismantle's
statement of claim because the arguments of the anti-cruise groups
were mere speculation. There was no evidence that foreign powers
were almost certain to act in the way hypothesized by the groups
opposed to the cruise. According to Dickson, it could just as easily
be supposed that

> lack of verification would have the effect of enhancing
> enforceability [rather] than of undermining it, since an
> inability on the part of nuclear powers to verify systems
> like the cruise could precipitate a system of enforcement
> based on cooperation rather than surveillance .... In brief,
> it is simply not possible for a court, even with best avail-
> able evidence, to do more than speculate upon the
> likelihood of the Federal Cabinet's decision to test the
> cruise missile resulting in an increased threat of nuclear
> war.

Justice Wilson gave different reasons for agreeing that the anti-
cruise groups did not have a case. She said that section 7 of the
Charter protects individual rights. In order for a claim to go to trial
under section 7, the claimants would have to argue that a cabinet
decision threatened the lives, liberties or personal security of specific
individuals.

Did the anti-cruise groups actually expect to stop the testing of the
cruise through Charter litigation, or did they use the case to generate

publicity for their cause? It is likely that those in the coalition with some legal training saw the challenge mainly as a publicity measure, while many of the rank-and-file members believed that they might actually win their case. There is a lesson here about how Canadians perceive civil liberties. Canadians unfamiliar with the intricacies of the legal system may tend to believe that whatever is morally right is probably also legally right when set against the Charter. Although some of those with legal training may also believe that the Charter enshrines moral values, others might be more apt to see the Charter as just another opportunity for winning cases regardless of moral right or for generating publicity regardless of legal foundation.

The Right to Counsel and the Therens Decision [109]

The Charter not only protects the right to counsel as the Canadian Bill of Rights does, but it goes beyond the Bill to establish a right to be informed of the right to counsel. Exactly one week after the Charter came into effect in 1982, Paul Mathew Therens lost control of his motor vehicle and collided with a tree in Moose Jaw, Saskatchewan. The police, suspecting that Therens had been drinking, took him to the police station for a breathalyzer test. Therens cooperated in taking the test. He was not informed of his right to counsel, and he did not request to contact a lawyer. The breathalyzer test provided evidence for the crown to charge Therens with driving while having a blood alcohol content in excess of 80 milligrams of alcohol in 100 millilitres of blood.

The reason why Therens was not informed of his right to counsel was that the right to counsel takes effect, according to section 10(b) of the Charter, only "on arrest or detention." Therens was not arrested before the breathalyzer test, and the police did not consider that he was being detained. This is because Therens could have refused to take the breathalyzer test. Had he refused to take the test, however, he would have been charged with refusing to take a breathalyzer test, the penalty for which is the same as the penalty for driving with a blood alcohol content of "over 80." Nevertheless, the definition of "detention" formulated by the Canadian Supreme Court under the Canadian Bill of Rights did not include being requested to give a breath sample [26]. Thus, the police were acting on what they considered to be good legal authority by not informing Therens of a right to counsel at the stage of the breathalyzer test.

At trial, Therens's lawyer claimed that to admit the evidence against Therens would constitute a violation of the Charter. Section 24(2) of the Charter states that where "evidence was obtained in a manner that infringed or denied any rights or freedoms guaranteed by this Charter, the evidence shall be excluded if it is established that, having regard to all the circumstances, the admission of it in the proceedings would bring the administration of justice into disrepute." The trial judge agreed that the evidence should not be admitted, and dismissed the charge against Therens for lack of evidence. The crown lost its appeal in the Saskatchewan Court of Appeal in April 1983 and appealed to the Supreme Court. In May 1985 the Supreme Court handed down its decision.

The Supreme Court dealt with four key issues: the status of Bill of Rights precedents as applied to the Charter; the meaning of "detention" under the Charter; whether the failure to inform of and allow the right to counsel before the breathalyzer test is a reasonable limit; and whether refusing to admit the evidence in this case would bring the administration of justice into disrepute.

The Status of Canadian Bill of Rights Precedents

The crown argued that the framers of the Charter must have been aware of the meaning that the Supreme Court had given to "detention" under the Bill of Rights and that therefore it is that meaning which should apply to the Charter. Mr. Justice Le Dain, who wrote the decision for the majority about this issue, disagreed. He said that constitutional documents must necessarily use "general language which is capable of development and adaptation by the courts." He referred to the analysis of legal theorist Ronald Dworkin (3), who claimed that constitutional language contains broad "concepts" that should not be reduced to narrow interpretations based on particular "conceptions" of the broader concept. Then Le Dain explained that the Supreme Court had given a narrow interpretation to the Bill because of the desire to defer to the principle of legislative supremacy. Because the Charter represented a "new constitutional mandate for judicial review," the definitions established under the Bill should not be taken as reliable guides to the meaning of the Charter.

The Meaning of "Detention"

Having rejected the definition of "detention" developed under the Bill, the Court needed to develop a new approach. The crown claimed that a person was "detained" only when compelled to do something and that a person could not be compelled to take a breath test. Le Dain disagreed. Because the consequences for refusing to take a breath test are the same as for being convicted of drinking and driving, "it is not realistic to speak of a person who is liable to arrest and prosecution for refusal to [take a breath test] as being free to refuse to comply .... Any criminal liability for failure to comply with a demand or direction of a police officer must be sufficient to make compliance involuntary."

Le Dain then supplied a broad definition of "detention" that includes what we could call "psychological detention":

> Most citizens are not aware of the precise legal limits of police authority. Rather than risk the application of physical force or prosecution for wilful obstruction, the reasonable person is likely to err on the side of caution, assume lawful authority and comply with the demand. The element of psychological compulsion, in the form of a reasonable perception of suspension of freedom of choice, is enough to make the restraint of liberty involuntary.

Because "detention" was defined to include Therens's situation, the Court concluded that a breach of the Charter had occurred when Therens was given a breath test without first being told of his right to counsel.

Reasonable Limits to the Right to Counsel

On this issue, Mr. Justice Le Dain examined the relevant breathalyzer provisions of the Criminal Code and could find no express or implied limitation to the right to counsel. He noted that breath samples must be taken within two hours from the time that the offence was allegedly committed and that this time period does not "preclude any contact at all with counsel prior to the breathalyzer test." Because there were no limits "prescribed by law," section 1 arguments could not be entertained.

Whether to Admit Evidence That Would Bring the Administration of Justice into Disrepute

The final question the Court had to decide was whether this violation of a Charter right had brought "the administration of justice into disrepute," so that the evidence should be excluded pursuant to section 24(2) of the Charter. The majority of the Court concluded that the evidence should be excluded. According to Mr. Justice Estey:

> Here the police authority has flagrantly violated a Charter right without any statutory authority for so doing. Such an overt violation as occurred here must, in my view, result in the rejection of the evidence thereby obtained. To do otherwise than reject this evidence on the facts and circumstances in this appeal would be to invite police officers to disregard the Charter rights of the citizen and to do so with an assurance of impunity.

Mr. Justice Le Dain had suggested an alternative approach. For this particular case, the evidence should be admitted, but in all future cases where a person being requested to take a breathalyzer test was not told of his or her right to counsel, the evidence would be excluded. The majority rejected this approach, however, because it would not send a clear signal to the police that they must take the Charter seriously. Mr. Justice McIntyre took a polar-opposite view. From his perspective, to *exclude* the evidence so that Therens would go free on a technicality "would itself go far to bring the administration of justice into disrepute."

The disagreement among the judges about what it means to "bring the administration of justice into disrepute" underlines one of the problems of legal interpretation that has never been satisfactorily resolved. In interpreting vague phrases that seem to imply a community standard, judges often try to apply what they consider to be the standard of the average reasonable person who is informed of the relevant circumstances surrounding the issue. Professor Dale Gibson of the University of Manitoba has suggested that litigants could conduct public opinion polls about whether excluding a particular piece of evidence would bring the administration of justice into disrepute. The majority on the Court rejected this suggestion, both because it would increase the costs to litigants and because of the difficulty in explaining all the relevant circumstances to persons being polled. In the absence of hard evidence, then, the standard of the average reasonable person becomes a subjective standard set by the judges themselves. Because judges are specialized professionals who are drawn from the upper echelons of society, it is unlikely that they will be able accurately to guess the views of average, reasonable persons.

A less subjective standard is obviously needed, but our legal imaginations have not yet been capable of finding one.

In view of the *Therens* decision, readers may wonder whether persons who are asked to take a "roadside" breathalyzer test have a right to retain counsel before taking the test. (The roadside tests are used by police as an initial screening procedure; persons who "fail" the roadside test are asked to accompany a police officer to a police station, where breathalyzer evidence is collected that may be used as evidence in court.) In *Regina v. Thomsen* [110] (April 1988), the Supreme Court of Canada decided that the denial of the right to counsel before a roadside test is a reasonable limit under section 1. The Court pointed out an important difference between the Criminal Code provision governing roadside breath tests (*Thomsen*) and police station breathalyzer tests (*Therens*). The former Criminal Code provision states that a person shall provide a breath sample "forthwith" if requested to do so, whereas in the latter section, the breath test shall be provided "forthwith *or as soon as practicable*" (emphasis added). Thus, the roadside test does imply a limit "prescribed by law" to the right to counsel, since a breath sample could not be provided "forthwith" if counsel were contacted and consulted.

The Court decided that the limit implied by the roadside testing procedure was "reasonable" under section 1. The objective of the roadside testing procedure — "not only to increase the detection of impaired driving, but to increase the perceived risk of its detection" — is a pressing and substantial concern, and the means chosen to achieve the objective are proportional to it, particularly in view of the fact that the *Therens* decision guarantees that a person who fails the roadside test has a right to retain counsel before the police station test.

In another 1988 case, the Supreme Court decided that police spot checks on highways, while they do violate the Charter's section 9 right not to be arbitrarily detained, constitute a reasonable limit [91]. This is because of the importance of detecting and reducing impaired driving.

Since *Therens,* the Supreme Court has developed a test for the exclusion of evidence that would bring the administration of justice into disrepute — section 24(2). In the *Collins* decision [84], Mr. Justice Lamer, writing for the majority, declared that the admissibility of evidence obtained in violation of a Charter right depends on three factors. First, if the admission of such evidence would prejudice the fairness of a trial, it should be excluded. Second, the more serious the

Charter violation, the more compelling the need for the judges to exclude the evidence. Third, the evidence should *not* be excluded if to exclude would bring disrepute to the justice system. The Court has tended to exclude evidence when, as in the *Therens* case, there was a violation of the right to counsel [27, 95, 104], but has sometimes admitted evidence in such cases if the *Collins* test has been met [108, 111]. On the other hand, the Court has tended to admit evidence when there was an unreasonable search or seizure [90, 92, 105, 106], although such evidence may be exluded for compelling reasons [87, 89].

The B.C. Motor Vehicle Act Case and Fundamental Justice [69]

Because a large number of serious motor vehicle accidents in Canada are alcohol related, provincial governments have in recent years greatly increased the penalties for drinking and driving. The suspension of driving privileges is one penalty often required by provincial legislation. In addition, to encourage safer driving overall, some provincial governments suspend drivers' licences for a specific period upon the accumulation of a certain number of demerit points. Unless the suspension of licences can be enforced, however, these sanctions do not serve as an effective deterrent.

In 1982 the British Columbia legislature amended its Motor Vehicle Act to create an "absolute liability" offence for driving without a valid driver's licence. A first conviction would result in a mandatory minimum fine of $300 and a mandatory minimum jail sentence of seven days. For subsequent convictions, the minimum jail sentence would become fourteen days.

Normally, judges assume that Parliament does not wish accused persons to be convicted unless they intentionally committed an illegal act or acted recklessly. This principle, known as *mens rea,* has been developed through the common law (see chapter 1). An absolute liability offence is one for which the accused person cannot claim as a defence that he or she was not aware of committing the prohibited act. The B.C. Motor Vehicle Act created an absolute liability offence because it declared that a person charged with driving without a valid licence could not claim as a defence that he or she was not aware that the licence was suspended. Perhaps the government feared that if a finding of *mens rea* was required, some of those guilty of driving without a valid licence might escape conviction — for example, by refusing to claim registered mail notices informing them of their licence suspensions.

Before 1982, legislatures in Canada could create absolute liability offences simply by stipulating that *mens rea* is not an element of particular offences. After 1982, it was not clear whether the Charter prohibited legislatures from creating absolute liability offences. Section 7 of the Charter guarantees everyone "the right to life, liberty and security of the person" unless deprived thereof pursuant to "the principles of fundamental justice." It was possible that "fundamental justice" included *mens rea*. To settle this issue, the B.C. government sent a reference to the provincial Court of Appeal in 1982. The case was appealed to the Supreme Court, which rendered its decision in 1985.

The question of whether *mens rea* is included in section 7 of the Charter raises the question of whether section 7 is *substantive* or *procedural* in nature. A procedural interpretation would mean that a legislature could enact a law that would deprive people of their "life, liberty or security" as long as the correct procedures of fundamental justice were followed — for example, a fair hearing before an independent and impartial judge, adequate notice of the hearing, the right to counsel and so on. A substantive interpretation would mean that even if the correct procedures were followed, in certain instances a legislature could not deprive a person of his or her life, liberty or security.

The substantive-versus-procedural issue is a product of the U.S. Supreme Court's interpretation of the "due process" clause in the American Bill of Rights. The fifth and fourteenth amendments to the U.S. constitution protect "life," "liberty" and "property" unless persons are deprived of them through "due process of law." Between 1905 and 1937 (a period known as the *Lochner* era, after a decision that set the tone for the period), the American Supreme Court interpreted "due process" in a substantive way to strike down social policy laws that restricted anti-union activity and provided for maximum hours of work, minimum wages and maximum prices. The laws were considered by the judges to interfere with employers' "liberty" to contract with employees, and with "property" rights.

When President Franklin Delano Roosevelt's New Deal legislation was threatened, among other things, by this substantive interpretation of "due process," Roosevelt considered expanding the Court and "packing" it with judges who would interpret "due process" in a merely procedural way. The Court-packing scheme was never carried out, for in 1937 the Court changed its tactics. It overruled earlier decisions and abandoned the substantive interpretation of "due process" that had precluded some social welfare legislation. The Court has continued to interpret "due process" in a substantive way with regard to other matters, however. For example, in 1965 the Court struck down a law prohibiting the use of contraceptives, and in 1973 it struck down an anti-abortion law [118].

The framers of the Charter hoped to foreclose any possibility that the Canadian courts might indulge in a Canadian version of the *Lochner* era and thereby limit the potential of Canadian social programs. Thus, they carefully avoided any mention of "due process" in the Charter. Instead, they adopted the phrase "fundamental justice." This phrase is potentially synonymous with "due process." However, the Canadian Supreme Court had already defined "fundamental justice" in a purely procedural way in a case decided under the Canadian Bill of Rights [34]. In testimony before the Special Joint Committee on the Constitution in 1981, Jean Chrétien, minister of justice, B.L. Strayer, assistant deputy minister, and F.J.E. Jordan, senior counsel, said that the phrase "fundamental justice" had been carefully chosen for section 7 as a signal for the courts to interpret the section in a procedural rather than in a substantive way.

In spite of this background, in the *B.C. Motor Vehicle Act* decision the Supreme Court gave "fundamental justice" a substantive interpretation. Concerning the Bill of Rights precedent, Mr. Justice Lamer, who wrote the majority opinion, reminded his readers that in the *Therens* decision the Court had declared that before 1982 concern about legislative supremacy had prevented the Court from applying the Bill broadly. Therefore, Bill of Rights precedents could not be taken as reliable guides to Charter interpretation.

There were two issues related to the impact of the testimony of Jean Chrétien and his officials. The first was whether evidence from a parliamentary committee hearing should be entertained by judges. Traditionally, common-law courts did not consider such evidence when determining the "intent of the legislature" because such evidence was considered to be an unreliable guide to the thinking of MPs as a whole. The only reliable guide was considered to be the legislation itself. In 1976, however, the Supreme Court decided that a blanket exclusion of certain types of evidence is unwise; whether to admit evidence should be determined by its potential relevance [77]. Since that time, the Supreme Court has accepted legislative debates as evidence in two cases [2, 68]. Thus, the Court decided that to accept evidence from a legislative committee would be in keeping with the new approach to admitting evidence.

The second issue was how much weight should be given to the evidence. The Court assigned the evidence "minimal weight" for two reasons. First, there was no evidence that Jean Chrétien and his officials represented the views of most MPs and provincial legislators. Second, according to Mr. Justice Lamer,

> Another danger with casting the interpretation of s.7 in terms of the comments made by those heard at the Joint Committee Proceedings is that, in so doing, the rights, freedoms and values embodied in the Charter in effect become frozen in time to the moment of adoption with little or no possibility of growth, development and adjustment to changing societal needs.

Having given minimal weight to Jean Chrétien's recommendation for interpreting section 7, Lamer had no difficulty in deciding that section 7 should be given more than a procedural interpretation. He described the procedural-versus-substantive issue as an American one, not relevant to the Charter because of its different wording. From the purposive perspective, Lamer claimed that section 7 was intended to protect "the basic tenets of our legal system," such as "the dignity and worth of the human person" and "the Rule of Law." He claimed that sections 8-14 of the Charter are specific examples of how fundamental justice is to be applied, and he noted that some of these provisions go beyond the provision of mere procedural safeguards.

Lamer concluded that a combination of a mandatory prison term (which deprives a person of liberty) and an absolute liability offence violates fundamental justice. He noted that such a violation of section 7 might be shown to be a reasonable limit under section 1 but that lawyers for the crown had failed to produce any evidence as to why this violation of fundamental justice should be accepted as a reasonable limit. In the absence of such evidence, the Court could only hold that the existence of a "reasonable limit" had certainly not been "demonstrably justified."

Mr. Justice Lamer's opinion in this case seems to be full of paradoxes. He first claimed that the procedural-substantive debate is not relevant to section 7 of the Charter and then interpreted section 7 in a substantive way. He accepted uncontested evidence from a parliamentary committee hearing, and then assigned it minimal weight and decided contrary to that evidence. He claimed that the courts do not make policies but merely apply the law, and then proceeded to make a very important policy decision: that "fundamental justice" includes, and extends beyond, the legal safeguards in sections 8-14.

But these apparent paradoxes oversimplify a very complex issue. The interpretation of "fundamental justice" in the context of the Charter has been one of the Court's most difficult policy-making tasks to date.

Judicial Independence and the Valente Case [132]

In 1981 Walter Valente was charged with dangerous driving after an accident in which three children were killed. Dangerous driving is a serious Criminal Code offence that can result in a jail sentence. The case came before an Ontario Provincial Court judge in December 1982. In an effort to keep his client out of jail, Valente's lawyer argued that the trial violated Valente's right to an "independent and impartial" judge, which is guaranteed by section 11(d) of the Charter. The Provincial Court judge decided that the argument had enough merit for it to be heard by a judge of a higher court. The Ontario Court of Appeal heard the case involving judicial independence early in 1983. In the meantime, two other Ontario Provincial Court judges and a justice of the peace announced that they would decline jurisdiction whenever a lawyer questioned their independence. (This series of events, which became known as the "judges' revolt," has been described in more detail elsewhere by the author(1).

The Ontario Court of Appeal found that Provincial Court judges qualify as independent and impartial for the purposes of the Charter, and this decision was confirmed by the Supreme Court of Canada in December 1985. In order for one to understand the significance of the Supreme Court decision, some familiarity with the relevant background issues is necessary.

The Provincial Court is the basic workhorse court in each province. Over 90 per cent of all cases generated in Canada are heard at this level. The bulk of the workload of the Provincial Courts is composed of minor traffic and criminal cases, although Provincial Court judges can hear cases involving a number of serious offences, including several for which the maximum penalty is life imprisonment. Provincial Court judges also hear family cases (such as custody disputes), young offenders cases and small claims cases. Canadians who become involved with the justice system are much more likely to form their impressions of Canadian justice in the Provincial Court than in any other court.

In spite of the importance of the Provincial Court, the working conditions and salaries of Provincial Court judges are not nearly as good as for judges of district and superior courts in the provinces. There are historical reasons for this discrepancy. Before the 1960s, Provincial Court judges were known as "magistrates" or "police magistrates," and until recently, many had no legal training. The "real" judges were considered to be those in the district and superior courts. Over the past three decades, however, all provincial governments have raised the standards for appointments to their Provincial Courts; now almost all Provincial Court judges have legal training and have practised law for several years before becoming judges. Concurrently, the kinds of cases provincial court judges can hear have steadily increased in seriousness in terms of penal consequences in criminal cases or monetary value in civil cases.

The fact that Provincial Court judges are paid significantly lower salaries and have fewer benefits than judges in the higher courts has led to a good deal of resentment among some Provincial Court judges. Valente's lawyer, no doubt aware of this situation, built his argument on those aspects of the poorer working conditions of Provincial Court judges that might impinge judicial independence.

In part, the independence of superior court judges is protected by sections 99 and 100 of the Constitution Act, 1867. Section 99 protects the security of tenure of superior court judges by stipulating that they shall hold office until retirement "during good behaviour," which means they cannot be removed for making decisions the government disapproves of. Moreover, they may only be removed with the approval of both the Senate and the House of Commons, a public process intended to protect judges from arbitrary firings. Section 100 states that the salaries of the superior and district court judges must be set by an act of Parliament rather than by cabinet order, and it implies that the salaries of judges may not be lowered except during a general economic crisis. Valente's position was that, in order to be independent, Provincial Court judges required the same constitutional guarantees of their independence. In addition, counsel for Valente argued that superior court judges have their own benefit plans — presumably to protect their independence — while Provincial Court judges are enrolled in ordinary public service benefit plans.

Mr. Justice Le Dain wrote the opinion of the unanimous Supreme Court panel. The decision is an important one for two reasons. First,

Le Dain distinguished between judicial independence and judicial impartiality. Impartiality, he wrote, is a "state of mind," while independence concerns the relations between judges and others — relations that ought to be regulated so as to promote impartiality. Second, Le Dain declared that there are three "essential conditions" for the existence of judicial independence: security of tenure, financial security and institutional independence. All ought to be secured through reasonable measures such as legislation; however, Le Dain considered that constitutional guarantees, like sections 99 and 100 of the Constitution Act, 1867, were useful but not absolutely necessary. The security of tenure of judges could be guaranteed by ordinary statutes as long as the statutes stipulated that judges held their appointments "during good behaviour" and as long as the removal process required an independent inquiry. The requirement of financial security could be met as long as a statute guaranteed judges a salary. And institutional independence could be achieved if judges could control those aspects of court administration directly related to decision-making.

Valente lost his case, but what emerged from the Supreme Court's decision was a working definition of "judicial independence" for the purposes of section 11(d) of the Charter. "Judicial impartiality," however, did not receive a clear definition because counsel for Valente chose not to raise impartiality issues. Therefore, the constitutional definition of "judicial impartiality" will await future litigation.

The Oakes Case [129]

As noted in chapter 1, one of the presumptions developed through the common law to protect civil liberties is that an accused person should be presumed innocent until proven guilty. Like all common law, this presumption may be reversed in specific instances with appropriate legislation. Such reversals of the presumption of innocence are known as "reverse onus clauses."

The Canadian Narcotic Control Act contains a reverse onus clause. A person who is proven to be in possession of a narcotic is also presumed to be guilty of trafficking unless he or she can prove otherwise. In other words, the traditional presumption of innocence applies to a person charged with possession of an illegal narcotic. However, once possession is proven, the onus is reversed and there is a presumption of guilt with regard to trafficking. The purpose of this reverse onus clause is, of course, to curtail the use of illegal drugs, which has become a very serious social problem.

David Edwin Oakes was charged with trafficking in narcotics in Ontario in 1981. At his trial, it was proven that he had been in possession of eight one-gram vials of hashish oil. It was then up to Oakes to prove that he was not also guilty of trafficking. Oakes claimed that he had bought the hashish oil for his own use and claimed that the reverse onus clause in the Narcotic Control Act violated section 11(d) of the Charter. Section 11(d) states that any person charged with an offence has the right to be presumed innocent until proven guilty according to law in a fair and public hearing by an independent and impartial tribunal.

Oakes won his case in the Ontario Court of Appeal in 1983, and the crown appealed to the Supreme Court of Canada. It was clear that the reverse onus clause in the Narcotic Control Act violated section 11(d), but the crown claimed that this provision was a reasonable limit pursuant to section 1. This was because of the serious problem of drug trafficking in Canada and the need of law enforcement agencies to have effective means to suppress it.

As noted in chapter 2, the Supreme Court developed a two-part test for reasonable limits in its decision in this case. The first part of the test was that the government objective in violating a Charter right must be of sufficient importance. Chief Justice Dickson, writing for a unanimous seven-judge panel, declared that the government's objective — "curbing drug trafficking by facilitating the conviction of drug traffickers" — was of sufficient importance to pass part one of the test.

The second part of the analysis, known as the proportionality test, has three prongs: (a) the rational connection test, (b) the least impairment test and (c) the general proportionality test (that is, the cure must not be worse than the disease). The chief justice failed the reverse onus clause on the first prong of part two of the test:

> In my view, [the reverse onus clause] does not survive the rational connection test .... [P]ossession of a small or negligible quantity of narcotics does not support the inference of trafficking. In other words, it would be irrational to infer that a person had an intent to traffic on the basis of his or her possession of a very small quantity of narcotics .... In light of the seriousness of the offence in question, which carries with it the possibility of imprisonment for life, I am further convinced that the first component of the proportionality test has not been satisfied by

the Crown. Having concluded that [the reverse onus clause] does not satisfy this first component of proportionality, it is unnecessary to consider the other two components.

It should be noted that the issue Dickson was considering in the above passage was whether the reverse onus clause would result in irrational conclusions in *any* case, not just in this particular one. Obviously, Oakes had been in possession of more than a "negligible quantity" of hashish oil. According to the rule of law, laws must be applied equally to everyone. Therefore, if a law violates the Charter rights of some but not others, it cannot be declared inoperative for some but upheld for the others. Laws must be framed so as to be fair to all. Therefore, laws that violate the Charter rights of some, and cannot be saved under section 1, must be struck down.

The Court has made other important decisions about section 11(d). In the *Vaillancourt* decision [113], the Court declared that the Criminal Code offence of "culpable homicide," a type of murder, violates the presumption of innocence. (Persons are guilty of culpable homicide if they act recklessly in a manner that may cause death and a death results, even if unintended.) The Court has also upheld the reverse onus clause in the Criminal Code that states that a person proven to have occupied the driver's seat in a vehicle is presumed to have "care and control" of the vehicle unless he or she can prove otherwise [115]. As a result, persons who are intoxicated and who are found in a driver's seat can be convicted of impaired driving whether or not their vehicle was in motion.

The Morgentaler Case [100]

In 1985 Dr. Henry Morgentaler and two other doctors were convicted of procuring abortions contrary to section 251 of the Criminal Code. They appealed to the Supreme Court of Canada on the grounds that section 251 violated the rights of pregnant women to "liberty" and "security of the person" contrary to the principles of fundamental justice in section 7 of the Charter. The Supreme Court rendered its decision in January 1988.

Section 251 prohibits abortions unless they are carried out by a qualified medical practitioner in an approved hospital, and unless such abortions have been sanctioned by the majority of members of the hospital's abortion committee on the grounds that an abortion is necessary to safeguard a woman's "life or health." Approved hospitals are those which are designated by the provincial minister of health (who is under no obligation to approve any hospitals) and which provide specified services. There must be at least three doctors on the abortion committee, none of whom do abortions. Because of these restrictions, only about 40 per cent of Canadian hospitals are eligible to provide abortions. Moreover, only about half of the eligible hospitals have actually established abortion committees. The result is that women could obtain abortions in about only 20 per cent of Canadian hospitals.

The seven-judge panel that heard the *Morgentaler* case was seriously divided. Five judges decided in favour of Morgentaler's appeal, but for three very different sets of reasons, as outlined below.

Section 251 Violates the Procedural Rights of Women (Dickson, Lamer Concurring)

Chief Justice Dickson began by pointing out that it would be necessary only to consider the procedural implications of fundamental justice in relation to section 251; a substantive review would not be necessary because the case could be decided on procedural grounds alone. (See the *B.C. Motor Vehicle Act* case, above, regarding the procedural and substantive approaches.)

True to the purposive approach to Charter adjudication developed by the Court, the chief justice reasoned that the purpose of the guarantee of "security of the person" was, at the very least, to prevent "state interference with bodily integrity and serious state-imposed psychological stress." He concluded that section 251 violates security of the person because

> every pregnant woman is told by the section that she cannot submit to a generally safe medical procedure that might be of clear benefit to her unless she meets criteria entirely unrelated to her own priorities and aspirations. Not only does the removal of decision making power threaten women in a physical sense; the indecision of knowing whether an abortion will be granted inflicts emotional stress .... Forcing a woman, by threat of criminal sanction, to carry a foetus to term unless she meets certain criteria unrelated to her own priorities and aspirations, is a profound interference with a woman's body and thus a violation of security of the person.

In addition, Dickson noted that the delays caused by the elaborate decision-making procedure required to obtain abortions, and the psychological stress caused by the decision-making procedures, also contributed to the violation of security of the person. For all these reasons, section 251 was held to violate the right to security of the person. (He left unanswered the question of whether section 251 violated the right to liberty.) Section 7, however, stipulates that certain violations of "life, liberty and security of the person" are acceptable: those that conform with "fundamental justice." Dickson therefore proceeded to a consideration of whether the violation of security of the person in section 251 conformed with fundamental justice.

Dickson reasoned that section 251 failed to meet the procedural standards for fundamental justice for several reasons. First, the administrative system established by section 251 is so cumbersome that the great majority of hospitals in Canada do not provide abortions. In other words, section 251 prohibits some abortions but permits others under certain conditions. These conditions, however, are difficult to meet in most locations. Therefore, the legal protection that section 251 supposedly provides to women whose life or health would be endangered by continuing a pregnancy does not in fact exist in many parts of the country.

Another difficulty, according to Dickson, is that section 251 provides no definition of "health." The evidence before the court was that

> therapeutic abortion committees apply widely differing definitions of health. For some committees, psychological health is a justification for therapeutic abortion; for others it is not. Some committees routinely refuse abortions to married women, while [others do not] . . . . It is not typically possible for women to know in advance what standard of health will be applied by any given committee . . . . It is no answer to say that "health" is a medical term and that doctors . . . must simply exercise their professional judgment . . . . [T]he absence of any clear legal standard to be applied by the committee in reaching its decision is a serious procedural flaw.

In other words, if a woman must meet a certain standard in order to obtain an abortion, she must know what that standard is. And the same standard, under the rule of law, must be applied to everyone.

Having concluded that section 251 failed to provide fundamental justice, Dickson considered whether the provision could be saved under section 1. In defining Parliament's objective in enacting section 251, Dickson accepted the statement of purpose in the abortion law itself: to protect the "life and health" of pregnant women. He accepted this statement of purpose as being sufficiently important to pass the first part of the *Oakes* test. (Dickson noted that section 251 says nothing about protecting the fetus.) However, he concluded that section 251 failed all three prongs of the second part of the *Oakes* test. The complex administrative machinery was arbitrary and not rationally connected with the objective of the section. It infringed women's rights far more than necessary. And its negative effects were generally out of proportion to its benefits.

Section 251 Violates the Procedural Rights of Women, but Parliament Is Justified in Protecting the Fetus (Beetz, Estey Concurring)

Mr. Justice Beetz agreed with Chief Justice Dickson that "if an effective and timely therapeutic abortion may only be obtained by committing a crime, then s.251 violates the pregnant woman's right to security of the person." Therefore, section 251 would pass muster only if it met the requirements of fundamental justice, or failing that, if it were considered a reasonable limit under section 1.

Beetz also agreed that section 251 violated fundamental justice, but for different reasons than those advanced by Dickson. Beetz noted that section 251 provided women with a limited right to therapeutic abortions, and in addition he claimed that the "right to liberty" in section 7 of the Charter entrenched some minimum right to an abortion. However, he concluded that the crown had failed to demonstrate that it was necessary for all abortions to be performed in a hospital. As well, he could find no justification for the requirement that committees established to approve abortions must consist of medical doctors practising at the hospital where the abortion would be performed. Nevertheless, he did think that the requirement for a second opinion about the necessity for an abortion was a reasonable one, given the possible conflict between the state's interest in protecting the fetus and a woman's interest in her liberty, security and health.

> The risk resulting from the delay caused by [the in-hospital provision and the resident committee provision] is unnecessary. Consequently, the requirement violates the

> principles of fundamental justice . . . . [These are] by no means a complete catalogue of all the current system's strengths and failings. It demonstrates, however, that the administrative structure put in place by Parliament has enough shortcomings so that [the abortion law] violates the principles of fundamental justice.

Beetz disagreed with Dickson, however, about whether the abortion law required a clearer definition of "health." He felt that a certain amount of flexibility was required in framing such a law and that medical doctors were entitled to exercise medical judgment. He regarded as having exceeded their authority those committees that routinely refused abortions unless approved by the woman's spouse, refused abortion requests from married women or refused to consider second abortions. Such decisions could therefore be reviewed by a court as exceeding the legal jurisdiction of the committees.

The most important aspect of the disagreement between the reasons of Beetz and Dickson, however, concerns the section 1 analysis. Whereas Dickson had taken the wording of the abortion law at face value and had considered its objective as protecting the "life and health" of women, Beetz concluded that this was only a secondary purpose. The primary purpose, he claimed, was to protect the fetus. From this perspective, Beetz found that the objective of section 251 was of sufficient importance to pass the first part of the *Oakes* test. However, he failed section 251 on the first prong of the second part of the *Oakes* test. Because section 251 contained unnecessary restrictions (like the in-hospital and resident committee provisions), the limit to a woman's section 7 rights was *not* rationally connected either with the primary objective of protecting the fetus or the secondary objective of protecting a woman's life or health.

Although Beetz and Dickson reached the same conclusion about the fate of section 251, their emphasis is quite different. Both condemned section 251 for its procedural shortcomings, but Dickson's criticisms were harsher. Beetz stressed the legitimacy of Parliament's desire to protect the fetus, while Dickson emphasized the rights of women. Moreover, Beetz hinted that if Parliament corrected the procedural deficiencies that he had pointed out, the abortion law might be found constitutional: "It is possible that a future enactment by Parliament along the lines of the laws adopted in [other] jurisdictions could achieve a proportionality which is acceptable under s.1."

Section 251 Is a Flagrant Violation of
Women's Rights (Wilson)

Madame Justice Wilson was far more critical of the civil liberties abuses contained in section 251 of the Criminal Code than any of the other judges on the panel, although even she concluded that the state had the constitutional authority to regulate abortions some time in the second trimester.

Wilson agreed with Dickson and Beetz that section 251 violated a woman's right to security of the person, but for her the deficiencies of section 251 were more than procedural:

> [T]he flaw in the present legislative scheme goes much deeper than that. In essence, what [section 251] does is assert that the woman's capacity to reproduce is not to be subject to her own control . . . . She is truly being treated as a means — a means to an end which she does not desire but over which she has no control. She is the passive recipient of a decision made by others as to whether her body is to be used to nurture a new life. Can there be anything that comports less with human dignity and self-respect?

Wilson considered that section 251, in addition to violating "security of the person," infringed the right to "liberty" in section 7. In coming to this conclusion, she analyzed the right to liberty from a purposive perspective and looked to the political theory of liberalism for support. She referred to John Stuart Mill and the jurisprudence of the U.S. Supreme Court concerning abortion [118] and wrote that the guarantee of liberty is

> tied to the concept of human dignity . . . [which] finds expression in almost every right and freedom guaranteed in the Charter. Individuals are afforded the right to choose their own religion and their own philosophy of life, the right to choose with whom they will associate and how they will express themselves, the right to choose where they will live and what occupation they will pursue. These are all examples of the basic theory underlying the Charter, namely that the state will respect choices made by individuals and, to the greatest extent possible, will avoid subordinating these choices to any one conception

of the good life . . . . The fact that the decision whether a
woman will be allowed to terminate her pregnancy is in
the hands of a committee is just as great a violation of the
woman's right to personal autonomy in decisions of an
intimate and private nature as it would be if a committee
were established to decide whether a woman should be
allowed to continue her pregnancy. Both these arrangements violate the woman's right to liberty.

Having decided that section 251 breached both liberty and security
of the person, Wilson considered whether it did so in conformity with
fundamental justice. She proposed that an infringement of a section
7 right that also infringed another Charter right could not possibly be
considered to be in accord with fundamental justice. From her
perspective, section 251 violated the guarantee of freedom of conscience contained in section 2(a) of the Charter. The decision about
whether to have an abortion is a matter of conscience for the mother,
and therefore no set of procedures will justify its abrogation. From
Wilson's perspective, the right of women to decide about the continuance of a pregnancy is a substantive right that could only be
limited if the state could make a case under section 1.

Wilson agreed with Beetz that the primary government objective
in section 251 was to protect the fetus. She considered this objective
to be of sufficient importance to pass the first part of the *Oakes* test.
But to meet the requirements of proportionality, the second part of
the *Oakes* test, valid abortion legislation could not interfere with a
woman's conscience during the first trimester of pregnancy. The
appropriate point at which the state could begin to regulate or prohibit
abortions would most probably occur some time during the second
trimester: "The precise point in the development of the foetus at
which the state's interest in its protection becomes 'compelling' I
leave to the informed judgment of the legislature which is in a position
to receive guidance on the subject from all the relevant disciplines."
Wilson did not deny "that the foetus is potential life from the
moment of conception." However, she noted that "[i]t is a fact of
human experience that a miscarriage or spontaneous abortion of the
foetus at six months is attended by far greater sorrow and sense of
loss than a miscarriage or spontaneous abortion at six days or even
six weeks."
Canadian women have widely divergent views about the issue of
abortion. It is not surprising that Wilson's opinion had a far more

passionate tone than the other decisions and that it outlined in more detail the ways in which section 251 affected the liberty, dignity and security of women. Her emphasis on the primacy of a woman's conscience during the first trimester should not be taken as an endorsement of the "pro-choice" movement, but rather as an acknowledgment that in matters of conscience, no point of view can be "proven" correct. Therefore, when courts are called upon to give meaning to the vague and general phrases of the Charter — which after all is an entrenchment of liberal-democratic values — those values must guide the courts' deliberations.

Let Parliament Decide the Difficult Issue of Abortion (McIntyre, La Forest Concurring)

Mr. Justice McIntyre, supported by Mr. Justice Le Dain, would have upheld section 251. McIntyre based his reasoning on a narrow interpretation of the rights to "liberty and security of the person" in section 7 of the Charter and on a procedural interpretation of "fundamental justice."

McIntyre was distressed at the possibility that the Court might give the Charter meanings its framers never intended it to have:

> [T]he courts must confine themselves to such democratic values as are clearly found and expressed in the Charter and refrain from imposing or creating other values not so based .... The Court must not resolve an issue such as that of abortion on the basis of how many judges may favour "pro-choice" or "pro-life" .... But there is a problem, for the Court must clothe the general expression of rights and freedoms contained in the Charter with real substance and vitality. How can the courts go about this task without imposing at least some of their views and predilections upon the law? [According to Mr. Justice Harlan of the U.S. Supreme Court, it is a] "mistaken view of the Constitution ... that every major social ill in this country can find its cure in some constitutional 'principle,' and that this Court should 'take the lead' in promoting reform when other branches of government fail to act."

McIntyre suggested that the Canadian Supreme Court had found a way to minimize writing the judges' own views into the constitution, and that was to pay strict attention to the "purposive approach" to

Charter interpretation. The purpose of section 7, he claimed, was to protect specific rights clearly included in the concepts of life, liberty and security of the person. He could find no right to abortion specifically included in these concepts. Moreover, he reviewed the history of abortion legislation in the United Kingdom and Canada to show that there never had been a right to abortion recognized in our political tradition.

As further evidence that Canadian legislatures had not intended there to be a right to abortion included in section 7, McIntyre quoted the testimony of Jean Chrétien, then minister of justice, when he appeared before the Special Joint Committee on the Constitution in 1981:

> Parliament has decided a certain law on abortion and a certain law on capital punishment, and it should prevail and we do not want the courts to say that the judgment of Parliament was wrong . . . . [W]e do not want the words "due process of law." [This is because] it is a danger, according to legal advice I am receiving that [the phrase "due process"] will very much limit the scope of the power of legislation by Parliament and we do not want that.

Clearly, it was the former justice minister's hope that the insertion of "fundamental justice" into section 7 instead of "due process" would signal the courts to give section 7 a merely procedural interpretation, thus leaving Parliament's abortion law intact.

Because McIntyre found that section 251 did not infringe either the right to liberty or security of the person, it was unnecessary for him to consider whether section 251 abridged fundamental justice. Nevertheless, he considered this issue in *obiter* to refute some of the conclusions of the majority. He agreed with Beetz that the word "health" was not too vague a standard to meet the requirements of fundamental justice. However, he disagreed with Beetz and Dickson that the administrative procedures established by section 251 unnecessarily restricted access to abortions. This is because he gave little weight to the evidence contained in the research studies cited by Dickson and Beetz; rather, he felt that the Court should "place principal reliance upon the evidence given under oath in court." None of the testimonies of medical doctors who had performed abortions produced examples of abortion applications ultimately refused, and no woman testified that her application for an abortion had been refused. Therefore, to McIntyre it was not clear that section 251 unnecessarily restricted access to abortions, and "the Court's role is not to second-guess Parliament's policy choice as to how broad or how narrow" the access to abortions should be.

Clearly, McIntyre's position is that unless the Charter is *very* clear, the Court should defer to the judgment of Parliament concerning policy issues such as access to abortion, as in this case, or concerning the right to strike. The three majority opinions, however, presented strong reasons for finding an infringement of security of the person in Parliament's abortion law. In the end, none of these approaches can be classified as the *right* one; the *best* one is probably the one that Canadians, over time, find the most convincing.

Each of the four opinions in the *Morgentaler* case raises cogent points. The decision of the Court should not be regarded as settling the issue, but rather as contributing towards a solution that is appropriate to our times. The judges' opinions are worthy of careful reflection by citizens and government policy-makers as a stimulus to further consideration of the issue.

The Supreme Court and Legal Rights

At the beginning of this chapter, it was noted that a number of observers thought that the Supreme Court's decisions about sections 7-14 would be among the least controversial from the perspective of judicial policy-making. Of all the decisions considered in this chapter, that conclusion fits only the *Southam* and *Valente* cases. Moreover, even the *Southam* and *Valente* cases were landmark decisions in that they defined important Charter phrases: "unreasonable search and seizure" and "judicial independence."

The *Operation Dismantle* case proved to be difficult because of the need for the Court to develop an approach towards the "justiciability" issue. As well, the loss suffered by the anti-cruise groups has not discouraged them from launching another major Charter challenge to the Canadian government's nuclear weapons policy. The Nuclear Weapons Legal Action is currently seeking a court declaration that Canada's support for the NATO (North Atlantic Treaty Organization) policy of reserving the right to "first use" of nuclear weapons is illegal under the Charter and international law. The *Therens* case demonstrated that the Court has decided to consider the Charter as a whole new ball game; the familiar definitions of legal terms that existed before the time of the Charter will not necessarily remain the same. Moreover, the legal rights sections of the Charter contain new terms, such as "bringing the administration of justice into disrepute." Thus, there is plenty of opportunity for the courts to make policy, as opposed to merely applying the law, even in the legal rights sections of the Charter.

The *Singh* decision demonstrates just how much potential the Charter has for encouraging the development of higher standards of procedural fairness in the public service. At the same time, it is possible that not many public servants are familiar with the rationale, based on the theory of liberalism, for high standards of procedural fairness. As a result, judicial attempts to give a broad scope to the rights and freedoms in the Charter — or to a resurrected Bill of Rights — might cause executive branch policy-makers to devise strategies that will insulate their programs from judicial review, rather than to create policies that respect procedural rights.

In the *B.C. Motor Vehicle* decision, the Court surprised observers by accepting a substantive interpretation of "fundamental justice." The *Oakes* case provided the Court with the opportunity to create a test for the application of section 1 of the Charter. Finally, in the *Morgentaler* case, the Court struck down the controversial federal abortion law.

It is clear that the legal rights part of the Charter has enhanced the policy-making role of courts far more than would have been predicted several years ago.

6

Equality

The current concern for equality in our society can be traced in part to the effects of liberal ideology. But there have been other influences on the thinking about equality in the liberal democracies. The equality principle in Western political thought has had a wide range of interpretations.

The various theories of equality, as Ployvios Polyviou has written, can be divided into three rough categories: formal equality, numerical equality and normative equality. Put very simply, formal equality urges treating equals equally and unequals unequally. It has its origins in the writing of Aristotle. The Supreme Court's decision in *A.G. Canada v. Lavell* [4] (see chapter 1), in which it was decided that there had been no breach of equality under the Canadian Bill of Rights as long as all Indian women were treated equally, is an example of the formal equality approach. If judges employ this perspective, they could apply the law unevenly so long as they were consistent within groups of "equals" — for example, Indian women, seniors, pregnant women and so on.

Theories of numerical equality begin with the proposition that because *all* human beings have traits in common, they deserve to be treated by and large as equals. There are many variations of this theory. The most conservative approach is that the rules of the economic system should apply equally to everyone. A more radical view is that an equality of *conditions,* such as offered by affirmative action programs, must come about before the rules of the marketplace can apply equally. There are even some who advocate close to absolute equality in the distribution of goods and services.

Those who support normative equality, like the advocates of numerical equality, accept that under ideal conditions human beings should be treated equally. Instead of asking, as the theories of numerical equality do, how *far* equality of treatment should extend, they attack the problem from the opposite direction. Normative theorists, such as Ronald Dworkin, have attempted to establish acceptable conditions for justifiable deviations from equality. Because theories of numerical and normative equality have so much in common, I refer to them together as "social equality." At the basis of social equality is the idea that all human beings deserve to be treated as equals and that departures from that principle require convincing justification.

Canadians are more likely to favour social equality than formal equality. This is indicated by the results of a recent survey of the attitudes of Canadians towards civil liberties conducted by Paul Sniderman and his colleagues. The survey found that 72 per cent of Canadians disagreed with the statement "Some people are better than others" and 73 per cent disagreed with the proposition "All races are certainly not equal."

It appears that during the past century, the attitudes of Canadians about equality, like those of citizens of other liberal democracies, have shifted from a formal equality perspective to one of social equality. From the 1960s to the late 1970s, more radical notions of social equality became popular, such as those advocating affirmative action programs for women, visible minorities and other disadvantaged groups. According to Patricia Marchak, however, the present neo-conservative trend may be moving Canadians towards an approach to social equality that merely advocates economic rules that apply uniformly.

The wording of the equality clause in the Charter of Rights and Freedoms (section 15) is in tune with the more radical concepts of social equality of the late 1970s. It was an attempt to broaden the scope of legally enforceable equality provisions in Canada in reaction to the more limited equality provisions in the Canadian Bill of Rights, which were interpreted according to the formal equality approach by the Supreme Court. In particular, it should be noted that section 15(1) guarantees the "equal benefit of the law," which according to Anne Bayefsky makes it one of the most far-reaching equality clauses of any modern bill of rights. If this clause were taken in a rigid and literal sense, it would seem to imply a very radical theory of numerical equality that would mandate government to enforce absolute equality in the provision of services and benefits. However, as chapter 1 argued, no right in the Charter can be considered absolute, and judges are usually reluctant to apply legal principles the results of which are markedly out of step with popular expectations.

It is in this context that the Supreme Court of Canada is making decisions about the scope of section 15. Because section 15 did not become operative until April 17, 1985, the Supreme Court has rendered only two decisions about its meaning — in the *Andrews* and *Turpin* cases. In another case, involving the extension of funding to Ontario Roman Catholic high schools, section 15 issues were raised, but the Court decided that section 15 could not take precedence over the denominational school rights in the constitution. Then there was the case of Joseph Borowski, who sought a declaration from the Supreme Court that a fetus is entitled to the full protection of the Charter, including equality rights under section 15. These cases are considered below.

The Andrews Case [11]

Lawyers constitute a self-governing profession. The provinces have the power to regulate the professions under the Constitution Act, 1867, and every provincial government has delegated to its provincial law society the power to make regulations regarding the practice of law. This means that the provincial law societies act as agents of the government when they establish these regulations. Therefore, the Charter applies to the provincial law societies to the extent that they exercise authority delegated to them by the provincial governments.

In three provinces, including British Columbia and Ontario, the provincial law society requires lawyers to be citizens. As noted in chapter 2, the first Charter challenge that came to the Supreme Court of Canada was brought by a South African citizen who had fulfilled all the requirements for the practice of law in Ontario except that he had not lived in Canada long enough to become a citizen. He challenged the constitutional validity of the Law Society of Upper Canada regulations under section 6 of the Charter (mobility rights) and lost [47].

Mark David Andrews, a U.K. citizen, brought a similar suit against the Law Society of British Columbia in 1985, except that he based his challenge on section 15. While taking his law degree in the United Kingdom, Andrews had met a Canadian woman; they decided to marry and to move to Canada. Andrews then completed all the requirements for the practice of law in B.C., but he did not meet the citizenship requirement, and he could not apply to become a Canadian

citizen until after having lived three years in Canada. He claimed in
the B.C. Supreme Court that the regulation of the Law Society of
British Columbia requiring lawyers to be citizens discriminates
against non-citizens and thus violates section 15. Section 15 states
that "[e]very individual is equal before and under the law and has the
right to the equal protection and equal benefit of the law without
discrimination."

The trial court judge in the B.C. Supreme Court decided against
Andrews's claim. He concluded that there was a "rational connection" between the citizenship requirement and the duties of a lawyer
in that lawyers have responsibilities that require a special commitment to the community. Thus, he could find no discrimination. However, Andrews appealed to the B.C. Court of Appeal and won. The
unanimous decision of the three-judge panel was written by Madame
Justice McLachlin (who was later appointed to the Supreme Court of
Canada). She concluded that the proper definition of "equality" in
section 15 was formal equality, and that Andrews, as an applicant for
admission to the bar, was not being treated the same as other ap-
plicants. The discrimination could not be justified under section 1 of
the Charter. The Law Society then appealed to the Supreme Court of
Canada, which rendered its judgment in February 1989.

Andrews won again in the Supreme Court, but the Court interpreted equality differently from how the B.C. Court of Appeal had.
The six-judge panel, consisting of Dickson, McIntyre, Lamer, Wilson, La Forest and L'Heureux-Dubé, all agreed about the general
principles that should govern judicial interpretation of section 15,
although they disagreed about how the principles should be applied
to the case at hand. Mr. Justice McIntyre wrote the opinion that
described how the Court would adjudicate equality claims.

McIntyre was critical of Madame Justice McLachlin's conclusion
that the courts should apply the formal equality approach to section
15. He noted how this approach had led to unacceptable results in
several Bill of Rights cases, such as *Lavell* [4] and *Bliss* [19]. (As
chapter 1 recounted, the *Lavell* decision found no violation of equality
in section 12 of the Indian Act, which entitled Indian men to more
benefits than Indian women, because the equality provision in the Bill
merely implied treating all Indian women equally in this case. In
Bliss, the Court found that the unemployment insurance regulations
of the time did not violate equality as long as all pregnant people were
treated equally.) He emphasized that the formal equality interpreta-

tion had been explicitly rejected in the *Drybones* decision. He said that the formal equality test

> is seriously deficient in that it excludes any consideration of the nature of the law. If it were to be applied literally, it could be used to justify the Nuremberg laws of Adolf Hitler. Similar treatment was contemplated for all Jews. The similarly situated test would have justified the formalistic separate but equal doctrine of *Plessy v. Ferguson* [65] a doctrine that [entrenched racial discrimination in the U.S. until the case of *Brown v. Board of Education* [23], which overruled *Plessy* in 1954].

Having rejected formal equality, McIntyre adopted a definition of equality similar to what was referred to above as "social equality." He reached this result by conducting a purposive analysis, concluding that descriptions of "equality" in section 15, especially the references to equality "under" the law, the "equal protection" of the law and the "equal benefit" of the law — all of which went beyond the definition of equality in the Bill of Rights — were intended to signal to the courts that a broader definition of equality than formal equality was intended:

> It is clear that the purpose of s.15 is to ensure equality in the formulation and application of the law. The promotion of equality entails the promotion of a society in which all are secure in the knowledge that they are recognized at law as human beings equally deserving of concern, respect and consideration.

McIntyre then explained that the equality referred to in section 15 could not have been intended to require the elimination of all distinctions (like a radical version of numerical equality):

> If the Charter was intended to eliminate all distinctions, then there would be no place for sections such as 27 (multicultural heritage); 2(a) (freedom of conscience and religion); 25 (aboriginal rights and freedoms); and other such provisions designed to safeguard certain distinctions. Moreover, the fact that identical treatment may frequently

produce serious inequality is recognized in s.15(2), which [allows affirmative action programs].

Like the theorists of numerical equality, McIntyre then tackled the question of how far equality should extend. He approached this issue by focusing on the words "without discrimination" in section 15. In other words, equality should extend far enough so as to preclude discrimination: "Discrimination is unacceptable in a democratic society because it epitomizes the worst effects of the denial of equality, and discrimination reinforced by law is particularly repugnant . . . . It is against this evil that s.15 provides a guarantee."

McIntyre was then faced with having to define "discrimination." After reviewing several approaches, he concluded that

discrimination may be described as a distinction, whether intentional or not but based on grounds relating to personal characteristics of the individual or group, which has the effect of imposing burdens, obligations, or disadvantages on such individual or group not imposed upon others, or which withholds or limits access to opportunities, benefits, and advantages available to other members of society. Distinctions based on personal characteristics attributed to an individual solely on the basis of association with a group will rarely escape the charge of discrimination, while those based on an individual's merits and capacities will rarely be so classed.

The "personal characteristics" upon which unacceptable discrimination is based would include all of the enumerated categories in section 15 — race, national or ethnic origin, colour, religion, sex, age and mental or physical disability — and categories analogous to these. This is what McIntyre referred to as the "enumerated and analogous grounds" method of defining discrimination. He stressed that not all unequal treatment based on these classifications violated equality, but only those which *discriminated,* that is, imposed disadvantages not imposed on others, or withheld benefits available to others. Discrimination could result directly from the wording of a law, or it could be indirect and unintentional, that is, the unintended result of legislation that happened to place unfair disadvantages on members of one of the enumerated or analogous categories in section 15. (Such unintentional discrimination is also known as "systemic" discrimination.)

McIntyre's approach is close to the one recommended by the Women's Legal Education and Action Fund (LEAF), which advocated a definition of equality that stressed the protection of the disadvantaged rather than allowing the advantaged to gain further ground. (LEAF had been allowed by the Court to "intervene" in this case. An intervenor is a party that is not one of the original litigants but that has a stake in the outcome of the case and can present the Court with useful evidence.)

Once discrimination is established, the onus is on the party seeking to maintain the inequality to demonstrate that it is a reasonable limit under section 1. Unless the inequality can be justified under section 1, the discriminatory law must be struck down.

With regard to the case at hand, all the judges agreed that by creating a distinction based on citizenship (a category analogous to "national origin"), the Law Society of British Columbia had imposed a burden on permanent residents, thus discriminating against them. Justices Dickson, Wilson, L'Heureux-Dubé and La Forest concluded that the citizenship requirement did not pass the *Oakes* test because there was no rational connection between the citizenship requirement and the objective of ensuring that lawyers have a knowledge of and commitment to the principles of government in Canada. McIntyre and Lamer dissented on this point. They agreed that citizenship was neither a necessary nor a sufficient condition to ensure the requisite knowledge of and commitment to the country's political system. However, McIntyre pointed out that the law against theft is neither a necessary nor a sufficient condition to prevent stealing, and yet it does help to promote the goal of protecting private property. McIntyre concluded that a "reasonable limit" must be one which "it was reasonable for the legislature to impose. The courts are not called upon to substitute judicial opinions for legislative ones as to the place at which to draw a precise line."

The *Andrews* decision is one of the most important ones the Supreme Court has made to date. As McIntyre pointed out, "The section 15(1) guarantee is the broadest of all guarantees [in the Charter]. It applies to and supports all other rights guaranteed by the Charter." From this perspective, it is somewhat disconcerting to realize that the Canadian judiciary below the Supreme Court level had generally defined equality according to the very narrow approach of formal equality, in spite of the clear signals in the wording of section

15 itself that the drafters of the Charter intended the courts to move beyond formal equality. This situation helps to illustrate that the task of analyzing theories of equality, and then applying them to policy-making, is not something most judges are appropriately trained for.

It is a little ironic that the first Supreme Court case involving section 15 — the section heralded as having the greatest potential to protect the disadvantaged in society — would be brought by a member of one of the least disadvantaged groups in Canada (lawyers) and that he should win his case. Nevertheless, the way in which the Court has decided to approach section 15 has at least provided disadvantaged groups with much more hope of overcoming discrimination through judicial review than had been the case with judicial interpretations of the equality clause in the Canadian Bill of Rights.

The Turpin Case [112]

On May 4, 1989, the Supreme Court rendered its second decision based on section 15. The case concerned the sections of the Criminal Code which require that an accused person charged with murder must be tried by a judge and jury in all provinces except Alberta, where the trial may be by judge alone. Sharon Turpin and her co-accuseds, who had been charged with first-degree murder in Ontario, made a pre-trial motion in 1985 to be tried by a judge alone. They argued that they had a right to choose either a jury trial or a trial by judge alone under either section ll(f) of the Charter (which provides a right to trial by jury for serious offences) or under section 15. The guarantee of equality before the law in section 15, they claimed, means that advantages granted to accused persons in Alberta under a federal law must also be available in the rest of the country.

The judge accepted the argument that section 11(f) allowed an accused to elect whether to be tried by judge and jury or by judge alone. Turpin was subsequently tried by judge alone and acquitted. The crown appealed on the grounds that the judge had erred in interpreting the Charter. In a 1987 decision, the Ontario Court of Appeal agreed with the crown, and ordered a new trial before judge and jury. Turpin appealed this decision to the Supreme Court and lost.

The judgment of the unanimous Court was written by Madame Justice Wilson. After holding that section 11(f) simply provides a right to a jury trial, and not a right to elect either a jury trial or a trial by judge alone, Wilson turned to the section 15 argument. She applied the two-step test developed in *Andrews* about whether a law has violated section 15(1). The first step is to determine whether there has been a violation of any of the four equality rights that section 15(1) enumerates. In this case, Turpin claimed that her right to equality before the law had been infringed. Wilson emphasized that this right must be given a broader interpretation than it was given under the Canadian Bill of Rights:

> The guarantee of equality before the law is designed to advance the value that all persons be subject to the equal demands and burdens of the law and not suffer any greater disability in the substance and application of the law than others. This value has historically been associated with the requirements of the rule of law that all persons be subject to the law impartially applied and administered.

Because the Criminal Code treats accused persons outside of Ontario more harshly than those charged in Alberta, Wilson concluded that the code violates equality before the law.

The second step is to determine whether there has been a discrimination. Wilson stressed that "it is only when one of the four equality rights has been denied with discrimination that the values protected by section 15 are threatened and the courts' legitimate role as a protector of such values comes into play."

Wilson affirmed the definition of discrimination provided by Mr. Justice McIntyre in *Andrews*, and advanced the definition a little further. She wrote that one question that ought to be considered is whether the group that is a victim of the inequality has suffered an historical disadvantage because of the inequality. In this case, accused persons outside of Alberta are not members of a "discreet and insular minority" who have been socially disadvantaged because of the inequality in the Criminal Code. To conclude that the impugned section of the Criminal Code discriminated, she claimed,

> would not, in my view, advance the purposes of section 15 in remedying or preventing discrimination against groups suffering social, political and legal disadvantage in our society. A search of indicia of discrimination such as stereotyping, historical disadvantage or vulnerability to political and social prejudices would be fruitless in this case . . . . [It would] "overshoot the actual purpose of the right of freedom in question": See *Regina v. Big M. Drug Mart.*

Wilson admitted that there might be some examples of inequalities in the criminal law and procedure, based on provincial variations, that might result in discrimination. She said that the Court would have to examine the discrimination issue on a case-by-case basis.

In denying that Turpin and her co-accuseds had been discriminated against, the Supreme Court reiterated that it intends to interpret section 15 to help clearly disadvantaged groups in society. The judges provided an example of a group that, although subjected to unequal treatment, is not disadvantaged: accused persons outside of Alberta.

The Ontario Roman Catholic High School Funding Case [78]

The funding of Roman Catholic high schools has been an issue in Ontario since the early part of this century. Part of the Confederation bargain of 1867 was an agreement that Protestants in Quebec and Roman Catholics in Ontario would be guaranteed the right to operate denominational schools with public funding at the same level as that which existed in 1867. Members of denominations who felt that their rights had been eroded could appeal to the federal government for redress under section 93 of the BNA Act (now the Constitution Act, 1867). If such an appeal failed to produce results, Parliament could enact remedial legislation to redress the grievances. Similar denominational school provisions were written into the terms of entry of new provinces after 1867. As noted in chapter 1, Parliament has never acted to protect the erosion of denominational school rights because of the political risks involved.

In 1915 the Ontario government decided to fund Roman Catholic high schools only to the end of what we now call grade 10. In addition, the government decided to reduce funding for the Roman Catholic schools up to and including grade 10 so that it would be up to 10 per cent less than that for public schools. Sentiment in some quarters against the Roman Catholic Church was partly responsible for this decision.

The Roman Catholic school board in Ontario's Tiny Township launched a court challenge to the provincial government's funding cutbacks. The case eventually reached the Judicial Committee of the Privy Council in 1928 [130]. The Privy Council upheld the provincial cutbacks with some questionable reasoning. The Judicial Committee declared that the provincial government, in funding only up to the grade ten level, had not reduced the funding of Roman Catholic schools below the 1867 level, because in 1867 schools only taught what in the 1920s would be referred to as grade 10 level. Moreover, the cutbacks in the level of funding up to grade 10 were acceptable because the government was merely regulating education in the province, and besides, the differential funding did not result in undue hardship. As unpersuasive as this reasoning is, it may have reflected the Judicial Committee's reading of the political reality of the time. A decision in favour of the Roman Catholic schools might actually have inflamed the anti-Roman Catholic feeling in the province even more. Judges are sometimes reluctant to stray too far from majority public sentiments, even in the face of an obvious constitutional violation.

In 1984 the provincial Conservative government did an about-face — it decided that henceforth it would fund Roman Catholic high schools right up to grade 13 and at the same level of support as public schools. The Liberals and NDP decided to support this initiative. However, a number of public school boards opposed the new policy because it would lead to the closing of some public high schools and the transfer of buildings and personnel to the Roman Catholic system. There was fear that this would lead to lowering the standards of education in the public school system. The legislation putting the new policy into effect was not passed until shortly after section 15 of the Charter came into effect in 1985. Those opposed to the policy change, including the Metropolitan Toronto School Board, claimed that the new legislation was unconstitutional because it violated section 15 of the Charter. The board alleged that the extension of funding provided Roman Catholics with more benefits under the law than members of other religions or those without a religion, and that this constituted a violation of equality contrary to section 15.

In order to settle the doubts created by the claims of the Metro Toronto School Board, the Ontario government sent a reference question to its Court of Appeal concerning the constitutional validity of Bill 30, the legislation that extended the funding of Roman Catholic high schools. A five-judge panel heard the case in 1986, and a majority of three concluded that Bill 30 was constitutional. This decision was upheld by the Supreme Court of Canada in 1987. In both courts the key to upholding the legislation was section 29 of the Charter, which states that "[n]othing in this Charter abrogates or derogates from any rights or privileges guaranteed by or under the Constitution of Canada in respect of denominational, separate or dissentient schools." Obviously, this means that the "rights or privileges" enjoyed by Roman Catholics in Ontario in 1867 with regard to their schools were to be continued. But in the *Tiny* case, the Privy Council had declared that Roman Catholic schools were not entitled to funding beyond grade 10. The argument of those opposed to Bill 30 was that the *extension* of funding beyond grade 10 was not rendered immune from section 15 by section 29 of the Charter.

The majority on the Ontario Court of Appeal gave a broad interpretation to the phrase "under the Constitution" in section 29. Their view was that this phrase referred to additional privileges granted to denominational schools after 1867 "under" the constitutional powers that the provinces have over education. The minority on the court disagreed; the two dissenting judges thought that even if "under the Constitution" could be interpreted in this way, at the most it could only refer to privileges granted between 1867 and the coming into force of the Charter. Because Bill 30 was not enacted prior to April 17, 1985, it would have to conform to section 15. To the minority, it was obvious that Bill 30 violated section 15 because it discriminated on the basis of religion, one of the prohibited categories. The crown's argument to justify the discrimination under section 1, that the government was merely redressing historical grievances, was not persuasive to the minority. The situation in 1985 is entirely different from that in the 1920s; a 1920s wrong cannot be "corrected" in 1988, according to the minority.

The minority view did not impress the Supreme Court of Canada. The Supreme Court gave even stronger reasons for upholding Bill 30 than the Court of Appeal had. In fact, the Supreme Court overruled the *Tiny* decision. With the *Tiny* precedent gone, Bill 30 simply restored to Roman Catholics what they should rightly have received all along. Moreover, the majority opinion, written by Madame Justice Wilson, stated that even without section 29, Bill 30 would have been found constitutional. Wilson's reasoning is as follows:

> It was never intended, in my opinion, that the Charter could be used to invalidate other provisions of the constitution, particularly a provision such as s.93 which represented a fundamental part of the Confederation compromise. As the majority of the Court of Appeal concluded . . . , "The incorporation of the Charter into the *Constitution Act, 1982* does not change the original Confederation bargain. A specific constitutional amendment would be required to accomplish that."

Section 93 of the Constitution Act 1867, clearly implies that the provinces have the power to grant special privileges with regard to denominational schools. The privileges granted at the time a province entered into Confederation cannot be reduced, but new privileges can be created. These new privileges, however, can be reduced back to their time-of-Confederation level at the discretion of the provincial legislature. This interpretation of section 93 relied heavily on historical evidence about the "Confederation bargain."

Although the Supreme Court did not, for these reasons, deal with the section 15 issue, the case illustrates that section 15 cannot be used by litigants to challenge inequalities built into the constitution itself. These can be changed only with a constitutional amendment.

The Borowski Case [20]

Joseph Borowski is one of the leading spokesmen for the "pro-life" movement in Canada. He is a former NDP member of the Manitoba legislature, but he broke with his party over the abortion issue. In 1978 he began his legal battle in favour of fetal rights in Saskatchewan's Court of Queen's Bench by challenging the constitutionality of section 251 of the federal Criminal Code — the section dealing with abortion. Because Borowski was not directly affected by section 251, his case went to the Supreme Court of Canada in 1981 for determination of whether he had "standing" to proceed with his case. Standing refers to the legal right of a litigant to have a case heard in a court. In 1981 the Supreme Court determined that Borowski had standing to challenge the abortion provisions [56].

In 1984 Borowski failed in his bid to obtain a declaration from the Saskatchewan Court of Queen's Bench that the Criminal Code provisions that allow for abortions in certain circumstances are contrary to the Charter and therefore of no force and effect. His position was that the right to life of the fetus is protected under section 7 of the Charter.

Borowski appealed to the Saskatchewan Court of Appeal. Because section 15 of the Charter was in effect by the time the appeal case was argued, Borowski contended that the abortion law also violated section 15 of the Charter, because it denied the fetus the equal protection of the law. The court rendered its decision on April 30, 1987, and Borowski lost again.

Borowski appealed to the Supreme Court of Canada. However, before his case could be heard, the Supreme Court struck down section 251 of the Criminal Code — the abortion law Borowski was challenging — in the *Morgentaler* decision in January 1988 (see chapter 5). It would then have been logical for the federal attorney general to have petitioned the Supreme Court to quash the appeal on the grounds that because section 251 of the Criminal Code had been struck down, Borowski no longer had standing. However, such a move might have been interpreted by some voters as a government stand against fetal rights. Instead, the government of Canada petitioned the Supreme Court to delay the Borowski hearing until after new abortion legislation had been passed by Parliament. This was obviously a strategy to keep the abortion issue out of the public spotlight until after the imminent federal election. However, the petition to delay was dismissed by the Supreme Court in September. On October 1, 1988, Prime Minister Mulroney called an election for November 21. Thus, when Borowski's case came before the Court on October 3, Canada was in the midst of an election campaign.

The Women's Legal Education and Action Fund, an intervenor opposed to Borowski's position, argued in court that the case had become "moot," a legal term meaning that the causes of the original controversy had disappeared, and therefore the original issue should not be decided because this would be of no practical value. LEAF took this position because the abortion law had already been struck down. Lawyers for the Canadian government refused to take a stand on this point, probably out of fear that any stand could cost the government votes. Borowski, however, continued to seek a declaration that the references to "everyone" in section 7 and to "every individual" in section 15 include the fetus, and he requested permission to proceed. The Court took the unusual step of agreeing to hear arguments from both sides, while reserving its decision (until after the election) about whether the case was moot. One can sympathize with the Court's position. If the judges had made a decision on the "mootness" of the case during an election campaign, it would have been interpreted as a victory for one side or the other, whether or not this actually was the case. The nation's top court, which desperately needs to maintain an image of neutrality to maintain its legitimacy, could only lose respect by becoming the centre of focus during an election.

To put the issue in perspective, it is useful to review the reasoning of the Saskatchewan Court of Appeal in dismissing Borowski's claim. The court could find no example of a fetus having the rights of a "person" in any common-law jurisdiction. In several instances, a person had successfully sued for damages caused to him or her while a fetus. However, the fetus had already attained "personhood" by virtue of having been born. No court had ever entertained a suit by a fetus before birth, and a fetus that was not born alive had never been considered to be a "person." Outside the common-law world, only in West Germany did the fetus have the status of a legal person in some respects. However, the court attributed this to West Germany's distinct legal tradition, and especially to the current regime's reaction to the former Nazi regime's flagrant disregard for the fetus. Thus, from a legal perspective, the Charter could not be presumed to have changed the legal definition of "person."

With regard specifically to section 7, the Court of Appeal recalled that in the *B.C. Motor Vehicle* decision (see chapter 5), the Supreme Court had determined that sections 8-14 of the Charter are examples of the kinds of rights protected by section 7. Sections 8-14 protect, for example, the right of "everyone" to be secure against unreasonable search or seizure and not to be arbitrarily detained or imprisoned. Because it is impossible to imagine these rights applying to the fetus, Parliament could not have intended section 7 to apply to the fetus.

The court also noted that a 1981 statement in the House of Commons by Robert Kaplan, the solicitor general, supported the view that the words "everyone" in section 7 and "every individual" in section 15 were not intended to include the fetus. Kaplan declared that the inclusion of these words in the Charter had not shifted "any responsibility away from Parliament to deal with [the abortion] question." As well, the judges noted that Canadian courts, in interpreting the Canadian Bill of Rights, had rejected the argument that "an unborn person is a human being from the moment of conception, or shortly thereafter, and that abortions result in [denying the fetus] equality before the law."

The Court of Appeal concluded that "the Charter is neutral in relation to abortion; it remains for Parliament, reflecting the will of the Canadian people, to determine without reference to the Charter in what circumstances the termination of pregnancy will be lawful or unlawful."

When the case reached the Supreme Court, the arguments put by those for and against Borowski's position clearly show that the Court was being asked to decide a question of policy rather than a legal issue. Morris Shumiatcher, Borowski's lawyer, showed the judges a series of anti-abortion films, including "The Hiccup Film" and "Jumping for Joy." Borowski came to the courthouse with two jars containing pickled fetuses. "It was my hope that by passing it from judge to judge ... they would see very clearly it is a perfect baby," said Borowski. The Interfaith Coalition on the Rights and Wellbeing of Women and Children, one of the intervenors, reminded the Court that the preamble to the Charter states that Canada is founded on principles that recognize the supremacy of God: "The Court should not be afraid — and lawyers should not be afraid — to turn to religious principles that underlie our society and say human life in all its stages must be protected" (*Globe and Mail,* October 5, 1988).

On the other side, the Women's Legal Education and Action Fund emphasized that the fetuses the judges had seen on film were inside a woman's body. In its factum (written submission to the Court), it criticized the films for "portraying the foetus as an autonomous 'space-hero' and the pregnant woman as the 'empty space' in which he floats." LEAF argued that the abortion issue is a sexual equality issue:

> The social context of sex inequality has denied women control over the reproductive uses of their bodies ....
> Women's reproductive capacity is thus an integral part of women's "equality problem," along a spectrum of situations .... For women of reproductive age, the guarantee of sex equality should be interpreted so as to reduce or minimize state-sanctioned interference with women's full development as human beings, socially, economically and politically .... Forced maternity in this broader sense must be clearly understood as a problem of sex inequality. Access to abortion is necessary as a means for women to survive in their unequal circumstances.

In March 1989 the Supreme Court of Canada rendered its decision. The Court declared that Borowski's case was moot and therefore the question of whether the fetus had a right to equality and to life could not be decided. The unanimous decision was written by Mr. Justice John Sopinka, and concurred in by Justices Dickson, McIntyre, Lamer, Wilson, La Forest and L'Heureux-Dubé. Sopinka outlined the two-step approach the Court would adopt in deciding how to approach the question of mootness. "The first stage in the analysis requires a consideration of whether there remains a live controversy," he wrote. In this case, the controversy had disappeared because the sections of the Criminal Code Borowski was challenging had been struck down by the Court in the *Morgentaler* decision. But the absence of a live controversy would not settle the issue. The second stage, which becomes relevant only if there is no live controversy, is to decide whether the Court should exercise its discretion to hear the case anyway. In making this decision, the Court ought to consider three factors, Sopinka wrote. The three factors would, on balance, have to mitigate in favour of the Court exercising discretion to hear the case.

The first factor is whether the adversaries in the case still have a stake in the outcome. Sopinka noted that they did: "The appeal was fully argued with as much zeal and dedication on both sides as if the matter were not moot," indicating that both sides were very concerned about how the Supreme Court would decide the issue.

The second factor is "judicial economy, which requires that a court examine the circumstances of a case to determine if it is worthwhile to allot the required judicial resources to resolve the moot issue." From this perspective, Sopinka implied that even if the Court were to decide that a fetus could claim Charter protection, such a decision would not make future litigation on the same issue unnecessary. It would still be necessary for the Court to consider the new abortion legislation, and to balance a woman's right to security of the person against a fetal right to life. Thus, such a decision could result in uncertainty that would not be in the public interest, and so this factor augured against the Court exercising discretion to hear the case.

The third factor is that the judiciary "should be sensitive to the extent that it may be departing from its traditional role." In this case, Sopinka observed that if the Court were to answer the abstract question about fetal rights, this "would in effect sanction a private reference." (It will be recalled that cabinets may send reference questions to the appropriate court. Sopinka is wary of private citizens gaining the ability to do the same through requiring the courts to answer moot questions.) This third factor, therefore, also suggested that the Court should not hear the case. Taking into account all three factors, therefore, Sopinka decided that on balance it would be unwise for the Court to hear the case.

In addition, Sopinka declared that Borowski no longer had standing to pursue the appeal. He noted that there had been two significant changes in the nature of the case since Borowski was originally granted standing by the Supreme Court in 1981: section 251 of the Criminal Code had been struck down in the *Morgentaler* decision, and Borowski's claim had shifted since 1981 to one primarily based on the Charter. Moreover, standing could be based neither on section

24(1) of the Charter (which provides standing only to those whose
rights have been personally infringed or denied) nor on section 52(1)
of the Constitution Act, 1982 (which provides standing to those challenging an actual law).

In concluding the judgment, Sopinka had some harsh words for the
federal crown for refusing to take a stand on whether the litigation
should proceed before and during the election campaign:

> In my opinion, in lieu of applying to adjourn the appeal,
> the [crown] should have moved to quash. Certainly, such
> a motion should have been brought after the adjournment
> was denied. Failure to do so has resulted in the needless
> expense to [Borowski] of preparing and arguing the appeal
> before this Court. In the circumstance, it is appropriate that
> the [crown] pay to [Borowski] the costs of the appeal.

In spite of the minor victory of being awarded costs, Borowski was
extremely disappointed by his loss. He made the following comments
to the press:

> I'm glad I did not come to Ottawa for the decision I
> probably would have gone into the court and punched the
> judges in the nose. It looks to me like it (hearing the case)
> was a gimmick, a charade, a trick they played on us . . . .
> I think it would be a waste of my time to ever go back
> before those gutless . . . judges who wasted 10 years of
> our time. (*Globe and Mail,* March 10, 1989)

With regard to being awarded costs, Borowski revealed that the
Alliance Against Abortion, of which he is president, had spent
$850,000 in ten years on the litigation. The costs awarded by the
Supreme Court, in the neighbourhood of $1,000, were no consolation
to him.

If Borowski had won, no doubt the pro-choice supporters would
have been equally as disappointed. This situation underlines how
much the Supreme Court stands to lose in terms of legitimacy and
prestige when deciding controversial moral issues framed as Charter
claims — no matter how it decides them.

One day, however, the Court may have to tackle the issue of fetal
rights. First, however, Parliament must enact new abortion legislation.
Even then, consideration of the issue by the Court could be further

postponed if the judges decide, like the Saskatchewan Court of Appeal, that a fetus is not protected by sections 7-15 because it is not a legal "person." In that case, it would be possible for Parliament and seven provincial legislatures to change the definition of "person" and "everyone" in the Charter to include the fetus. If this were done, the Court would then have to balance the rights of the fetus against those of pregnant women. The judges would have to decide whether the approach to the relation between equality rights and abortion suggested by LEAF is appropriate.

It should be kept in mind that even if the fetus never attained legal personhood, Parliament might still enact legislation to protect the fetus. Such legislation would provide "rights" to the fetus, but *legislated* rights, not Charter rights.

Other Equality Cases

A major equality case has recently been heard by the Supreme Court of Canada. This is the *McKinney* case, which deals with the issue of whether compulsory retirement provisions at universities violate section 15. Because the Court's decision may have important implications for the interpretation of section 15, some details of the case are presented here.

In 1986 an application was made in the Ontario High Court by several professors that compulsory retirement provisions at York University, the University of Guelph, the University of Toronto and Laurentian University violated section 15 of the Charter. The professors and the librarian lost their case and appealed. The Ontario Court of Appeal handed down its decision in December 1987.

There were three major issues: whether the Charter applies to the personnel policies of universities; if so, whether compulsory retirement is a violation of the Charter that cannot be upheld under section 1; and whether the provisions of the Ontario Human Rights Code that permit compulsory retirement constitute a violation of the Charter that cannot be justified under section 1.

With regard to the first issue, the Court of Appeal decided that the Charter does not apply to the personnel policies of universities because no government action is involved there. The judges claimed that there was an insufficient link between the government control and the private nature of university personnel policies to invoke the Charter. "With respect to employment of professors, they are masters in their own houses." Because the Charter did not apply, the second issue became irrelevant.

The third issue, which concerned the Ontario Human Rights Code, became the most important. The Human Rights Code prohibits discrimination on the basis of age in the private sector between the ages of eighteen and sixty-five. The five-judge panel agreed that the exclusion of those over sixty-five from the protection of the code violates section 15 of the Charter. However, four of them concluded that the violation is a reasonable limit under section 1.

In applying the *Oakes* test for reasonable limits, the majority wrote that the objectives of the exclusion of the over-sixty-five age group from the protection of the code were twofold: to strike a compromise between, on the one hand, the right to work regardless of age and the right to retire with a guaranteed pension and, on the other, the need to promote renewal of the work force through providing employment opportunities to younger persons. After reviewing evidence from social scientists, the majority concluded that these objectives were "pressing and substantial" and that therefore the requirements of part one of the *Oakes* test had been met.

With respect to the rational connection test, the majority found that the exclusion of those over sixty-five from the protection of the code was a sensible way to achieve the two objectives. With regard to the second factor — minimal impairment of the right to equality — the judges noted that many "free and democratic" countries have legislated provisions for compulsory retirement, including the United Kingdom, Ireland, West Germany, Japan and Norway. In the United States, the Supreme Court has found that federal and state laws that provide for compulsory retirement meet the equal protection requirements of the U.S. Bill of Rights. In Canada, about half of the work force is subject to contractual provisions that provide for mandatory retirement, usually at age sixty-five. As a result, tax reductions apply at sixty-five, as well as a number of other benefits for seniors. The judges concluded:

> In the university context, bearing in mind the extent to which 65 years of age has been adopted as the normal age of retirement both by the universities and generally, the extent to which the financing of pension plans has been based upon it, and the impact which the elimination of mandatory retirement would have on faculty renewal, the impairment of the right to freedom from discrimination on the basis of age by [the Human Rights Code] was as little as possible.

The majority also concluded that the exclusion of over-sixty-fives passed the third test — overall proportionality. They pointed out that no one is exempt from the aging process, so that compulsory retirement provisions are liable to affect everyone. Moreover, they noted that the universities are free to make special arrangements to retain certain faculty who are over sixty-five.

Mr. Justice Blair dissented over the section 1 issue. He was of the opinion that the Ontario Human Rights Code "does not merely limit or restrict the appellants' Charter rights under s.15(1). It eliminates them because, under the *Code*, no protection against age discrimination in employment is provided after the age of 65." Thus, according to Blair, the code fails to meet the minimal impairment requirement of the *Oakes* test.

The Supreme Court's decision on this issue is bound to create controversy no matter which way it goes. Like other Charter issues, this one boils down to a question of how best to promote interpersonal respect. Are those over sixty-five shown the greatest respect by not having to agree to retire at a particular age or by being exempted from tests to measure their continued competence? Or as Samuel LaSelva has argued, it is a question of balancing the rights of seniors — who have already had the chance to enjoy employment — with the rights of the younger generation — who haven't.

Two Supreme Court decisions concerning the equality provisions in the human rights codes are significant because they indicate how the Court may treat the concept of "systemic discrimination" — that is, indirect and unintentional discrimination — in Charter cases. In the *Bhinder* decision of 1985 [16], the Supreme Court held that a Sikh who was fired from his job for refusing to replace his turban with a hard hat was the victim of systemic discrimination contrary to the Canadian Human Rights Code. Although the regulations of Bhinder's employer, Canadian National, concerning the wearing of hard hats had not been established to discriminate against Sikhs, they had that effect. Bhinder had hoped to be reinstated in his job through the litigation. The Court did not order Bhinder reinstated, however, because the code allowed discrimination in the case of a "bona fide occupational requirement," and the regulation requiring the wearing of a hard hat was such a requirement.

In another case also decided in 1985, *Ontario Human Rights Commission and O'Malley v. Simpsons-Sears Ltd.* [60], the Court considered whether an employee of Simpsons-Sears who had been demoted for refusing to work on Saturdays when she became a

Seventh Day Adventist had been subjected to systemic discrimination contrary to the Ontario Human Rights Code. O'Malley claimed that the policy of Simpsons-Sears to require employees at certain levels to work on Saturdays had the effect of discriminating against Seventh Day Adventists, even though the company had not deliberately set out to discriminate. Because the Ontario Human Rights Code has no "bona fide occupational requirement" clause, O'Malley won her case. The Court concluded that in instances where a company's policies resulted in systemic discrimination, the company had a duty to accommodate disadvantaged employees up to the point of undue hardship for the company.

The Charter was not in effect when the litigation began in these two cases, so that the issue of whether the two codes conformed with the Charter did not arise. In the *Andrews* case, the Supreme Court indicated that discrimination under section 15 includes systemic discrimination. Rainer Knopff has suggested that to interpret section 15 as prohibiting systemic discrimination may have an enormous impact on public policy. This is because the extent of systemic discrimination is unknown precisely because it is unintentional.

A final case involving human rights codes deserves mention because it overruled the *Bliss* decision — the infamous Bill of Rights case about pregnancy decided in 1979 [17]. It will be recalled from chapter 1 that in *Bliss*, the Supreme Court gave the stamp of approval to discrimination based on pregnancy because such discrimination could not be considered discrimination based on sex. In the *Brooks* case [??], decided in May 1989, the Supreme Court considered a claim under the Manitoba Human Rights Act. Women employees claimed that a company's group insurance plan, which provided weekly benefits for loss of pay because of accident or illness but which excluded pregnancy, constituted discrimination based on sex. The Supreme Court agreed. Chief Justice Dickson's judgment, which all judges on the panel supported, declared that "those who bear children and benefit society as a whole should not be eonomically or socially disadvantaged." Holding that pregnancy cannot be separated from gender, the Court overruled *Bliss*.

Because the Court has attempted to interpret words that appear in both the Charter and the human rights codes similarly — like "discrimination" — the *Brooks* decision signals that "discrimination" in section 15 of the Charter will include discrimination based on pregnancy.

The Courts and Equality

The question of how much social equality Canadians should enjoy and how to resolve conflicting equality claims is one of the fundamental policy questions every Canadian politician and citizen must grapple with. It is tempting for politicians to avoid this difficult issue by leaving it to the courts. But equality becomes a truly legal issue only after its scope has been defined and after some guidelines are established for resolving conflicting equality claims.

In general, the courts are not well equipped to settle these policy questions, although some judges are able to make useful contributions to the analysis of these issues. For example, the Supreme Court's decision in the *Andrews* case contains some perceptive insights into our country's quest for social equality. If we now had the same Supreme Court that decided the *Lavell* and *Bliss* cases, however, judicial interpretation could well have done more to retard the careful consideration of these issues than to advance it. For this reason, the development of policies about the application of the Charter should not be left entirely to the judicial process. Moreover, as the *Borowski* decision so vividly illustrates, leaving the resolution of divisive social equality issues to the courts is likely to harm the legitimacy of the Supreme Court as a neutral arbiter of legal disputes.

7

Language Rights

Language rights (sections 16-23), unlike most of the other civil liberties the Charter was designed to protect, are not rights in the traditional liberal sense. Rather, they represent a cultural compromise designed to enable two linguistic communities to coexist in one federal country. The language rights in the Charter extend the language rights created in 1867 by section 133 of the Constitution Act, 1867. Section 133, which was part of the Confederation bargain, permitted the use of either English or French in Parliament and the Quebec National Assembly, and in the courts of Quebec and those created by Parliament.

Since 1982, the Supreme Court has made six major decisions dealing with language rights. Only two of these directly concern the language rights in the Charter. (This is because not all of the constitutional language rights in Canada are contained in the Charter.) The first is the *Quebec Protestant School Boards* case, in which the Court resolved the collision between the "Canada clause" in the Charter and the "Quebec clause" in the Quebec Charter of the French Language by striking down the Quebec clause. The second is the *Société des Acadiens* case, in which the Court decided that section 19(2) of the Charter, which states that "[e]ither English or French may be used by any person in . . . any court . . . of New Brunswick," does not entitle litigants to have judges who are fluent in the official language of the litigant. A judge may rely on an interpreter.

Four other cases are given consideration in this chapter because they help to illustrate the approach the judges are developing towards language rights. The first of these is the *Manitoba Language Rights* case. It concerns section 23 of the Manitoba Act, 1870, which provides the same kinds of guarantees for the use of English and French in Manitoba as are provided with regard to Quebec in section 133 of the Constitution Act, 1867, and with regard to New Brunswick in sections 18 and 19 of the Charter. Next, the *MacDonald* and *Bilodeau* cases decided that the clause in section 133 that authorizes the use of either English or French in the courts of Quebec, and the parallel clause in the Manitoba Act, do not imply that court summonses must be printed in both official languages. Finally, the *Mercure* case decided that the language rights of francophones protected by the Saskatchewan Act (and by implication, the Alberta Act) must be respected by the provincial legislature but that they may be changed without a constitutional amendment.

The "Quebec Clause" and the Quebec Protestant School Boards Case [8]

This case concerns the constitutional validity of the sections of the Quebec Charter of the French Language (Bill 101) that restrict English-language schooling to children of long-time anglophone Quebeckers, that is, anglophone parents who had received their primary or secondary school education in Quebec.

Bill 101, enacted in 1977, was the culmination of several attempts by successive provincial governments since the beginning of the Quiet Revolution to prevent the disappearance of the French culture in Quebec. In the 1960s the birth rate of native francophone Quebeckers declined dramatically. At the same time, the great majority of new immigrants were opting to join the anglophone culture because of the perceived economic benefits of this choice. In 1968 a violent conflict occurred involving a school board that tried to force children of Italian immigrants to attend French schools. As a result, in 1969 the provincial government enacted Bill 63, the Act to Promote the French Language in Quebec.

The legislation authorized the ministers of education and immigration to "take the measures necessary" to encourage new immigrants to "acquire the knowledge of the French language upon arrival." As Quebec nationalism grew and there was no apparent increase in the proportion of immigrants who assimilated into the francophone culture, the permissive approach of Bill 63 was considered inadequate. In 1974, Bill 63 was replaced by Bill 22, the Official Language Act. Bill 22 declared the "official language" of Quebec to be French. The section dealing with education prevented the expansion of English-language instruction in schools unless authorized by the minister of education, who had to be satisfied that there was a sufficient number of students whose *mother* tongue was English to justify such an expansion. In other words, English-language schooling was to be provided only to children of native anglophones, not to children of immigrants whose mother tongue was not English. In addition, Bill 22 prevented francophone children not already fluent in English from attending English-language public schools, and anglophone children not already fluent in French from attending French-language public schools. In 1976 the Parti Québécois came to power in Quebec. The PQ had been critical of Bill 22 for not going far enough to protect and promote the French language. In 1977, Bill 22 was replaced by Bill 101, the Charter of the French Language. The section of Bill 101 dealing with education restricted English-language instruction to children of persons who had received their primary education in English in Quebec, or to children with an older sibling who had received primary education in English in Quebec. These restrictions became known as the "Quebec clause."

When the Canadian Charter of Rights and Freedoms came into effect in 1982, it guaranteed that citizens who had received a French primary education anywhere in Canada could have their children educated in French anywhere in the country and that citizens who had received an English primary education anywhere in Canada could have their children educated in English anywhere in the country. In addition, children with siblings who had received primary or secondary education in English anywhere in Canada could attend English-language schools anywhere in the country, and children with siblings who had received primary or secondary education in French anywhere in Canada could attend French-language schools anywhere in the country. These provisions became known as the "Canada clause." It is noteworthy that René Lévesque, premier of Quebec at the time, had at one time agreed to the Canada clause because he was convinced that the premiers of the other nine provinces would not accept it. He withdrew his agreement, however, when the constitution was patriated without the consent of Quebec.

There was an obvious contradiction between the Canada clause in section 23 of the Charter and the Quebec clause in Bill 101. Shortly after the Charter came into effect in 1982, the Quebec Association of Protestant School Boards applied to the Quebec Superior Court for a declaration that the Quebec clause in Bill 101 was inoperative. The major issue before the Superior Court was whether the Quebec clause could be justified as a reasonable limit pursuant to section 1 of the Charter. A great deal of sociolinguistic evidence was presented to the trial judge, Chief Justice Jules Deschênes, to the effect that the replacement of the Quebec clause by the Canada clause would result in higher enrollments in the English school system in Quebec and that this would seriously threaten the survival of the French language. After carefully considering the evidence, Deschênes concluded that the increased enrollments that would result from the Canada clause — in the order of less than 5 per cent — would not be enough to threaten the continued existence of the French language in Quebec. It is clear that Deschênes would have accepted the Quebec clause as a reasonable limit had there been evidence that the Canada clause would have resulted in substantially increased enrollments in English schools in Quebec.

The Quebec attorney general appealed to the Quebec Court of Appeal, lost again and then appealed to the Supreme Court of Canada. The Supreme Court rendered one decision attributed to "The Court." This was a technique that allowed the Court, when dealing with divisive issues, both to display unanimity and to conceal the identity of the justice who wrote the decision. The panel consisted of Ritchie, Dickson, Beetz, Estey, McIntyre, Lamer and Wilson. The Court's decision was much briefer than that of Deschênes. The judges simply concluded that the Quebec clause was not a mere "limit" of section 23 of the Charter, but a complete denial of it:

> The provisions of s.73 of *Bill 101* [the Quebec clause] collide directly with those of s.23 of the Charter, and are not limitations which can be legitimized by s.1 of the Charter. Such limitations cannot be exceptions to the rights and freedoms guaranteed by the Charter.

The importance of this decision to the judicial interpretation of section 1 is that any legislation that completely denies a Charter right can never be justified under section 1. However, it may be difficult for the judges always to be able to distinguish clearly between a limitation and a complete denial.

The Issue of Judicial Bilingualism and the Société des Acadiens Case [126]

In 1982 the Société des Acadiens du Nouveau-Brunswick became embroiled in a dispute with a school board in Grand Falls, New Brunswick. The board wished to offer French immersion programs to francophone students in English schools, a measure that the Société des Acadiens considered contrary to the New Brunswick Schools Act. The Société brought an action in the New Brunswick Court of Queen's Bench for an injunction to prevent the board from offering the courses.

The Queen's Bench judge made a decision in favour of the Société, and the board decided not to appeal. However, a number of parents of the students affected banded together to form the Association of Parents, and this association filed an application with the New Brunswick Court of Appeal for leave (permission) to appeal the Queen's Bench decision. Arguments were presented in both English and French. The association's application for leave to appeal was granted by a three-judge panel, which included two bilingual judges and an anglophone judge who claimed that he understood enough French to be able to hear the case. The Société appealed the panel's decision to the Supreme Court of Canada, in part on the grounds that the hearing violated section 19(2) of the Charter, which stipulates that "[e]ither English or French may be used by any person in . . . any court . . . of New Brunswick." The Société claimed that section 19(2) guarantees the right to be understood in either official language in the courts of New Brunswick and that the anglophone judge, Mr. Justice Stratton, did not comprehend enough French to be able to understand the arguments presented in French.

The Société des Acadiens lost in the Supreme Court, and in the process it was decided that the right to use either English or French in a court does *not* include the right to be understood in the language of choice. (It should be pointed out, however, that litigants do have a right to be understood, but this right stems not from section 19[2], but from the common-law principles of natural justice that are affirmed in sections 7, 11(d) and 14 of the Charter and in section 2[e] of the Canadian Bill of Rights.) It is worth comparing the judgments of the majority and the minority, as they contain very different views about the purpose of the language rights sections of the Charter.

The Majority Decision

The majority decision was written by Mr. Justice Beetz, with Estey, Chouinard, Lamer and Le Dain concurring. Beetz grounded his approach to the issue on the assumption that there is a fundamental difference between the language rights and the legal rights protected by the Charter:

> [L]egal rights tend to be seminal in nature because they are rooted in principle . . . . Language rights, on the other hand, although some of them have been enlarged and incorporated into the Charter, remain nonetheless founded on political compromise.

Because language rights are the result of political compromises made by two linguistic communities attempting to coexist with each other, Beetz considered that any broadening of these rights should be effected by the political process rather than by the courts. He noted that the language rights part of the Charter was clearly designed so that provinces in addition to New Brunswick could opt into it. All that would be required would be the consent of the legislature of the province involved and of the Senate and House of Commons. He was afraid that if the Supreme Court took an approach to language rights that indicated the language rights would be continually broadened, other provinces would be discouraged from opting in.

Beetz gave two additional reasons for interpreting the Charter's language rights narrowly. First, he compared section 19, which concerns language rights in courts, with section 17, which protects language rights in Parliament and the New Brunswick legislature. Section 17 states that "[e]veryone has the right to use English or French in any debates and other proceedings of Parliament . . . [and] the legislature of New Brunswick." The wording of section 17 is parallel to that of section 19 except that section 17 deals with the legislative process. Beetz reasoned that section 17 could not possibly contain the assumption that anyone speaking in the legislature had a right to be understood by all other legislators in whatever language was being spoken. Because section 17 merely protected the right to speak, not the right to be understood, section 19 should be interpreted in the same way.

Second, Beetz argued that if section 19 had been meant to include a right to be understood in the language of the litigant's choice, the drafters of the Charter could have clearly indicated this intention. For example, section 20 of the Charter, which concerns the right of Canadians to receive services in French or English, refers to the right to "communicate." To Beetz, the word "communicate" plainly indicates the right to be understood. Because the drafters chose not to word section 19 in such a fashion, Beetz deduced that the right to be understood had deliberately been left out of section 19.

Beetz therefore concluded that section 19 simply protects the right to use either English or French in court, and not the right to be understood in that language. He noted that litigants have a right to be heard by judges who "are capable by any reasonable means of understanding the proceedings . . . [but] this entitlement is derived from the principles of natural justice . . . and not from s.19(2) of the Charter." On the question of whether Mr. Justice Stratton had sufficient knowledge of French to fulfil the natural justice requirements, Beetz wrote that "in the absence of any system of testing, it is for the judge to assess in good faith . . . his or her level of understanding of the language." It was not appropriate for the Supreme Court to question Stratton's judgment in this matter.

The Minority View

Justices Dickson and Wilson agreed with the majority that the Société des Acadiens must lose the appeal, but each issued a separate opinion. Both would have preferred a broader interpretation of section 19. But even given a more generous interpretation of the constitution, both Dickson and Wilson felt that the decision about whether Mr. Justice Stratton understood enough French to satisfy a beefed-up section 19 should be left to the judge himself. Dickson and Wilson were concerned about the proper interpretation of section 19, not about the outcome of this particular case.

Chief Justice Dickson stressed the importance of language rights in the Confederation bargain:

> Linguistic duality has been a longstanding concern in our nation. Canada is a country with both French and English solidly embedded in its history. The constitutional language protections reflect continued and renewed efforts in the direction of bilingualism . . . . In the words of André Tremblay . . ., "a broad, liberal and dynamic interpretation of the language provisions of the Constitution would be in line with the exceptional importance of their function."

Dickson would have preferred that the Court had given such a "broad and liberal" interpretation to section 19 by finding that it implied a right to be understood in the preferred language. He asked, "What good is a right to use one's language if those to whom one speaks cannot understand?"

Madame Justice Wilson's opinion was similar to Dickson's in its "broad and liberal" thrust, but she went further. For her, the language rights in the Charter imply that bilingualism is a goal Canadians are steadily moving towards but have not yet achieved. The courts must take this reality into account, she wrote, so that "[w]hat may be adequate to-day in terms of protection for the litigant's right under s.19(2) may not be adequate tomorrow . . . . We are looking at a process which will call for a progressively expansive interpretation of the litigant's right under s.19(2) to meet gradually increasing social expectations." For her, section 19(2) implies a right for litigants to be understood in the official language of their choice, and the appropriate level of understanding at the present time is "receptive bilingualism." This means that the listener can understand the "full flavour of the argument" in the litigant's language of choice, but may not necessarily speak that language fluently. Judges could legitimately use a translator to make comments to litigants in the language that they were not fluent in. Ultimately, however, the goal should be that judges understand and speak both languages equally well.

The Contrasting Approaches Adopted by the Judges

It would be difficult to find a better illustration than the *Société des Acadiens* case of judges differing over how the broad and general phrases in the Charter should be interpreted or of judges allowing their political views to influence their conclusions. Beetz opted for a narrow interpretation of language rights so that the judges would not upset the delicate political compromise that had been worked out and so as to encourage politicians, not judges, to continue the process of developing more appropriate compromises on the language issue. In contrast, Dickson chose a broad interpretation of language rights because he perceived them to be central to Canada's existence. Wilson, too, supported a broad interpretation but also suggested that the judges themselves should gradually expand the scope of the language rights sections of the Charter as social expectations about bilingualism, and the practical means of satisfying them, increased.

One could speculate that two competing images of Canada were contending for the loyalty of the judicial mind. One is the notion that Canada should eventually reach such a high state of bilingualism that both francophones and anglophones can feel at home in any province. This perception has been associated with the views of Pierre Trudeau. The other image is of a Canada in which two separate linguistic communities find ways of coexisting as "two solitudes" without many in either community becoming bilingual. From this perspective, Quebec will become more unilingual as a francophone society and the other nine provinces will remain (or become more) unilingual as anglophone societies. This view has been associated with the Parti Québécois, Robert Bourassa and the western premiers.

Clearly, the opinions of Justices Dickson and Wilson were consistent with the Trudeau vision. It is tempting to think that the majority decision was based on the two solitudes notion. This may well be the case, although an alternative explanation is that some judges favouring the Trudeau ideal feared that judicially enforced bilingualism might lead to a backlash that would actually retard the dawning of the Trudeau vision. In any case, it is noteworthy that the three Quebec judges, as well as a bilingual Ontario judge (Le Dain), all preferred the narrow approach.

The Manitoba Language Rights Case [73]

In 1985 the Supreme Court of Canada declared that Manitoba statutes would not be valid unless enacted in both French and English and that all English-only statutes that had been created since 1890 were invalid. To understand this historic decision, some background is necessary.

Background

Manitoba became a province of Canada under the Manitoba Act, 1870, which was entrenched in the British North America Act, 1871. The Manitoba Act, 1870, is part of the formal Constitution of Canada as defined by section 52 of the Constitution Act, 1982.

Section 23 of the Manitoba Act, 1870, was for Manitoba what section 133 of the Constitution Act, 1867, was for Quebec. It declared, among other things, that the acts of the Manitoba legislature shall be printed and published in both English and French. Up to 1890 the francophones and anglophones in Manitoba were roughly equal in number, but in that year a clear majority of anglophones gained control of the government in a provincial election. In 1890 the Manitoba legislature enacted the Official Language Act, which proclaimed English as the only official language of the province and declared that henceforth statutes would be printed and published only in English.

In 1892 a francophone litigant challenged the constitutionality of the Official Language Act in a county court and won [64]. The act was obviously *ultra vires,* and the judge declared this to be the case. The government simply ignored the decision and carried on enacting legislation only in English. Although the decision was technically binding on the government, the government decided not to appeal to a higher court. Thus, there were no precedents in a superior court to indicate that the Official Language Act was *ultra vires,* and county court decisions, according to the doctrine of *stare decisis,* are not binding on superior courts (see chapter 2). The litigant who won in the county court could not appeal because of the fact that he had won. Litigants successfully challenged the Official Language Act again in 1909 and 1976 with the same results: they won in the county court but the decisions were ignored by the government. In 1976 the Manitoba attorney general simply announced that the government did not accept the ruling of the court, but the decision was not appealed because of the fear that the government would lose. These events should provide a good antidote to the belief that constitutional rights can always be successfully enforced by the courts.

The francophone litigant who won the 1976 case adopted a new strategy in 1978. He brought an application in the Manitoba Court of Queen's Bench that the Official Language Act was invalid. This time, in Peter Hogg's (1) words, he was "fortunate enough to lose." Thus, he was able to appeal to the Manitoba Court of Appeal, where he won. This was a decision that the Manitoba government could not ignore, and it appealed to the Supreme Court of Canada in order to settle the issue. In 1979, in the *Forest* decision [6], the Supreme Court declared the Official Language Act to be unconstitutional. The Court did not discuss the broader consequences of this declaration regarding the validity of Manitoba statutes enacted since 1890 only in English.

At the same time as it rendered judgment in *Forest,* the Court released its decision on the constitutionality of the sections of Quebec's Bill 101 that declared that statutes would be enacted only in French. The Court had no difficulty in finding that these provisions were unconstitutional, as they violated section 133 of the Constitution Act, 1867. The case became known as *Blaikie No. 1* [9]. (Later, in

Blaikie No. 2 [10], the Supreme Court further clarified the scope of section 133 by proclaiming that, in addition to the requirement that statutes must be enacted in English and French, regulations that were subject to the approval of the cabinet, the rules of practice in courts and the rules of quasi-judicial tribunals had to be produced in both official languages.)

The attorneys general of Manitoba and Quebec, during the hearings for *Forest* and *Blaikie No. 1,* had argued that a provincial government was entitled to amend its own internal constitution under section 92(1) of the Constitution Act, 1867, which gave the provinces the power to amend the "Constitution of the province, except as regards the Office of Lieutenant Governor." The Court rejected this view. It proclaimed that the language rights in the constitution were an essential part of the Confederation bargain and were designed to prevent provincial legislatures from destroying minority language rights.

Within twenty-four hours of the Supreme Court's decisions in *Blaikie No. 1* and *Forest,* the Quebec legislature had re-enacted in both official languages all of the statutes that had been passed only in French since 1977. This task was made easy by the fact that the government had continued to produce unofficial English versions of the statutes. The Manitoba legislature was not so quick. It began to enact some statutes in both official languages, but many statutes continued to be enacted only in English. Francophones in Manitoba became impatient. Roger Bilodeau, a francophone who had been charged with a traffic offence, developed a strategy designed to spur the legislature along. He pleaded not guilty on the grounds that his summons had been issued only in English and that the Highway Traffic Act and Summary Convictions Act themselves were unconstitutional, having been enacted only in English. The results of the *Bilodeau* case are discussed in the next section.

Before the *Bilodeau* case could be heard by the Supreme Court, the federal government decided to send a reference question to the Court about the status of Manitoba laws. This was because of the fear that the *Bilodeau* decision might address only the narrow issue of the status of the Highway Traffic Act and the Summary Convictions Act. The reference asked, among other things, whether all the Manitoba statutes published only in English since 1890 were invalid, and if so, under what circumstances they might have some legal force and effect. The Supreme Court heard arguments on both the *Bilodeau* case and the *Manitoba Language Reference* at the same time in 1984. The judgment on the *Manitoba Language Reference* was released in 1985, and on the *Bilodeau* case in 1986.

The Decision

One opinion was presented for the entire panel, which consisted of Justices Dickson, Beetz, Estey, McIntyre, Lamer, Wilson and Le Dain. By following the precedents established by the *Blaikie* and *Forest* decisions, the Court had no difficulty in declaring that all of Manitoba's statutes enacted in English only after 1890 were invalid.

This conclusion presented a dilemma around the question about how Manitoba statutes could regain legal force. Because all statutes from 1890 were invalid, the current Manitoba legislature had no legal standing, having been elected under an invalid electoral law. For the same reason, Manitoba had no legal courts, public service or police force. What existed in the province was a legal vacuum, and there was no obvious way to remedy the situation because a legal government did not exist and could not be created. In a strictly legal sense, Manitoba was under the control of an unconstitutional regime.

The Supreme Court looked for guidance to the decisions of other common-law courts that had had to contend with the effects of governments acting unconstitutionally. For example, for several years after Pakistan's independence in 1947, laws were enacted without royal assent, and all of them were eventually deemed to be ineffective. In 1963 in Cyprus, normal legislative procedures proved impossible because an insurrection physically prevented most Turkish Cypriots from participating in the government. In 1965 Ian Smith, representing Southern Rhodesia's white minority, illegally declared the country independent. In legal matters arising out of each of these cases, courts found the "doctrine of necessity" helpful.

According to the doctrine of necessity, civilization cannot exist without the rule of law. Therefore, the courts cannot tolerate a legal vacuum. The doctrine of necessity holds that the laws of an illegal government must be deemed to be effective to the extent that they do not violate the constitution. That particular interpretation of the doctrine of necessity was only partly helpful to the Canadian Supreme Court, because all of Manitoba's laws from 1890 definitely violated the constitution by being enacted only in English. Therefore, the Supreme Court developed its own version of the doctrine of necessity:

> The Constitution will not suffer a province without laws.
> Thus the Constitution requires that temporary validity and

force and effect be given to the current Acts of the
Manitoba Legislature from the date of this judgment, and
that rights, obligations and other effects which have arisen
under these laws . . . are deemed *temporarily* to have been
and continue to be effective and beyond challenge. It is
only in this way that legal chaos can be avoided and the
Rule of Law preserved. [Emphasis added]

After hearing more evidence, the Court decided to give the
Manitoba legislature until December 31, 1988, to re-enact in French
and English the current statutes, regulations and rules of court, and
until December 31, 1990, all other Manitoba laws.

The Implications of the Manitoba Language Reference

This fascinating case and its predecessors — *Forest* and the two
Blaikie cases — illustrate the close connection between section 133
and the Charter, as well as some aspects of the ongoing politics of
language in Canada. It is clear that sections 16-23 of the Charter are
really extensions of the language rights contained in Canada's first
"little bill of rights," section 133 of the Constitution Act, 1867. For
the sake of simplicity, it is perhaps unfortunate that section 133, as
well as section 23 of the Manitoba Act, was not moved into the
Charter.

The fate of section 23 of the Manitoba Act, from 1890 to 1985,
illustrates both the limits and potential of constitutionally entrenched
language rights. Section 23 was no help at all to franco-Manitobans
during that time period. Their political influence was simply not great
enough to ensure that their constitutional rights would be respected,
and judicial remedies are often ineffective in the face of overpowering
political forces. As well, the fact that language rights were *not* enforced in Manitoba for almost a century probably goes a long way
towards explaining why so many franco-Manitobans assimilated into
the anglophone community, and why most francophone Quebeckers
stopped emigrating to Manitoba. If some way had been found in the
1890s to protect the constitutional rights of franco-Manitobans, the
Trudeau vision of Canada might well be closer to reality today.

The MacDonald and Bilodeau Cases [51, 17] and Bilingual
Summonses

In 1980 Roger J.A. Bilodeau received a summons for speeding contrary to Manitoba's Highway Traffic Act. The summons was issued

in English only. In 1981 Duncan Cross MacDonald received a summons for speeding contrary to a Montreal city by-law. His summons was in French only. Both pleaded not guilty in their respective provinces on the grounds that the summonses were ineffective unless issued either in both official languages or in the language of choice of the recipient of the summons. In addition, Bilodeau argued that the Manitoba Highway Traffic Act and Summary Convictions Act were *ultra vires* because they had been enacted only in English. Both Bilodeau and MacDonald were convicted. They appealed and lost in their provincial court of appeal. The Supreme Court of Canada granted both litigants leave to appeal because of the importance of the constitutional issues they raised. The judgments were released on the same day in 1986.

MacDonald based his claim on section 133 of the Constitution Act, 1867, which states that "either English or French . . . may be used by any Person or in any Pleading or Process in or issuing from any Court of Canada established under this Act, and in or from all or any of the Courts of Quebec." Bilodeau's case was founded on section 23 of the Manitoba Act, 1870, which is almost identical to section 133 except that "Manitoba" is substituted for "Quebec." Both argued that because they have the right to plead in their official language of choice, the state has a correlative duty to respect the language of choice by issuing a summons in the language of choice or by issuing a bilingual summons. The appellants also drew on the *Blaikie* (No.2) decision, which settled that the rules of practice for the courts of Quebec must be issued in both languages. If the rules of practice had to be in both official languages, then other official court documents, such as summonses, logically had to be in both official languages as well.

The majority on the Supreme Court did not accept this argument. In *MacDonald,* the opinion was written by Mr. Justice Beetz, with Estey, McIntyre, Lamer and Le Dain concurring entirely, and Dickson concurring on the constitutional question. In *Bilodeau,* Chief Justice Dickson wrote the majority opinion, with Beetz, Estey, McIntyre, Lamer and Le Dain concurring. Madame Justice Wilson wrote a dissenting opinion in both cases.

The Majority Opinions

The majority looked closely at the wording of sections 133 and 23 and determined that there were language rules in the constitution of two kinds: (1) those that impose a duty to use both official languages and (2) those that permit the use of one or both of the languages at the discretion of the speaker. They concluded that sections 133 and 23 *require* the use of both official languages only for the enactment and publication of statutes and the creation and publication of regulations (including the rules of practice in court). The permissive parts of sections 133 and 23 concern the debates in Parliament and in the Quebec or Manitoba legislatures, and pleadings and processes in the courts of Canada, Quebec or Manitoba. The permissive sections allow people to use either language at their discretion, but *do not require* the use of both languages. According to the majority, the authorities responsible for establishing the courts in the provinces — that is, the provincial legislatures — are permitted to decide whether English or French or both should be used in court processes such as summonses, just as litigants have the discretion to speak English or French or both in court.

In the *MacDonald* decision, the majority noted that MacDonald had based his entire submission on section 133. He had not argued that the right to a fair hearing (as protected by the common-law principles of natural justice, sections 7, 11(d) and 14 of the Charter and section 2 of the Canadian Bill of Rights) required that he receive a translation of the summons. Therefore, the majority did not decide this issue. In *obiter,* however, the majority hinted that if MacDonald had requested a translation of the summons, the court would be obliged to provide it, not because of section 133, but pursuant to fair hearing rights:

> It is axiomatic that everyone has a common law right to a fair hearing, including the right to be informed of the case one has to meet and the right to make full answer and defence. Where the defendant cannot understand the proceedings because he is unable to understand the language in which they are being conducted, or because he is deaf, the effective exercise of these rights may well impose a consequential duty upon the court to provide adequate translation.

MacDonald had not requested a translation of the summons from the court, but had obtained his own translation. In court he had presented his case in English and had been understood in that language. Therefore, his right to a fair hearing was not in question. His conviction stood.

In the *Bilodeau* case, the majority held that pursuant to the doctrine of necessity (discussed above under the *Manitoba Language Reference*) the Highway Traffic Act and Summary Convictions Act remained temporarily valid. Therefore, Bilodeau's conviction also stood.

The Dissent

Madame Justice Wilson anchored her dissent in both cases on an analysis of the relation between rights and duties (see chapter 1). She stressed that in legal theory, when a person is granted a right in law, then another person or body has a correlative duty to respect or meet that right. For example, section 10 of the Charter states that persons detained by the police have a right to be informed of the right to counsel. This means that the police have a duty to inform persons they detain of their right to counsel. Wilson's opinion is a scholarly analysis of the legal theory; she refers to leading theorists, including Hart, Hohfeld, Austin, Hegel, Salmond and, in the Canadian context, Lederman and McRuer.

The majority of the Court had concluded that the phrase in sections 133 and 23 — "either [English or French] may be used by any Person or in any Pleading . . . in any Court" — gave the state the right to one or other of the official languages in issuing summonses. The state in this sense was regarded as a legal person, and the court was considered as acting on behalf of the state. Wilson claimed that this interpretation was wrong. She pointed out that in constitutional theory the state is assumed to possess all possible powers of government and the constitution limits those powers in order to protect the rights of citizens. A constitution, therefore, does not confer rights on the state. The phrase quoted above must therefore confer rights on *citizens* to use either English or French in their relations with courts. Because citizens have this right, the court has a correlative duty to respect this right by communicating with citizens in the official language of their choice.

Wilson noted that the courts could fulfil their section 133 and 23 duties in this situation in at least two ways: by issuing bilingual summonses or by issuing unilingual summonses that also state, in the other official language, that the court will provide a translation at the request of the recipient of the summons. After reviewing the history of section 133, she concluded that the latter method would fulfil the court's obligation. (Prior to Confederation, bilingual summonses had been required at one time, but this requirement was eventually repealed.)

Because neither the court in Montreal nor the court in Manitoba had proceeded against the appellants by issuing proper summonses, Wilson concluded that these courts had no jurisdiction to convict.

The Significance of the MacDonald and Bilodeau Decisions

The decisions of the majority in these two cases are in the same vein as in the *Société des Acadiens* decision. They present a narrow interpretation of the language rights in the constitution so as to avoid antagonizing linguistic majorities in Manitoba and Quebec and to allow politicians to work out compromises that will expand language rights, if they are to be expanded.

It is noteworthy that even Chief Justice Dickson sided with the majority view in these cases, whereas in the *Société des Acadiens* decision he took the broader view. Consistent with his position to interpret language rights as narrowly as reasonably possible, in the *Société des Acadiens* case it may have seemed unreasonable that a right to speak in the language of choice in court would not include the right to be understood. In *MacDonald* and *Bilodeau,* however, he may have felt that a narrower interpretation of language rights was possible without seeming to stretch credulity.

Wilson's analysis is complex because of her reliance on legal theory. From this perspective, her approach seems the most convincing. It makes more sense to interpret the phrase "either [English or French] may be used by any Person or in any Pleading . . . in any Court" as conferring a right on citizens rather than on the state. Her position — that once a right is imposed, the state has a correlative duty — is compelling.

Nevertheless, the majority decision may be preferable from a political perspective if it is true that an overly expansive interpretation of language rights might result in a backlash that could diminish the chances of minority language survival. The majority decision may be an example of one which is legally questionable but politically astute.

The Mercure Case [98] and Language Rights in Saskatchewan and Alberta

Father André Mercure, a francophone priest in Saskatchewan, was charged with speeding in 1981. When he appeared in court, he applied for permission to proceed with his trial in French. He claimed he had a right to enter a plea and to proceed in French pursuant to section 110 of the North-West Territories Act, which became part of the law of Saskatchewan pursuant to section 16 of the Saskatchewan Act, 1905. Section 110 provides for the protection of French and English language rights parallel to those provided for Quebeckers in section 133 of the Constitution Act, 1867, and for Manitobans in section 23 of the Manitoba Act. (The Saskatchewan Act brought Saskatchewan into Confederation, and it is now part of the formal Constitution of Canada defined by section 52 of the Constitution Act, 1982.) Section 16 of the act provides for the continuance of the laws of the old North-West Territories in Saskatchewan until they are amended or repealed by the new legislature of Saskatchewan. Section 110 of the North-West Territories Act had never been amended or repealed. (The legislature of the North-West Territories had made an attempt to repeal section 110 in 1891, but the effort failed because the correct procedures were not followed.)

Father Mercure was denied permission to enter a plea and to proceed in French, and he appealed this decision all the way to the Supreme Court of Canada. The Court rendered a decision in his favour in 1988, but by then he had died. (Although the issue of the speeding ticket was moot because of Father Mercure's death, the Court decided to hear the case anyway because the judges felt it would be in the public interest to settle the constitutional issue.)

All nine judges heard the appeal, which indicates the importance of the case. The decision of the majority was written by Mr. Justice Gérard La Forest and concurred in by Dickson, Beetz, Lamer, Wilson and Le Dain. Mr. Justice Estey wrote a dissenting opinion, which McIntyre concurred in. Mr. Justice Julien Chouinard sat on the appeal but became ill and resigned before the decision was prepared.

The Majority Opinion

The majority held that section 110 of the North-West Territories Act still applied in Saskatchewan. Therefore, Saskatchewan was in a similar position to Manitoba after the *Manitoba Language Reference:* none of its laws were valid, as none had been enacted in both languages. As in Manitoba, Saskatchewan laws were declared temporarily valid pursuant to the doctrine of necessity, and the province was given a reasonable time to make amends.

Section 110 of the North-West Territories Act, however, differed in one important respect from section 133 of the Constitution Act, 1867, and section 23 of the Manitoba Act. In 1890 some anglophone members of Parliament had pressed for amendments to the North-West Territories Act that would make the territories unilingual. These members had a vision of Canada in which the French language would be eliminated throughout the country. The majority in Parliament, however, felt that the language issue should be resolved by the legislature of the territories, not by Parliament. As a result, section 110 was amended to allow the territorial legislature to abolish the bilingual provisions if it chose to do so. La Forest reasoned that because section 110 contained this provision for its own amendment, the Saskatchewan legislature could, if it chose, simply repeal section 110:

> Accordingly, the Legislature may resort to the obvious, if ironic, expedient of enacting a bilingual statute removing the restrictions imposed on it by s.110 and then declaring all existing provincial statutes valid notwithstanding that they were enacted, printed and published in English only.

The Court had been invited by Mercure to declare that the language rights in section 110 were entrenched in the constitution and could only be changed pursuant to the amending formula described in section 43 of the Constitution Act, 1982 — the agreement of Parliament and the provincial legislature concerned. Section 43 covers "any amendment to any provision that relates to the use of the English or the French language within a province." The majority rejected this suggestion, however, because the Saskatchewan Act stated that laws inherited from the North-West Territories could be amended by the new provincial government.

It remained for the majority to determine "the reasonable means necessary to ensure that the [judges] understand the proceedings [if they do not speak the preferred official language of the litigants]." This was an issue that had not been determined in the *MacDonald, Bilodeau* or *Société des Acadiens* cases, since in each of these cases the judge or judges involved were deemed to have comprehended the language used by the litigant. La Forest noted that regardless of section 110, witnesses may address the court in the language they are most comfortable with, and the court has a duty (presumably under common law and sections 7, 11(h) and 14 of the Charter) to provide a translator. In addition he concluded that litigants at least deserve to have proceedings recorded in the official language they use in court. He pointed out that "the proceedings, for example, may continue in the Court of Appeal where the judges may quite properly wish to refer to the exact words used by a person at trial, words that person has a right to use." Because Father Mercure had not been allowed to enter a plea in French, the majority held that the conviction should be quashed.

The Minority Opinion

Justices Estey and McIntyre considered that section 110 of the North-West Territories Act was of even less assistance to francophones in Saskatchewan than the majority thought. Their approach seemed to be to "let sleeping dogs lie." They concluded that section 110 of the North-West Territories Act was inapplicable after 1905. Estey claimed that the Saskatchewan Act created a new legislature and new courts; this meant that section 110, which referred to the old legislature and the old courts, is not relevant. Even if it were assumed that section 110 had been incorporated into the laws of Saskatchewan, section 110 would have become spent with the termination of the old legislature of the North-West Territories and the old courts of the territories. From this perspective, Father Mercure had no right to plead in French at his trial.

The Political Consequences of the Mercure Decision

Until 1885, the majority of settlers in what is now Saskatchewan and Alberta were francophone. That proportion has now dropped to about 3 per cent. One reason for this was that government policies encouraged the settlement of the West by non-francophones. In addition, since 1890, the territorial and then the provincial governments have supported policies that have encouraged the assimilation of the francophones. The *Mercure* decision merely restored to prairie francophones a few of the rights they should have enjoyed all along.

Those restored rights, as might be expected, were short-lived. Two months after the February 1988 Supreme Court decision, the Saskatchewan legislature repealed section 110 of the North-West Territories Act. However, the government announced that some statutes would be translated into French and that French would be allowed to be spoken in the legislature and used in the courts. In June the federal government agreed to pay for most of the cost of translating statutes into French and for most of the other costs incurred in the provision of additional translators and francophone court reporters. As well, the federal government agreed to help fund a prairie language institute. The institute would help to train provincial public servants to develop a capacity in French, and in addition it would provide instruction in nineteen other minority languages spoken on the prairies. By including the other minority languages in the language institute, the package of reforms became politically more palatable in a province where francophones constitute one of the smaller ethnic minorities.

The *Mercure* decision also had implications for Alberta, which was in exactly the same position as Saskatchewan regarding section 110 of the North-West Territories Act. In June Premier Getty announced that Alberta would take measures similar to those in Saskatchewan by repealing section 110 but providing limited services to Alberta's 63,000 francophones.

Although most francophone associations in Alberta and Saskatchewan were critical of the provincial governments for not restoring francophone rights to the same level as existed in Manitoba after the *Manitoba Language Rights Reference,* Quebec's premier, Robert Bourassa, praised the two prairie governments for at least providing a small improvement to services for francophones. He said that he recognized that it was impractical to provide a greater range of rights to such a small proportion of the population. Once again, Bourassa was promoting the "two solitudes" concept of Canada. Moreover, some suggested that Bourassa's comments might be intended to help justify future provincial government action in Quebec to limit the rights of Quebec anglophones. The Supreme Court was soon to render judgment in the *Ford* and *Devine* cases concerning the English-only signs provisions of Bill 101. If Saskatchewan and Alberta reduced the rights of their francophone minorities by repealing section 110 of the North-West Territory Act, Quebec would be equally justified in using the Charter's override clause, section 33, to limit the rights of the anglophone minority in Quebec. As we saw in chapter 3, this is precisely what happened in December 1988.

Judicial Interpretation of Language Rights

From the six cases discussed above, it is clear that the Supreme Court has decided to uphold language rights where their existence is unquestionable in the Charter or other parts of the constitution — an approach particularly evident in the *Quebec Protestant School Board* case, and the *Manitoba Language Reference*. However, the Court has also decided to interpret language rights narrowly so as to signal that if basic language rights are to be extended, this should come about as a result of political solutions, not judicial ones.

The decisions in *Société des Acadiens, Bilodeau, MacDonald* and *Mercure* illustrate the restrained approach towards language rights. In the first case, it was decided that the right to speak the minority language in court does not include the right to be understood in that language. The second and third cases settled that summonses need only be issued in one of the official languages in the provinces with bilingual guarantees emanating from section 133, the Charter, or another part of the constitution (Quebec, New Brunswick and Manitoba). Although the *Mercure* decision did extend section 133-like guarantees to Alberta and Saskatchewan for a few months, the majority decision in a sense invited the provinces to repeal the minority language rights.

Although the narrowness of these decisions will disappoint the proponents of the Trudeau vision of Canada, it is difficult to come to a firm conclusion at this time about the wisdom of the "political" strategy adopted by the judiciary in these cases. The decisions could be an incentive for those espousing the Trudeau vision to redouble their lobbying efforts to encourage provincial governments to provide more services and facilities for the minority language groups. In the long run, such political action might be more effective in promoting bilingualism than judicial decisions could be. Judicial pronouncements about the rights of minority language groups will not necessarily bring about a greater degree of respect in society for these groups, nor an improved atmosphere of tolerance, so important if minority language groups are to succeed in maintaining their languages.

On the other hand, there is also the danger that restrictive judicial decisions regarding language rights might be accepted as definitive "constitutional wisdom." This approach might encourage the proponents of greater bilingualism, like the losers in any court battle over the meaning of the constitution, to give up and accept the "superior" wisdom of the judiciary. But it would be sad if this occurs, because the judges intended their narrow decisions regarding language rights to promote more comprehensive consideration of language issues through the democratic process.

8

Conclusion:
The Charter and Human
Rights

In the Introduction, I quoted Donald Smiley's assertion that "the degree to which human rights are safeguarded is the final test by which any polity should be judged." Has the Charter improved Canada's prospects for a favourable judgment? I will now try to provide a framework that may be useful in answering this question. I will first summarize my perspective on human rights. Next, I will present my impressions about how the Charter has affected thinking about human rights in Canada. Finally, I will suggest some ways in which the positive effects of the Charter can be enhanced and its direct or indirect negative influences minimized.

Human Rights

At the most basic level, human rights can be thought of as considerations which are owed to every human being and which every person owes to others, in recognition that all persons are equally deserving of respect, a sense of self-worth, and fair treatment. The liberal democracies have pursued this goal by endeavouring to maximize individual liberty, and through providing procedural safeguards, promoting a degree of social equality and facilitating at least minimal political participation.

The concept of interpersonal respect implies that everyone both is owed respect and owes respect to others. If there is a conflict between the two in a specific instance, it is necessary to make a value judgment about which is to be given preference. For example, are human rights promoted most effectively by respecting the desires of Ernst Zundel and James Keegstra to disseminate their beliefs freely or by promoting the self-worth of the Canadian Jewish community by banning the publication of materials that suggest stereotypes and advocate hatred? Does fair treatment mean that procedural safeguards in the criminal justice system should be rigorously enforced so that there is almost no chance that an innocent person will be mistreated? Or should less emphasis be placed on procedural safeguards so that the police will be able to prevent crime more effectively?

These kinds of value conflicts are often presented as a tension between the promotion of individual human rights and a commitment to the larger community. My own view is that it is not very useful to think of human rights in terms of individual claims devoid of corresponding responsibilities. The concept of civil rights makes no sense except in respect to *relations* among people. A hermit has no use for civil rights until he or she interacts with others.

From this perspective, I suggest that a commitment to human rights, or rights-consciousness, is supported by the belief that the consideration one owes to others is as important as the consideration owed to oneself. Such an attitude will not automatically yield "correct" decisions about how to act, but it is likely to lead to certain tendencies regarding both beliefs and actions.

For example, a person committed to human rights is likely to be more tolerant of the diversity of beliefs in the community (except sometimes with regard to others who are intolerant) than someone not so committed. As Paul Sniderman has noted, such tolerance is associated with higher levels of education. The more people know about different cultures, religions and ideologies, the less their inclination to accept false stereotypes and the greater their willingness to tolerate the existence of beliefs and life-styles outside their own culture and that they do not necessarily agree with.

A "mixed" attitude to authority is probably also conducive to a commitment to human rights. Persons who are tolerant are unlikely to acquiesce unquestioningly to authority figures simply because of a belief that submission to authority is the right thing to do. In their eyes, legitimate authority figures must earn esteem, for example, by respecting human rights (Sniderman, Fletcher, Russell and Tetlock).

Finally, building on C.B. Macpherson's views, a commitment to human rights means being as interested in promoting the self-fulfilment of others as in developing one's own creative potentials.

There are some who would consider the Charter simply as a means of protecting individuals from unreasonable encroachments on their rights and liberties by governments. While this is one function of the Charter, it could also serve a more fundamental objective — to promote higher levels of rights-consciousness in society. This is certainly not a goal that the Charter can be expected to achieve on its own, but it can be hoped that the Charter will at least make a contribution to this end. From this perspective on civil rights, I will speculate about the impact the Canadian Charter of Rights and Freedoms may have had on the beliefs and actions of Canadians. My comments will be organized around four dimensions affected by the Charter: national unity, liberal-democratic values, the political process and the legal system.

The Charter's Impact on Thinking about Human Rights

National Unity

According to the Trudeau government's strategy for nation-building, the Charter's primary purpose was to promote national unity. It was hoped that the Charter would encourage national debates about important issues, and that these debates would cut across regional and ethnic cleavages. It was also hoped that the Charter would cultivate national rather than regional loyalties through providing a common base of language and mobility rights.

The Promotion of National Debates

As a vehicle for fostering national debates and diverting attention away from ethnic and regional divisions, the Charter has had mixed results. For example, the Supreme Court's decisions on Sunday closing, abortion and the right to strike have all generated controversies that have produced more of a liberal-conservative split than divisions along regional or ethnic lines. This result may have drawn our attention away from a preoccupation with regional and ethnic issues, at least temporarily. On the other hand, the Supreme Court's decisions about the commercial signs provisions of Quebec's Bill 101 and minority language education rights in Quebec have generated disputes that have divided Canadians according to both language and region.

At a more basic level, the central question is whether the public debates the Charter has given rise to have encouraged more interpersonal respect and understanding. I suspect they have not. For example, members of the pro-life and pro-choice movements seem no closer to tolerating the views of their opponents than they were before. Western Canadians are probably no more sympathetic towards the francophone community because of a new awareness — stemming from Supreme Court decisions — of the history of suppression of francophone language rights in the West. Few would-be Sunday shoppers have stopped to consider whether the social need for a common pause day might outweigh their acquisitive desires, and those who favour existing Sunday-closing laws have probably not thought more deeply about how such laws might be framed so as to penalize as little as possible those whose holy day is other than Sunday.

If the Charter has not engendered more interpersonal respect and tolerance through the debates it has generated, this result is not by and large the fault of the judges. In contrast to the narrow, legalistic approach to the interpretation of the Canadian Bill of Rights the Supreme Court adopted during the 1960s and 1970s — which was unlikely to give rise to a society more respectful of civil liberties — a number of the Charter decisions of the Supreme Court could be considered as at least having the potential to encourage a greater overall commitment to human rights among those who read them. However, if judicial decisions about human rights are to affect society as a whole, ways must be found to disseminate effectively the judges' reasoning, and not just the "bottom line" of who wins or loses court decisions.

Language and Mobility Rights

The policy of extending bilingual services has continued in the federal public service and in New Brunswick. However, most of the progress that has occurred was not required by sections 16-22 of the Charter. It occurred largely because of the policy priorities of the governments in power. In Ontario, since 1982, the provincial government has probably made even more progress than the federal government or New Brunswick in providing government services in French, although Ontario has not opted into the language rights section of the Charter.

The only Supreme Court decision concerning sections 16-22, the *Société des Acadiens* case, interpreted language rights in a restricted fashion. Likewise, the Court has interpreted other language rights in the constitution narrowly, except when a broad interpretation could not be avoided, as in the *Manitoba Language Rights* case. The strategy of the Court has been to leave the extension of language rights to future political compromises. Thus, sections 16-22 of the Charter have had little impact on the state of language rights in Canada, and therefore little bearing on the rights-consciousness of Canadians.

In contrast, section 23 of the Charter, which has created new minority language education rights for both francophones and anglophones, has had repercussions in several ways. First, provincial governments in the anglophone provinces have established more extensive French-language school facilities. Second, judicial decisions in the lower courts have promoted the advancement of these facilities in Ontario, Alberta and Saskatchewan. These reforms in the anglophone provinces may help to counteract the pressures towards assimilation experienced by the francophone minorities outside Quebec, but so far there has been no rush of immigrants from Quebec to the anglophone provinces to take advantage of the new rights. It is too soon to tell whether section 23 will foster a general atmosphere of bilingualism, so that francophones as well as anglophones will feel free to move to any province without fear of losing their linguistic heritage. If section 23 has this effect, it will certainly augment the sense of self-worth of francophone Canadians and thus will contribute to the advancement of human rights.

With regard to Quebec, the Supreme Court has struck down the section of Bill 101 that denied English-language education to children of anglophones from other provinces. Although this decision created some resentment among Quebec nationalists, the additional English-language school privileges thus established do not seem to have created a serious threat to the survival of the French language. No doubt, section 23 has contributed towards the sense of self-worth of anglophone Canadians who move to Quebec, thus enhancing human rights.

Section 6 of the Charter — mobility rights — has had very little impact, although there is some indication in the Supreme Court's recent decision in *Black* [18] that this may change. By affirming the ability of Canadians from each province to work in other provinces, section 6 could possibly foster a greater sense of self-worth among Canadians who seek work in other provinces.

Liberal-Democratic Goals

The liberal-democratic goals consist of the three traditional liberal values of optimum freedom, social equality, and procedural fairness, plus the more recent democratic goal of facilitating more meaningful public participation in the political process. In seven years the Charter has led to very few changes in how our society promotes these values. This is partly because of what F.L. Morton refers to as Canada's "excellent historical record on human rights and freedoms compared to other nations." Although our good comparative record certainly does not mean that we have nothing to improve on, it does mean that radical changes are not to be expected. What we look for is small adjustments that will reduce the likelihood of the recurrence of overly narrow judicial decisions like those rendered under the Canadian Bill of Rights.

Optimum Freedom

The Charter has resulted in very little change in the amount of freedom enjoyed by Canadians. The federal Lord's Day Act is gone, but the provinces have been left with a fairly wide mandate to enact secular Sunday-closing legislation. Unions have failed to persuade the Supreme Court that the Charter implies the freedom to strike. The Supreme Court declared that the Charter provides merchants in Quebec with the right to post bilingual outdoor signs — as long as French predominates — but the Quebec government was able to avoid the effects of this decision through the use of a section 33 override.

Social Equality

Because the Supreme Court handed down its first substantive decision on the equality rights in the Charter only in February 1989, it is too early to form conclusions about the effect of the Charter on social equality. However, the *Andrews* decision is a refreshing departure from the narrow approach to equality the Supreme Court took under the Bill of Rights. At the same time, the Court has declared that it will refrain from striking down legislation as a violation of equality unless such an action will assist the socially disadvantaged. It is likely, therefore, that the Charter will promote social equality, but it is difficult to predict the extent of its effect.

Procedural Fairness

It is with regard to procedural safeguards that judicial decisions about the Charter's treatment of liberal-democratic values have had the greatest impact. As Morton has pointed out,

> The most heavily affected area of public policy [by Charter decisions] has been that of criminal law enforcement. To date 74 per cent of all Charter litigation has involved criminal law enforcement. Individuals have enjoyed a success rate of 31 per cent in these cases .... The result has been many instances of evidence being excluded from trial, re-trials, dropping of charges, and a large number of acquittals . . . .
>
> Prior to the Charter criminologists consistently characterized Canada as conforming to the "crime control" model of criminal law rather than the "due process" model. Canadian criminal law, like most European systems, has consistently struck the balance in favour of more effective law enforcement as opposed to the rights of the accused . . . . While the wording of the Charter carefully preserved some of the "crime control" elements of Canadian criminal law, judicial interpretation of the Charter has embraced some of the core concepts of the "due process" model.

The *Therens* decision, which resulted in the exclusion of breathalyzer evidence whenever the police had not informed recipients of the breathalyzer tests of their prior right to counsel, provides the most dramatic illustration of Morton's conclusion. The *B.C. Motor Vehicle Act* decision demonstrated that the Supreme Court would not necessarily interpret the "crime control" elements of the Charter as the framers of the Charter had hoped. The *Southam, Morgentaler* and *Singh* decisions all sent signals to governments that closer attention must be paid to procedural safeguards.

The Supreme Court's interpretation of legal rights has resulted in the legal system treating accused persons with more respect. On the other hand, it is possible that the publicity surrounding judicial decisions on procedure may have reinforced the view that rights consist more of considerations owed to individuals than of considerations individuals owe to others. To the extent that this has happened, the new procedural safeguards may not have had an entirely positive effect on rights-consciousness.

Democratic Rights

The democratic rights sections of the Charter have also resulted only in minor adjustments. Some of the mentally ill and mentally handicapped in institutions, as well as a limited number of prisoners, have gained the right to vote. There have been minor changes made to voting procedures, and some restrictions on candidacy have been removed. But overall, the democratic rights sections have not led to a significant increase in the proportion of persons qualified to vote or to run for office. This result is not surprising, because the democratic rights protected by the Charter were generally already in place before 1982.

Political participation in democracies, according to political theorists like John Stuart Mill and Jean Jacques Rousseau, requires far more than voting. For them, citizen participation in policy-making can have an educative value that can promote a more tolerant society. Because the Charter protects only basic democratic rights, it is not realistic to think that it will promote democracy in this broader sense.

Patrick Monahan has urged the judiciary to interpret the entire Charter from the perspective of promoting democracy and community. Wherever possible, he suggests, judges should decide cases in a way that would encourage more public participation in the resolution of policy issues. The judiciary could implement the Monahan ideal by avoiding policy decisions in cases where the Charter quite clearly provides the judiciary with no guidance. A non-decision by the judiciary could force a decision by the legislature, a procedure more likely to engage citizen participation. The Supreme Court has taken this approach in the right-to-strike cases, in language rights cases and in the *Borowski* decision. It is not evident, however, that this approach has actually promoted more political participation.

In general, then, it appears that the Charter has had little effect on democratic beliefs or practices. It may be unwise to rely on the Charter as a vehicle for advancing political participation.

Public Officials

It is useful to think of the Charter not only as a guide to judges conducting judicial review, but also as a set of instructions to legislators, cabinet ministers and public servants, as Brian Slattery has suggested. Therefore, members of these groups could be expected to take an active role in considering the implications of the principles behind the Charter by attempting to ensure that these principles are reflected in legislation, policies and actions.

Politicians

There are no obvious examples of how the Charter may have had a direct impact on politicians' thinking about human rights in their policy-making roles. The Charter, however, has had a fairly important indirect impact on their behaviour in two respects. First, politicians must develop strategies for reacting to politically sensitive judicial decisions about the Charter, such as those on abortion or the commercial signs provisions of Quebec's Bill 101. To date, these reactions appear to have been calculated more to minimize potential damage in terms of public support than to promote greater respect for human rights. Second, there are indications that some politicians are using the Charter as a means of avoiding, in Morton's words, "political hot potatoes."

For example, in 1982 Premier William Davis of Ontario evaded taking a clear position about the extension of French-language schools by referring his province's Education Act to the Court of Appeal for an opinion about whether it conformed with section 23 of the Charter. In 1985 the Conservative government of Premier Grant Devine avoided the abortion issue by referring controversial anti-abortion legislation to the Court of Appeal. Also in 1985, Ontario's new premier, David Peterson, was able to deflect criticism about his support for the expansion of funding to Roman Catholic high schools by referring the legislation to the Court of Appeal. During the 1988 election campaign, Prime Minister Brian Mulroney said that he would announce his government's strategy on the abortion issue only after the Supreme Court announced its decision in the *Borowski* case. The government ensured that this decision would not occur until after the election by refusing to bring a motion before the Supreme Court to quash the appeal.

It appears that the Charter has done little to encourage politicians to take a more deliberate and active role in promoting higher levels of interpersonal respect in society than they otherwise would have. On the contrary, politicians have used the Charter to avoid taking a stand on sensitive human rights issues.

Public Servants

F.L. Morton has found that two-thirds of all Charter cases involve claims that public officials have violated the Charter, rather than challenges to the constitutional validity of a law. Such cases would include, for example, a claim that a police officer had failed to inform a detainee of the right to counsel, that a customs official used unreasonable search methods or that a social worker did not observe procedural safeguards when apprehending a neglected child.

The higher procedural standards the courts have discovered in the Charter may promote greater respect for individuals among public officials, as well as a higher sense of self-worth among those who have dealings with government officials. On the other hand, the new procedural safeguards may place burdensome and time-consuming demands on law-enforcement officials and public servants, with the consequence that victims of crime are less well protected and persons dealing with government officials are subjected to longer waits and poorer service in some respects. However, the new stress on procedure is not necessarily detrimental, on balance. For example, it does not seem unreasonable for a police officer to inform a detainee of the right to counsel before a breathalyzer test or to accommodate that right. The task of creating new rules governing abortions that would respect procedural safeguards ought to be well within the capacity of competent policy-makers. And according to the Canadian Bar Association and various refugee support groups, it should be possible to create refugee-determination procedures that would respect the new standards of procedural fairness *and* allow for the expeditious processing of refugee claims.

If there is resistance to the new procedural safeguards among public servants, it may be a result of the lack of appreciation of their central importance to our political system.

The Policy Process

There has been little systematic research conducted into how the Charter has affected the policy-making process in government. My own experience when working for the Alberta government from 1982 to 1985 was that the Charter had little impact in this area. There were several reasons for this. First, in most cases it was impossible to predict how the Supreme Court would interpret the Charter; the wisest course of action was to wait until a relevant Charter decision at the Supreme Court level came along and *then* consider the implications of the Charter on policy. There were very few attempts by policy-makers, as far as I could determine, to reason about the implications of the Charter independently of judicial decisions. Second, most policy analysts had little background or training in public law or human rights, and they often felt out of their depth where Charter considerations were concerned. Third, there was a separation between "policy" and "legal" matters in the policy-making process. What typically happened was that departmental staff would develop a policy with little or no consideration of Charter implications. The draft policy would then be reviewed by lawyers employed by the government's legal department. These lawyers would suggest how the policy could be "Charter-proofed" (drafted into law so that the chances of a successful Charter challenge could be minimized). In other words, the emphasis was on *avoiding* the inconveniences of the Charter rather than considering how the ideals behind the Charter could be given effect.

The tendency of many in the policy-making process to try to avoid Charter considerations is illustrated by the reaction of the federal Department of Employment and Immigration to the *Singh* decision. Rather than trying to develop expeditious and fair methods of handling refugee claimants in Canada, policy-makers focused on developing strategies for keeping refugee claimants from coming to Canada in the first place so that fewer Charter claims would arise.

In order for the Charter to have a positive influence on the policy-making process, policy-makers will need a better understanding of the nature of human rights, as well as of the policy implications of the Charter.

The Legal System

Judges

The Canadian judiciary has adopted a dramatically different approach to the interpretation of human rights legislation since 1982. Prior to that year, judges at all levels were reluctant to give a broad interpretation to the Canadian Bill of Rights and other human rights legislation because of the fear of interfering with legislative supremacy. The 1982 constitutional changes gave the judiciary a clear mandate to interpret the Charter liberally and to apply these interpretations even if it meant striking down statutes. Although the courts have accepted this responsibility, the new role has not turned the judges into ardent social reformers. The Supreme Court of Canada, which sets the tone for the entire judicial system, has been described as only "moderately activist" by Peter Russell (1).

One measure of the degree to which judges might be considered social reformers is the proportion of human rights cases in which the judges uphold the right claimed by an individual litigant. From 1960 to 1982, of a total of thirty-five Bill of Rights cases that came before the Supreme Court, there were only five "individual wins" of this sort (14 per cent). From 1982 to early December 1988, eighteen of sixty Charter cases in the Supreme Court of Canada resulted in individual wins, a success rate of 30 per cent. In addition, Morton reports that the success rate of individual Charter claims in the courts below the Supreme Court climbed steadily from 26 per cent in 1982 to 32 per cent in 1985.

Russell (1) has divided the Supreme Court's treatment of the Charter into two periods. During the first period, from 1982 to April 1986, the Court decided fifteen Charter cases, nine of which represented individual wins (60 per cent). During the second period, from May 1986 to December 1988, there were another nine individual wins, although forty-five Charter cases were decided — an individual-win success rate of only 20 per cent. During the first period, the Supreme Court sent a clear signal to the courts below that judges should not hesitate to give the Charter a liberal interpretation. Having established the Charter's potential, during the second period — which began with the narrow interpretation of language rights in the *Bilodeau, MacDonald* and *Société des Acadiens* decisions and included the right-to-strike cases — the Court made an equally important point. The message of the second period is that judges must balance the good that might come from giving the Charter a liberal application against the drawbacks of judicial policy-making. If it appeared that the latter outweighed the former, then judicial restraint ought to be adopted.

When considering the implications of the Court's new approach during the second period, it is useful to keep in mind the nature of judicial policy-making under the Charter. The courts make human rights policies in two ways. The first is to define the specific content of general phrases: whether "freedom of association" contains a right to strike; whether the "right to life" covers a fetus; whether the "right to security of the person" includes the right of women to make decisions about abortions; and so on. The second is to decide whether a government objective that violates a right (once it is defined) can be considered a "reasonable limit" under section 1.

The legal reasoning skills judges have learned are of little use in making these kinds of decisions. A master's degree in public administration would be far more helpful. Take, for example, the *Edwards* case regarding Ontario's Sunday-closing laws. The Court had practically no empirical data about the importance to the people of Ontario of a common pause day. The judges had been presented with outdated information on which to base their decision about whether the method of implementing Sunday closing was rationally connected with the objective of a common pause day. When it came to considering whether other approaches might infringe the rights of non-Sabbatarians less, the Court had to work with limited information from counsel about different approaches that had been tried elsewhere. The Court might have benefited from a more comprehensive list of alternatives that professional public policy specialists could have produced.

One of the handicaps that judges labour under in making policy decisions is that they must rely primarily on information presented by counsel. Most lawyers have never had training in public policy analysis and are therefore not in a position to provide judges with the type of comprehensive information that is relevant to policy decisions. In several Charter decisions, Supreme Court judges have complained about the poor quality of section 1 arguments presented by counsel [47, 69, 125].

In short, judges have reluctantly accepted the policy-making role that was perhaps inappropriately thrust upon them by politicians more interested in national unity than the protection of human rights. Judges are now making human rights policy decisions more or less in a vacuum. It is difficult for them to make convincing policy-related decisions without access to appropriate public policy research resources.

Lawyers

Among lawyers, the Charter has undoubtedly had the greatest impact on those who practise criminal law. F.L. Morton and M.J. Withey report that 90 per cent of Charter arguments in all reported cases have been based on the legal rights sections (sections 7-14). The Charter has provided lawyers not only with additional tools for protecting innocent clients, but also with new methods of winning cases on technicalities, regardless of the guilt or innocence of their clients. The *Valente* case presents a good example of how lawyers, by pushing a complex Charter argument through the legal system, can postpone the inevitable.

According to Morton, 19,000 charges of driving with an "over 80" blood alcohol content were dropped in Alberta alone after the *Therens* decision. One criminal lawyer whom I interviewed in Alberta described the Charter as a "gold mine — the mainstay of my business, which consists mainly of defending drinking drivers." In young offenders cases, several Alberta Youth Court judges have observed that as a result of the combined effect of the Charter and the Young Offenders Act, more time is being spent in court by lawyers on "picky legal arguments and less time discussing the rehabilitative needs of the young offenders" (Gabor, Greene and McCormick). Obviously, there are some lawyers who welcome the new higher procedural standards, not primarily because human rights can be better protected, but because they can win more cases for their clients or charge higher fees for time spent researching Charter issues and presenting them in court. That type of approach has no positive impact on rights-consciousness and has a negative effect on the victims of crime.

I have also interviewed a number of lawyers whose ethical standards do not allow them to take unfair advantage of procedural standards. They pointed out that all lawyers are "officers of the court," and as such they have a responsibility to use their judgment not to exploit procedural safeguards. However, according to the results of a scientific sample of trial lawyers in Ontario and Alberta, only one-fifth of these lawyers think that the interests of justice and fairness — the duty to the court — always come before the interests of their clients (McCormick and Greene).

It is my view that the various provincial legal profession acts and the Canadian Bar Association code of professional conduct do not provide lawyers with clear ethical standards concerning the use of procedural safeguards. There is a need for more careful consideration by the legal profession of the ethical implications of the new procedural standards defined by the Supreme Court in the Charter. Otherwise, it may be difficult to persuade the public that the Charter has resulted in an acceptable balance between the rights of accused persons and the rights of victims of crime.

Was It Worth It?

In chapter 2, I noted that Charter skeptics had four major apprehensions: that the Charter would erode the democratic skills of ordinary Canadians and legislators alike; that the Charter would favour the powerful in society who can afford litigation; that the Charter would divert attention away from more serious threats to social well-being; and that, because the courts are inappropriate institutions for policy-making, their interpretations of human rights would likely be disappointing. On the other hand, supporters of the Charter cheerfully assumed that an entrenched Charter is bound to protect human rights better than the pre-1982 system had.

In 1985, Peter Russell (5) wrote, "After three years of living with a constitutional charter of fundamental rights and freedoms, the only safe thing to say is that it has turned out to be not nearly as bad as its opponents feared it might be nor nearly as great as its promoters promised it would be." This conclusion is still valid. Certainly the judicial system has done a better job of promoting rights than it had before the Charter, but it could be argued that this result owes as much to the quality of the leadership of the Supreme Court since 1982 as to the Charter itself.

There has not yet been a significant erosion of democratic skills, but neither has the Charter made us a more participatory democracy. Those who are already advantaged in society have won some cases (such as the National Citizens Coalition case concerning the Canada Elections Act [57], or the right-to-strike cases in the Supreme Court [79, 122, 66]), but have lost others (such as the *Lavigne* case [72] or the *Canadian Newspapers* case [83]). The Charter has not had much impact on social well-being either in terms of making it difficult for governments to assist the disadvantaged, or by distracting Canadians from addressing basic social issues which have little to do with Charter litigation. As critics predicted, Canadian judges have encountered problems dealing with human-rights policy-making, but it is fair to say that, at least at the level of the Supreme Court, the judges have handled their new responsibilities better than the critics expected they would.

The Charter, then, has so far been a mixed blessing. But it is too late in the day to re-assess whether Canada should have adopted the Charter in the first place; it is here to stay. It is more useful to devise strategies which may enhance the Charter's potential.

The Agenda for Reform

The following reforms would help to accentuate the potential of the Charter for promoting human rights; they would also minimize the possibility of it having an overall counterproductive effect in promoting interpersonal respect, self-worth and fairness.

Lawyers

There are two ways in which the legal profession could promote the Charter's positive potential. The first is to consider more carefully the relation between legal ethics and the possible abuse of procedural safeguards. This is a subject that might be given more attention in the law schools, and in the continuing education programs of the various lawyers' associations.

The second is for the legal profession to learn to make better use of the many resources generally available for researching policy-related questions, such as professional policy analysts who work for the universities or private consulting firms.

Judges

Judges would also benefit from having better access to public policy research. There are a number of ways in which this could be done. For example, judges who are frequently called upon to consider policy questions could pursue relevant courses in an MPA (master of public administration) program during the sabbaticals to which some of them will soon be entitled. Some courts could be provided with research assistants trained in public policy analysis to supplement the assistance that judges already receive from law clerks.

The Public Service

Public servants would have a more positive impact on civil liberties if they had a better background in the legal and ideological underpinnings of human rights and in Charter jurisprudence. Such a background would encourage a broad range of public servants, from the police to social workers to clerks handling public enquiries, to show more consideration and tolerance when pursuing their duties. Public servants engaged in the policy-making process might also place more emphasis on promoting fundamental freedoms, procedural safeguards and social equality when proposing new programs.

The civil liberties education of public servants can be enhanced in two ways: through appropriate in-house seminars and courses and through the inclusion of a civil liberties component in the public policy and administration programs at universities and colleges.

Legislatures

Canadian legislators have generally adopted a rather passive role concerning the Charter. Rather than considering the Charter as a prescription for action, they have tended to wait for the courts to tell them what they must do to in order not to infringe the Charter.

One way in which Canadian legislators could take a more active role in promoting human rights would be through permanent legislative committees with a mandate to consider human rights issues. For example, each provincial legislature, the House of Commons and the Senate could establish standing committees on human rights (or, more generally, on the constitution). These committees could systematically consider ways in which human rights might more effectively be promoted in their jurisdictions without waiting for sporadic pronouncements from the courts. As well, they could monitor judicial decisions about the Charter and hold public hearings about the most pressing human rights issues.

In chapter 3, I suggested that although section 33 of the Charter is a useful device that provides some flexibility in allowing governments to govern, decisions about whether to override the judicial interpretation of human rights are so important that they ought to be scrutinized through public hearings. If the legislative committees suggested above were established, they would be the logical vehicles for holding public hearings when governments are considering the use of a section 33 override or after emergency situations in which the override has already been invoked.

The most effective way in which legislatures can counteract inappropriate judicial interpretation of the Charter is through constitutional amendment. (Section 33 allows legislatures only to *postpone* judicial review for five-year periods. It does not permit them to *change* judicial interpretation.) For example, if a strong majority of Canadian legislators wanted "freedom of association" to contain a right to strike, then section 2(d) of the Charter could be amended to include a specific right to strike.

Because of the American example, Canadians often assume that our constitution is as difficult to amend as the U.S. constitution and therefore that judges do have the last word about the meaning of the constitution most of the time. This is not necessarily the case. In the United States, the least number of assemblies required to approve a constitutional amendment is 77 out of 101. (All but one of the states have bicameral legislatures.) In Canada, the agreement of only 8 of 11 legislatures is absolutely required for an amendment to the Charter. Because of responsible government (which has allowed cabinets to dominate legislatures) and "executive federalism" — which, as Donald Smiley (3) has shown, has led to mechanisms that allow federal and provincial cabinets to coordinate their strategies — constitutional amendments in Canada that employ the "seven/50 formula" (seven provinces representing 50 per cent of the population), such as amendments to the Charter, ought to be less cumbersome than amendments to the U.S. Bill of Rights.

The possibilities for legislative supervision of Charter interpretation do not end here. It would seem desirable if some way could be found for legislatures to "change" judicial interpretation of the Charter in cases where there is a clear need to do so, without having actually to change the wording of the Charter. Frequent constitutional amendments may make the wording of the Charter more awkward than it already is. In cases where the wording of the Charter is not the issue, but rather the judicial interpretation of that wording, there ought to be a way in which legislatures can signal their intent to the judiciary without having to foist on Canadians the inconvenience of a change in the Charter's wording. Such a result could be achieved through the device of interpretive resolutions.

For example, seven out of ten provincial legislatures plus Parliament could endorse resolutions that would instruct the judiciary about how to interpret some of the general phrases in the Charter. An interpretive resolution could read, "Section 2(d) of the Charter, 'freedom of association,' shall be deemed to include the right of employees in non-essential services to strike, except during emergencies." Such a resolution could even spell out fairly specifically the definition of a non-essential service and of an emergency. Thus, it could be more detailed than a formal constitutional amendment, which by its nature would tend to be phrased in rather cursory language.

The procedure for creating interpretive resolutions could be exactly the same as the procedure for a formal constitutional amendment, including "opting out" provisions. Thus, the major difference between an interpretive resolution and a formal constitutional amendment would be that the interpretive resolution would not actually change the wording of the Charter. The advantage of having the interpretive resolution procedure available is that legislators would be encouraged to take a more active role in refining and specifying the general phrases in the Charter. Over time, a constitutional document like the Charter comes to be viewed like an historic building: something that ought to be preserved in its present form for future generations to enjoy. Interpretive resolutions would allow legislators to continue adapting the specific meaning of the Charter to changing times and circumstances without interfering with the outward appearance of the document.

If this concept of interpretive resolutions has merit, it would make sense to implement it through a constitutional amendment. This amendment could contain a provision that would preclude the use of interpretive resolutions for what would amount to changes in the basic structure of the Charter. Their purpose would be to clarify what is already there rather than indirectly to bring about an important change in the Charter's structure. The enabling amendment should also contain a direction to the courts to take the resolutions into consideration when interpreting the Charter. There could be no enforcement mechanism for these interpretive resolutions; their implementation would depend on the judiciary. But this is probably sufficient. During the second period of Charter adjudication, the Supreme Court seems to be signalling to the legislative branch to take more responsibility for human rights policy development.

The Public

In many ways, the public has been left out of the ongoing process of Charter interpretation. As many pre-1982 critics of the concept of a constitutional bill of rights predicted, the task of Charter interpretation has been almost entirely co-opted by the legal profession. Is the "average reasonable person" whom judges are fond of referring to destined to stand by the sidelines and watch the drama of Charter interpretation unfold — for a fee — while his or her reasoning powers atrophy? There may be ways in which the average citizen can become involved in the process of defining, refining and extending human rights in Canada.

To begin with, the more Canadians know about the theory of human rights, the Charter and related subjects, the more they will be able to participate meaningfully in the human rights discourse, and the more clout they are likely to have in affecting the outcome of specific controversies. In order to become truly a "people's package," the Charter must have its cloak of legal mystery removed. For example, there is no reason why elementary and secondary school children cannot study the theory of human rights and, from that perspective, debate the strengths and weaknesses of Supreme Court decisions on the Charter. This would help to prepare them for more effective participation in democratic life.

If the standing legislative committees mentioned above were established, they would provide a potentially useful vehicle for public input into the interpretation of the Charter in that the committees could hold public hearings about important human rights issues. But if such hearings are to become more than opportunities for those with intransigent positions to vent their frustrations, there should be more information readily available to the public that could help to encourage a higher quality of public debate. Judicial decisions about human rights issues are often informative in terms of describing particular issues and various approaches to resolving them. The question is, how can these judicial insights be made more available to the public and be presented in a more appealing format?

A day or two after important Supreme Court decisions, the major newspapers in Canada will often print excerpts from the decisions. Although this is useful, without some accompanying explanation of the context of the judges' comments, their full significance may often be missed. Academics, including law teachers and political scientists, have a public duty, it seems to me, to contribute readable commentaries on Supreme Court decisions to the popular press. Some do this already, but there is room for more activity of this kind.

The print media, of course, is not nearly as influential today as radio and especially television broadcasting. Perhaps radio and television documentaries on human rights could be developed, with some of the leading Supreme Court decisions as central features. If these series were skilfully produced, there is no reason why they could not attract a wide audience, given the abiding interest of Canadians in human rights.

The Charter and Rights-Consciousness

In asking whether the Charter will have a positive effect on rights-consciousness, one should keep two points in mind. First, the job of promoting and protecting human rights belongs to everybody — politicians, public servants, members of interest groups, and the general public — in addition to the legal profession. Second, in the final analysis, the measure of our commitment to human rights is the degree to which we believe in and practise interpersonal respect, the extent to which we are all able to achieve a sense of self-worth and encourage it in others, and the success we have in treating each other fairly.

The ultimate effect of the Charter will depend primarily on the integrity of those who are involved in its application, secondly on the procedures through which it is interpreted and applied, and lastly on the nature of the instrument itself.

Appendix
Constitution Act, 1982, Part I
The Canadian Charter of Rights and Freedoms

Whereas Canada is founded upon principles that recognize the supremacy of God and the rule of law:

Guarantee of Rights and Freedoms

1. The Canadian Charter of Rights and Freedoms guarantees the rights and freedoms set out in it subject only to such reasonable limits prescribed by law as can be demonstrably justified in a free and democratic society.

Fundamental Freedoms

2. Everyone has the following fundamental freedoms:
(a) freedom of conscience and religion;
(b) freedom of thought, belief, opinion and expression, including freedom of the press and other media of communication;
(c) freedom of peaceful assembly; and
(d) freedom of association.

Democratic Rights

3. Every citizen of Canada has the right to vote in an election of members of the House of Commons or of a legislative assembly and to be qualified for membership therein.

4. (1) No House of Commons and no legislative assembly shall continue for longer than five years from the date fixed for the return of the writs at a general election of its members.

(2) In time of real or apprehended war, invasion or insurrection, a House of Commons may be continued by Parliament and a legislative assembly may be continued by the legislature beyond five years if such continuation is not opposed by the votes of more than one-third of the members of the House of Commons or the legislative assembly, as the case may be.

5. There shall be a sitting of Parliament and of each legislature at least once every twelve months.

Mobility Rights

6. (1) Every citizen of Canada has the right to enter, remain in and leave Canada.

(2) Every citizen of Canada and every person who has the status of a permanent resident of Canada has the right

    (a) to move to and take up residence in any province; and

    (b) to pursue the gaining of a livelihood in any province.

(3) The rights specified in subsection (2) are subject to

    (a) any laws or practices of general application in force in a province other than those that discriminate among persons primarily on the basis of province of present or previous residence; and

    (b) any laws providing for reasonable residency requirements as a qualification for the receipt of publicly provided social services.

(4) Subsections (2) and (3) do not preclude any law, program or activity that has as its object the amelioration in a province of conditions of individuals in that province who are socially or economically disadvantaged if the rate of employment in that province is below the rate of employment in Canada.

Legal Rights

7. Everyone has the right to life, liberty and security of the person and the right not to be deprived thereof except in accordance with the principles of fundamental justice.

8. Everyone has the right to be secure against unreasonable search or seizure.

9. Everyone has the right not to be arbitrarily detained or imprisoned.

10. Everyone has the right on arrest or detention

(a) to be informed promptly of the reasons therefor;

(b) to retain and instruct counsel without delay and to be informed of that right; and

(c) to have the validity of the detention determined by way of *habeas corpus* and to be released if the detention is not lawful.

11. Any person charged with an offence has the right

(a) to be informed without unreasonable delay of the specific offence;

(b) to be tried within a reasonable time;

(c) not to be compelled to be a witness in proceedings against that person in respect of the offence;

(d) to be presumed innocent until proven guilty according to law in a fair and public hearing by an independent and impartial tribunal;

(e) not to be denied reasonable bail without just cause;

(f) except in case of an offence under military law tried before a military tribunal, to the benefit of trial by jury where the maximum punishment for the offence is imprisonment for five years or a more severe punishment;

(g) not to be found guilty on account of any act or omission unless, at the time of the act or omission, it constituted an offence under Canadian or international law or was criminal according to the general principles of law recognized by the community of nations;

(h) if finally acquitted of the offence, not to be tried for it again and, if finally found guilty and punished for the offence, not to be tried or punished for it again; and

(i) if found guilty of the offence and if the punishment for the offence has been varied between the time of commission and the time of sentencing, to the benefit of the lesser punishment.

12. Everyone has the right not to be subjected to any cruel and unusual treatment or punishment.

13. Any witness who testifies in any proceedings has the right not to have any incriminating evidence so given used to incriminate that witness in any other proceedings, except in a prosecution for perjury or for the giving of contradictory evidence.

14. A party or witness in any proceedings who does not understand or speak the language in which the proceedings are conducted or who is deaf has the right to the assistance of an interpreter.

Equality Rights

15. (1) Every individual is equal before and under the law and has the right to the equal protection and equal benefit of the law without discrimination and, in particular, without discrimination based on race, national or ethnic origin, colour, religion, sex, age or mental or physical disability.

(2) Subsection (1) does not preclude any law, program or activity that has as its object the amelioration of conditions of disadvantaged individuals or groups including those that are disadvantaged because of race, national or ethnic origin, colour, religion, sex, age or mental or physical disability.

Official Languages of Canada

16. (1) English and French are the official languages of Canada and have equality of status and equal rights and privileges as to their use in all institutions of the Parliament and government of Canada.

(2) English and French are the official languages of New Brunswick and have equality of status and equal rights and privileges as to their use in all institutions of the legislature and government of New Brunswick.

(3) Nothing in this Charter limits the authority of Parliament or a legislature to advance the equality of status or use of English and French.

17. (1) Everyone has the right to use English or French in any debates and other proceedings of Parliament.

(2) Everyone has the right to use English or French in any debates and other proceedings of the legislature of New Brunswick.

18. (1) The statutes, records and journals of Parliament shall be printed and published in English and French and both language versions are equally authoritative.

(2) The statutes, records and journals of the legislature of New Brunswick shall be printed and published in English and French and both language versions are equally authoritative.

19. (1) Either English or French may be used by any person in, or in any pleading in or process issuing from, any court established by Parliament.

(2) Either English or French may be used by any person in, or in any pleading in or process issuing from, any court established by the legislature of New Brunswick.

20. (1) Any member of the public in Canada has the right to communicate with, and to receive available services from, any head or central office of an institution of the Parliament or government of Canada in English or French, and has the same right with respect to any other office of any such institution where

(a) there is a significant demand for communications with and services from that office in such language; or

(b) due to the nature of the office, it is reasonable that communications with and services from that office be available in both English and French.

(2) Any member of the public in New Brunswick has the right to communicate with, and to receive available services from, any office of an institution of the legislature or government of New Brunwsick in English or French.

21. Nothing in sections 16 to 20 abrogates or derogates from any right, privilege or obligation with respect to the English and French languages, or either of them, that exists or is continued by virtue of any other provision of the Constitution of Canada.

22. Nothing in sections 16 to 20 abrogates or derogates from any legal or customary right or privilege acquired or enjoyed either before or after the coming into force of this Charter with respect to any language that is not English or French.

Minority Language Educational Rights

23. (1) Citizens of Canada

(a) whose first language learned and still understood is that of the English or French linguistic minority population of the province in which they reside, or

(b) who have received their primary school instruction in Canada in English or French and reside in a province where the language in which they received that instruction is the language of the English or French linguistic minority population of the province, have the right to have their children receive primary and secondary school instruction in that language in that province.

(2) Citizens of Canada of whom any child has received or is receiving primary or secondary school instruction in English or French in Canada, have the right to have all their children receive primary and secondary school instruction in the same language.

(3) The right of citizens of Canada under subsections (1) and (2) to have their children receive primary and secondary school instruction in the language of the English or French linguistic minority population of a province

    (a) applies wherever in the province the number of children of citizens who have such a right is sufficient to warrant the provision to them out of public funds of minority language instruction; and

    (b) includes, where the number of those children so warrants, the right to have them receive that instruction in minority language educational facilities provided out of public funds.

24. (1) Anyone whose rights or freedoms, as guaranteed by this Charter, have been infringed or denied may apply to a court of competent jurisdiction to obtain such remedy as the court considers appropriate and just in the circumstances.

(2) Where, in proceedings under subsection (1), a court concludes that evidence was obtained in a manner that infringed or denied any rights or freedoms guaranteed by this Charter, the evidence shall be excluded if it is established that, having regard to all the circumstances, the admission of it in the proceedings would bring the administration of justice into disrepute.

General

25. The guarantee in this Charter of certain rights and freedoms shall not be construed so as to abrogate or derogate from any aboriginal, treaty or other rights or freedoms that pertain to the aboriginal peoples of Canada including

    (a) any rights or freedoms that have been recognized by the Royal Proclamation of October 7, 1763; and

    (b) any rights or freedoms that now exist by way of land claims agreements or may be so acquired.

26. The guarantee in this Charter of certain rights and freedoms shall not be construed as denying the existence of any other rights or freedoms that exist in Canada.

27. This Charter shall be interpreted in a manner consistent with the preservation and enhancement of the multicultural heritage of Canadians.

28. Notwithstanding anything in this Charter, the rights and freedoms referred to in it are guaranteed equally to male and female persons.

29. Nothing in this Charter abrogates or derogates from any rights or privileges guaranteed by or under the Constitution of Canada in respect of denominational, separate or dissentient schools.

30. A reference in this Charter to a province or to the legislative assembly or legislature of a province shall be deemed to include a reference to the Yukon Territory and the Northwest Territories, or to the appropriate legislative authority thereof, as the case may be.

31. Nothing in this Charter extends the legislative powers of any body or authority.

32. (1) This Charter applies
   (a) to the Parliament and government of Canada in respect of all matters within the authority of Parliament including all matters relating to the Yukon Territory and Northwest Territories; and
   (b) to the legislature and government of each province in respect of all matters within the authority of the legislature of each province.
(2) Nothwithstanding subsection (1), section 15 shall not have effect until three years after this section comes into force.

33. (1) Parliament or the legislature of a province may expressly declare in an Act of Parliament or of the legislature, as the case may be, that the Act or a provision thereof shall operate notwithstanding a provision included in section 2 or sections 7 to 15 of this Charter.
(2) An Act or a provision of an Act in respect of which a declaration made under this section is in effect shall have such operation as it would have but for the provision of this Charter referred to in the declaration.
(3) A declaration made under subsection (1) shall cease to have effect five years after it comes into force or on such earlier date as may be specified in the declaration.
(4) Parliament or the legislature of a province may re-enact a decla-

ration made under subsection (1).

(5) Subsection (3) applies in respect of a re-enactment made under subsection (4).

Citation

34. This Part may be cited as the Canadian Charter of Rights and Freedoms.

References

Agresto, John. *The Supreme Court and Constitutional Democracy.* 1984.

Axworthy, T.S. "Colliding visions: the debate over the Canadian Charter of Rights and Freedoms, 1980-81." *Journal of Commonwealth and Comparative Politics* 24 (1985): 239.

Bayefsky, Anne F., and Mary Eberts. *Equality Rights and the Canadian Charter of Rights and Freedoms.* 1985.

Beatty, D. "Constitutional Conceits." *University of Toronto Law Journal* 50 (1987): 183.

Bouthillier, Guy. "Profil du juge de la Cour superieure du Québec." *Canadian Bar Review* 55 (1977): 436.

Canada. Department of Justice. "A Canadian Charter of Human Rights." 1968.

Canada. Parliament. *Minutes of Proceedings and Evidence of Special Joint Committee of the Senate and of the House of Commons on the Constitution of Canada.* First Session of the Thirty-second Parliament, 1980-81.

Canadian Bar Association. *Report on the Appointment of Judges in Canada.* 1985.

Canadian Judicial Council. *Annual Report, 1987-88.*

Cheffins, Ronald, and Patricia Johnson. *The Revised Canadian Constitution.* 1986.

Claridge, Thomas. "Ontario's judge restores prisoners' voting rights after Charter challenge." *Globe and Mail,* July 20, 1988, A1.

Conklin, William E. *Images of a Constitution.* 1989.

Corelli, Rae. "How an Indian changed Canada's civil rights laws — the *Drybones* case." In Paul Fox, ed., *Politics: Canada,* 5th ed., 633. 1982.

Cushman, Robert F., with Susan P. Koniak. *Leading Constitutional Decisions,* 17th ed. 1987.

Delacourt, Susan. "Charter spurred more to fight for their voting rights in '88." *Globe and Mail,* November 24, 1988, A9.

Dicey, A.V. *Introduction to the Study of the Law of the Constitution.* c. 1885.

Diefenbaker, John. "Equality and the Bill of Rights." In *Those Things We Treasure.* 1972.

Drummond, Robert. "Comment on 'Mandatory Retirement . . . ' by Samuel LaSelva." *Canadian Journal of Political Science* 21 (1988): 585.

Dworkin, Ronald.
(1) *A Matter of Principle.* 1985.
(2) *Law's Empire.* 1986.
(3) *Taking Rights Seriously.* 1978.

Eberts, Mary. "Risks of Equality Litigation." In Sheilah Martin and Kathleen Mahoney, eds, *Equality and Judicial Neutrality.* 1987.

Ely, John Hart. *Democracy and Distrust: A Theory of Judicial Review.* 1980.

Flanagan, Thomas. "Age discrimination in Canada." Research unit for Socio-Legal Studies, University of Calgary, Occasional Papers Series, Reserach Study 1.3. 1985.

Fletcher, Frederick J., and Daphne F. Gottlieb, "The Mass Media and the Politics: An Overview." In Michael Whittington and Glen Williams, eds., *Canadian Politics in the 1980's,* 2nd ed., 193. 1984.

Fudge, Judy. "The Public/Private Distinction: The Possibilities of and the Limits to the Use of Charter Litigation to Further Feminist Struggles." *Osgoodge Hall Law Journal* 25 (1987): 485.

Gabor, Peter, Ian Greene and Peter McCormick. "The Young Offenders Act: The Alberta Youth Court Experience in the First Year." *Canadian Journal of Family Law* 5 (1986): 301.

Gall, Gerald. *The Canadian Legal System,* 2nd ed. 1983.

Gibson, Dale. "Determining disrepute: opinion polls and the Canadian Charter of Rights and Freedoms." *Canadian Bar Review* 61 (1983): 377.

Gold, Marc.
(1) "A Principled Approach to Equality Rights: A Preliminary Inquiry." *Supreme Court Law Review* 4 (1982): 131.
(2) "The Mask of Objectivity: Politics and Rhetoric in the Supreme Court of Canada." Supreme Court Law Review 7 (1985): 455.

Green, Leslie. "Are Language Rights Fundamental?" *Osgoode Hall Law Journal* 25 (1987): 639.

Greene, Ian.

(1) "The Doctrine of Judicial Independence Developed by the Supreme Court of Canada." *Osgoode Hall Law Journal* 26 (1988): 177.

(2) "The Myths of Legislative and Constitutional Supremacy." In David Shugarman and Reginald Whitaker, eds., *Federalism and Political Community: Essays in Honour of Donald Smiley*. 1989.

(3) "The Politics of Court Administration in Ontario." *Windsor Yearbook of Access to Justice* 2 (1982): 124.

Hart, H.L.A. *Definition and Theory in Jurisprudence*. 1954.

Hiebert, Janet. "Fair Elections and Freedom of Expression under the Charter: Should Interest Groups' Election Expenditures be Limited?" *Journal of Canadian Studies* 23 (1989).

Hogarth, John. *Sentencing as a Human Process*. 1971.

Hogg, Peter.

(1) *Constitutional Law of Canada*, 2nd ed. 1985.

(2) *The Meech Lake Accord Annotated*. 1988.

Hohfeld, W.N. *Fundamental Legal Conceptions As Applied in Judicial Reasoning*. 1919.

Hutchinson, Allan, and Andrew Petter. "Private Rights/Public Wrongs: The Liberal Lie of the Charter." *University of Toronto Law Journal* 38 (1988): 279.

Jennings, Ivor. *The Law and the Constitution*. 1959.

Knopff, Rainer. "What Do Constitutional Equality Rights Protect Canadians Against?" *Canadian Journal of Political Science* 20 (1987): 265.

Knopff, Rainer, and F.L. Morton. "Nation-Building and the Canadian Charter of Rights and Freedoms." In A. Cairns and C. Williams, *Constitutionalism, Citizenship and Society in Canada*, 133. 1985.

LaSelva, Samuel. "Mandatory Retirement: Intergenerational Justice and the Canadian Charter of Rights and Freedoms." *Canadian Journal of Political Science* 20 (1987): 149.

Lahey, Kathleen. "Feminist Theories of (In)Equality." In Sheilah Martin and Kathleen Mahoney, eds., *Equality and Judicial Neutrality*, 71. 1987.

Lederman, W.R.

(1) "The Nature and Problems of a Bill of Rights." *Canadian Bar Review* 4 (1959).

(2) "The power of the judges and the new Canadian Charter of Rights and Freedoms." *U.B.C. Law Review* 16 (1982): 1.

Levy, Leonard W., ed. *Judicial Review and the Supreme Court*. 1967.

Lipovenko, D. "Problems plague vote by retarded." *Globe and Mail*, October 22, 1988, A1.

Locke, John. *The Second Treatise of Government*. c. 1690.

Lyon, N. "The Charter as a mandate for new ways of thinking about law." *Queen's Law Journal* 9 (1984): 241.

Macpherson, C.B.
(1) "Berlin's Division of Liberty." In *Democratic Theory: Essays in Retrieval*. 1973.
(2) *The Real World of Democracy*. 1965.

Mandel, Michael. *The Charter of Rights and the Legalization of Politics in Canada*. 1988.

Manning, Morris. *Rights, Freedoms and the Courts*. 1982.

Marchak, Patricia. *Ideological Perspectives on Canada*. 1981.

Marshall, Geoffrey. *Constitutional Theory*. 1971.

Matas, David. "The working of the Charter." *Manitoba Law Journal* 16 (1986): 111.

McConnell, W.H.
(1) "The Canadian Charter of Rights and Freedoms: Commentary." *Canadian Bar Review* 61 (1983): 426.
(2) *Commentary on the British North America Act*. 1977.

McCormick, Peter. "Judicial Councils for Provincial Judges in Canada." *Windsor Yearbook of Access to Justice* 6 (1986): 160.

McCormick, Peter, and Ian Greene, "The Alberta Judiciary Study." Report prepared for the Canadian Institute for the Administration of Justice with financial assistance from the Alberta Law Foundation. 1989.

McWhinney, Edward.
(1) *Canada and the Constitution 1979-1982: Patriation and the Charter of Rights*. 1982.
(2) "The Canadian Charter of Rights and Freedoms: the lessons of comparative jurisprudence." *Canadian Bar Review* 61 (1983): 55.

Mill, John Stuart. *On Liberty*. c. 1859.

Milne, David. *The Canadian Constitution: From Patriation to Meech Lake*. 1989.

Monahan, Patrick. *Politics and the Constitution: The Charter, Federalism and the Supreme Court of Canada*. 1987.

Montesquieu, Charles de Secondat., baron de. *The Spirit of the Laws*. c. 1750.

Morton, F.L. "The Political Impact of the Canadian Charter of Rights and Freedoms." *Canadian Journal of Political Science* 18 (1987): 31.

Morton, F.L., and M.J. Withey. "Charting the Charter, 1982-1985: A Statistical Analysis." Research Unit for Socio-Legal Studies, University of Calgary, Occasional Papers Series, Research Study 2.1.

Mossman, J.J. "Equality rights and the Canadian Charter of Rights and Freedoms." *Canadian Bar Review* 66 (1987): 185.

Nash, Alan E., ed. *Human Rights and the Protection of Refugees under International Law.* 1988.

Nash, Alan. *International Refugee Pressures and the Canadian Public Policy Response.* 1989.

Olsen, Dennis. *The State Elite.* 1980.

Paine, Thomas. *The Rights of Man.* c. 1791-92.

Pal, L.A., and F.L. Morton. "Impact of the Charter of Rights on Public Administration." *Canadian Public Administration,* 1985, 221.

Panitch, Leo, and Donald Swartz. *The Assault on Trade Union Freedoms.* 1988.

Pateman, Carole. *Participation and Democratic Theory.* 1970.

Peck, Sidney R. "An Analytical Framework for an Application of the Canadian Charter of Rights and Freedoms." *Osgoode Hall Law Journal* 25 (1987): 1.

Petter, Andrew. "The Politics of the Charter." *Supreme Court Law Review* 8 (1986): 473.

Penton, M. James. *Apocalypse Delayed: The Story of Jehovah's Witnesses.* 1985.

Pilkington, M.L. "Damages as a remedy for infringement of the Canadian Charter of Rights and Freedoms." *Canadian Bar Review* 62 (1984): 517.

Pocklington, Thomas. "Against Inflating Human Rights." *Windsor Yearbook of Access to Justice* 2 (1982): 77.

Polyviou, Ployvios G. *The Equal Protection of the Laws.* 1980.

Purich, Donald J. *Our Land: Native Rights in Canada.* 1986.

Romanow, Roy, John Whyte and Howard Leeson. *Canada — Notwithstanding: The Making of the Constitution, 1976-1982.* 1984.

Russell, Peter H.
(1) "Canada's Charter of Rights and Freedoms: A Political Report." *Public Law* (U.K.), 1988, 385.

(2) "The Supreme Court Decision: Bold Statecraft Based on Questionable Jurisprudence." In P.H. Russel *et al. The Court and the Constitution*. 1982.

"The Constitutional Reference: Political Statesmanship, Questionable Jurisprudence." *The Courts and the Constitution*. 1982.

(3) "A Democratic Approach to Civil Liberties." *University of Toronto Law Journal* 19 (1969): 109.

(4) "The effect of a Charter of Rights on the policy-making role of Canadian courts." *Canadian Public Administration* 25 (1982): 1.

(5) "The first three years in Charterland." *Canadian Public Administration* 28 (1985): 367.

(6) *The Judiciary in Canada: The Third Branch of Government*. 1987.

(7) *Leading Constitutional Decisions,* 4th ed. 1987.

(8) "The Political Purposes of the Canadian Charter of Rights and Freedoms." *Canadian Bar Review* (Charter ed.) 61 (1983): 30.

(9) "The Political Role of the Supreme Court of Canada in its First Century." *Canadian Bar Review* 53 (1975): 577, 592.

Russell, Peter H., Rainer Knopff and F.L. Morton, eds., *Federalism and the Charter: Leading Constitutional Decisions,* 5th ed. 1989.

Saunders, Douglas. "Prior Claims." In Stanley M. Beck and Ivan Bernier, *Canada and the New Constitution*. 1983.

Salhany, Roger E. *The Origin of Rights*. 1986.

Sharpe, Robert J.

(1) "The Charter of Rights and Freedoms and the Supreme Court of Canada: The First Four Years." *Public Law*, 1987, 48.

(2) "Commercial expression and the Charter." *University of Toronto Law Journal* 37 (1987): 229.

Slattery, Brian J.

(1) "A Theory of the Charter." *Osgoode Hall Law Journal* 25 (1987): 701.

(2) "The Charter's relevance to private litigation: does Dolphin deliver?" *McGill Law Journal* 32 (1986-87), p. 905.

(3) "The hidden constitution: aboriginal rights in Canada." *American Journal of Comparative Law* 32 (1984): 361.

Slotnick, Lorne. "Use of union dues for political causes does not violate Charter, court rules." *Globe and Mail,* January 31, 1989, A1.

Smiley, Donald V.

(1) *The Canadian Charter of Rights and Freedoms*. 1981.

(2) "The Case against the Canadian Charter of Human Rights." *Canadian Journal of Political Science* 2 (1969): 277.

(3) *The Federal Condition in Canada*. 1988.

Smith, Jennifer.

(1) "Canadian Confederation and the Influence of American Federalism." *Canadian Journal of Political Science* 21 (1988): 443.

(2) "The Origins of Judicial Review in Canada." *Canadian Journal of Political Science* 16 (1983): 115.

Smith, Lynn, et al., eds. *Righting the Balance: Canada's New Equality Rights*. 1986.

Sniderman, Paul. *Personality and Democratic Politics*. 1975.

Sniderman, Paul M., Joseph F. Fletcher, Peter H. Russell and Phillip E. Tetlock. "Liberty, Authority and Community: Civil Liberties and the Canadian Political Culture." Paper delivered at the annual meetings of the Canadian Political Science Association and the Canadian Law and Society Association, University of Windsor, June 9, 1988.

Tarnopolsky, Walter S.

(1) *Discrimination and the Law*. 1985.

(2) "The Evolution of Judicial Attitudes." In Sheilah Martin and Kathleen Mahoney, eds., *Equality and Judicial Neutrality*. 1987.

(3) *The Canadian Bill of Rights*. 1966.

Tarnopolsky, Walter S., and Gerald-A. Beaudoin. *The Canadian Charter of Rights and Freedoms: Commentary*. 1982.

Taylor, Charles. "Legitimacy, Identity and Alienation in Late Twentieth Century Canada." In Alan Cairns and Cynthia Williams, *Constitutionalism, Citizenship and Society in Canada*, 183. 1985.

Tribe, Laurence. *American Constitutional Law*, 2nd ed. (editor) 1986.

Tribe, Laurence, ed. *Constitutional Choices*. 1985.

Trudeau, Pierre. *Federalism and the French Canadians*. 1968.

Vaughan, Frederick, and James Snell. *The Supreme Court of Canada: History of the Institution*. 1985.

Verney, Douglas. *Three Civilizations, Two Cultures, One State: Canada's Political Traditions*. 1986.

Weiler, Paul.

(1) *In the Last Resort*. 1974.

(2) "Rights and Judges in a Democracy: A New Canadian Version." *University of Michigan Journal of Law Reform*, 1984, 51.

Whitaker, Reginald. *Double Standard*. 1987.

Whyte, John D. "Fundamental justice: the scope and application of section 7 of the Charter." *Manitoba Law Journal* 13 (1983): 455.

Williams, Cynthia. "The Changing Nature of Citizen Rights." In Alan Cairns and Cynthia Williams, *Constitutionalism, Citizenship and Society in Canada,* 99. 1985.

Wilson, Bertha. "Decision-Making in the Supreme Court." *University of Toronto Law Journal* 36 (1986): 227.

Cases

The following abbreviations are frequently used in the list below:

CRD: Charter of Rights Decisions.
D.L.R.: Dominion Law Reports.
LCD: Peter H. Russell, Rainer Knopff and F.L. Morton, *Federalism and the Charter: Leading Constitutional Decisions,* 5th ed. 1989.
LCDSCC: Peter H. Russell, Rainer Knopff and F.L. Morton, eds. *Leading Constitutional Decisions of the Supreme Court of Canada.* Produced and distributed by the Research Unit for Socio-Legal Studies, Faculty of Social Sciences, University of Calgary.
O.R.: Ontario Reports.
SCR: Supreme Court Reports.
W.W.R.: Western Weekly Reports.

Cases

[1] A.-G. Can. and Dupond v. Montreal, [1978] 2 SCR 770; LCD, 5th ed., no. 36.
[2] A.-G. Can. v. Canadian National Transportation Ltd., [1983] 2 SCR 206.
[3] A.-G. Can. v. Gould,4] 1 F.C. 1133 (Federal Court of Appeal), on appeal from [1984] 1 F.C. 1119 (Federal Court, trial div.)
[4] A.-G. Can. v. Lavell and Isaac v. Bédard, [1974] SCR 1349; LCD, 5th ed., no. 38.
[5] A.-G. Man. et al. v. A.-G. Can. et al., [1981] 2 SCR 753; LCD, 5th ed., no. 62.
[6] A.-G. Man. v. Forest, [1979] 2 SCR 1032.
[7] A.-G. Que. v. A.-G. Can., [1982] 2 SCR 793.; LCD, 5th ed., no. 63.
[8] A.-G. Que. v. Association of Quebec Protestant School Boards et al., [1984] 2 SCR 66; LCD, 5th ed., no. 55; LCDSCC, no. 2.
[9] A.-G. Que. v. Blaikie (No. 1), [1979] 2 SCR 1016.
[10] A.-G. Que. v. Blaikie (No. 2), [1981] 1 SCR 312.

[11] Andrews v. Law Society of British Columbia, [1989] 1 SCR 143; LCD, 5th ed., no. 52A; LCDSCC, no. 57, on appeal from [1986] 4 W.W.R. 242.

[12] Argentina v. Mellino, [1987] 1 SCR 536; LCDSCC, no. 24.

[13] Badger et al v. A.-G. Man., [1986] 8 CRD 325.20-01 (Manitoba Queen's Bench). For subsequent developments, see [1988] 14 CRD 325.30-01 and [1988] 14 CRD 325.30-02.

[14] Basile v. A.-G. Nova Scotia, [1985] 5 CRD 685-02.

[15] Beauregard v. Canada, [1986] 2 SCR 56; LCDSCC, no. 940.

[16] Bhinder et al. v. Canadian National Railway Co. et al., [1985] 2 SCR 561.

[17] Bilodeau v. A.-G. Man. et al., [1986] 1 SCR 449; LCDSCC, no. 951.

[18] Black v. Law Society of Alberta, [1989] 1 SCR; LCDSCC, no. 59, on appeal from [1986] 3 W.W.R. 590.

[19] Bliss v. A.-G. Can., [1979] 1 SCR 183.

[20] Borowski v. A.-G. Can, [1989] 1 SCR; LCDSCC, no. 58; LCD, 5th ed., no. 51, on appeal from [1987], 4 W.W.R. 385 (Saskatchewan Court of Appeal).

[21] British Columbia Government Employees Union v. A.-G. of B.C., [1988] 2 SCR 214; LCDSCC, no. 45.

[22] Brooks v. Canada Safeway Ltd., [1989] 1 SCR.

[23] Brown v. Board of Education (1954), 347 U.S. 483.

[24] Canada v. Schmidt, [1987] 1 SCR 500; LCDSCC, no. 24.

[25] Christie v. York Corporation, [1940] SCR 139.

[26] Chromiak v. The Queen, [1980] 1 SCR 471.

[27] Clarkson v. The Queen, [1986] 1 SCR 383; LCDSCC, no. 13.

[28] Co-op Committee on Japanese Canadians v. A.-G. Can., [1947] A.C. 87 (P.C.).

[29] Corporation professionnelle des médecins du Québec v. Thibault, [1988] 1 SCR 1033; LCDSCC, no. 42.

[30] Cunningham v. Tomey Homma, [1902] A.C. 151 P.C.

[31] Devine v. A.-G. Quebec, [1988] 2 SCR 790, LCDSCC, no. 53.

[32] Dixon v. A.-G. B.C., [1989] 15 CRD 325.20-01 (Sup. Ct. Canada), and [1986] 9 CRD 325.20-01 (Sup. Ct. B.C.)

[33] Dubois v. The Queen, [1985] 2 SCR 350; LCDSCC, no. 9.

[34] Duke v. The Queen, [1972] SCR 917.

[35] Edwards v. A.-G. Can., [1930] A.C. 124, on appeal from [1928] SCR 276.

[36] Entick v. Carrington (1765), 19 St. Tr. 1030, 95 E.R. 807 (K.B.)

[37] Ford v. A.-G. Quebec, [1988] 2 SCR 712; LCD, 5th ed., no. 52; LCDSCC, no. 53.

[38] Franklin v. Evans (1924), 55 O.L.R. 349.

[39] Fraser v. A.-G. Nova Scotia, [1986] 9 CRD 400.30-01 (Supreme Court of Nova Scotia).

[40] Hedstrom v. Commissioner of Yukon Territory, [1986] 8 CRD 325.20-02 (Yukon Court of Appeal), on appeal from [1985] 6 CRD 325.30-02 (Yukon Supreme Court).

[41] Hoogbruin v. A.-G. of B.C., [1986] 7 CRD 325.30-01 (B.C. Court of Appeal), on appeal from [1984] 4 CRD 325.20-01 (Supreme Court of B.C.).

[42] Hunter et al. v. Southam Inc., [1984] 2 SCR 145; LCDSCC, no. 3.

[43] Johnson v. Sparrow, [1899] Q.S.C. 104.

[44] Jolivet et al. v. The Queen, [1983] 3 CRD 325.30-01 (Supreme Court of B.C.)

[45] Jonson v. County of Ponoka, [1988)] 12 CRD 400.10-01.

[46] Krug v. The Queen, [1985] 2 SCR 255; LCDSCC, no. 8.

[47] Law Society of Upper Canada v. Skapinker, [1984] 1 SCR 357; LCD, 5th ed., no. 40; LCDSCC, no. 1.

[48] Lévesque v. A.-G. Can., [1986] 2 F.C. 287.

[49] Loew's Theatres v. Reynolds (1921), Q.R. 30 B.R. 459.

[50] Lukes et al. v. Chief Electoral Officer, [1986] 8 CRD 325.30-01.

[51] MacDonald v. City of Montreal et al., [1986] 1 SCR 460; LCDSCC, no. 951.

[52] MacKay v. The Queen, [1980] 2 SCR 370.

[53] MacLean v. A.-G. Nova Scotia (1987), 35 D.L.R. (4th) 306.

[54] Mia v. Medical Services Commission of B.C., [1985] 6 CRD 5685-01.

[55] Mills v. The Queen, [1986] 1 SCR 863; LCDSCC, no. 15.

[56] Minister of Justice (Can.) v. Borowski, [1981] 2 SCR 575.

[57] National Citizens' Coalition v. A.-G. Can., [1984] 5 W.W.R. 436.

[58] Nova Scotia Board of Censors v. McNeil, [1978] 2 SCR 662.

[59] Oil, Chemical and Atomic Workers International Union v. Imperial Oil Ltd. and A.-G. B.C., [1963] SCR 584; LCD, 4th ed., 354.

[60] Ontario Human Rights Commission and O'Malley v. Simpsons-Sears Ltd. et al., [1985] 2 SCR 536.

[61] Operation Dismantle Inc. et al. v. The Queen et al., [1985] 1 SCR 441; LCD, 5th ed., no. 43; LCDSCC, no. 6, on appeal from [1983] 1 F.C. 745.

[62] OPSEU v. A.-G. Ontario, [1987] 2 SCR 2; LCDSCC, no. 28.

[63] Osborne v. The Queen, [1986] 9 CRD 400.30-02 (Federal Court, trial div.).

[64] Pellant v. Hebert (1981), 12 R.G.P. 242.

[65] Plessy v. Ferguson (1896), 163 U.S. 537.

[66] Public Service Alliance of Canada v. Canada, [1987] 1 SCR 424; LCDSCC, no. 27.

[67] Quong-Wing v. Regina (1914), 49 SCR 440.

[68] Re Authority of Parliament in relation to the Upper House Reference, [1980] 1 SCR 54; LCD, 5th ed., no. 61.

[69] Re B.C. Motor Vehicle Act, [1985] 2 SCR 486; LCD, 5th ed., no. 45; LCDSCC, no. 10.

[70] Re Blainey and Ontario Hockey Association (1986), 54 O.R. (2d) 513.

[71] Re Clifford Maltby et al., [1983] 2 CRD 300-01 (Saskatchewan Queen's Bench).

[72] Re Lavigne and Ontario Public Service Employees Union et al. (1986), 55 O.R. (2d), 449.

[73] Re Manitoba Language Rights (*Order*), [1985] 2 SCR 347; LCD, 5th ed., no. 56; LCDSCC, no. 950.

[74] Re McKinney and Board of Governors of the University of Guelph and seven other applications (1987), 63 O.R. (2d), 1, on appeal from (1986), 57 O.R. (2d) 1.

[75] Re Ontario Film and Video Appreciation Society and Ontario Board of Censors (1984), 45 O.R. (2d) 80, on appeal from (1983) 41 O.R. (2d) 583.

[76] Reference re Alberta Statutes, [1938] SCR 100; LCD, 5th ed., no. 32.

[77] Reference re Anti-inflation Act, [1976] 2 SCR 373; LCDSCC, no. 22.

[78] Reference re Bill 30, An Act to Amend the Education Act (Ont.), [1987] 1 SCR 1148; LCD, 5th ed., no. 58; LCDSCC, no. 34, on appeal from (1986), 53 O.R. (2d) 5B.

[79] Reference re Public Service Employee Relations Act (Alta.), [1987] 1 SCR 313; LCD, 5th ed., no. 49; LCDSCC, no. 22.

[80] Regents of the University of California v. Bakke (1978), 438 U.S. 265, 98 S.Ct. 2733.

[81] Regina v. Beare; Regina v. Higgins, [1988] 2 SCR 387; LCDSCC, no. 46.

[82] Regina v. Big M Drug Mart Ltd. et al., [1985] 1 SCR 295; LCD, 5th ed., no. 42; LCDSCC, no. 5.

[83] Regina v. Canadian Newspapers Co., [1988] 2 SCR 122; LCDSCC, no. 44.

[84] Regina v. Collins, [1987] 1 SCR 265; LCDSCC, no. 20.

[85] Regina v. Cornell, [1988] 1 SCR 461; LCDSCC, no. 36.

[86] Regina v. Drybones, [1970] SCR 282; LCD, 5th ed., no. 37.

[87] Regina v. Dyment, [1988] 2 SCR 417; LCDSCC, no. 47.

[88] Regina v. Edwards Books and Art Ltd., [1986] 2 SCR 713; LCD, 5th ed., no. 48; LCDSCC, no. 19.

[89] Regina v. Genest, [1989] 1 SCR 59.

[90] Regina v. Hamill, [1987] 1 SCR 301; LCDSCC, no. 25.

[91] Regina v. Hufsky, [1988] 1 SCR 621; LCDSCC, no. 37.

[92] Regina v. Jacoy, [1988] 2 SCR 548.

[93] Regina v. Jones, [1986] 2 SCR 284; LCDSCC, no. 17.

[94] Regina v. Lyons, [1987] 2 SCR 309; LCDSCC, no. 29.

[95] Regina v. Manninen, [1987] 1 SCR 1233; LCDSCC, no. 26.

[96] Regina v. Mannion, [1986] 2 SCR 272; LCDSCC, no. 16.

[97] Regina v. McKitka, [1987] 9 CRD 350.20-02.

[98] Regina v. Mercure, [1988] 1 SCR 234; LCDSCC, no. 952.

[99] Regina v. Milne, [1987] 2 SCR 512; LCDSCC, no. 31.

[100] Regina v. Morgentaler, [1988] 1 SCR 30; LCD, 5th ed., no. 50; LCDSCC, no. 35.

[101] Regina v. Murphy (John S.), [1988] 11 CRD 900.170-01.

[102] Regina v. Operation Dismantle Inc. et al, [1983] 1 F.C. 745. 300-01 (Saskatchewan Queen's Bench).

[103] Regina v. Rahey, [1987] 1 SCR 588; LCDSCC, no. 25.

[104] Regina v. Ross, [1989] 1 SCR 3.

[105] Regina v. Sieben, [1987] 1 SCR 295; LCDSCC, no. 21.

[106] Regina v. Simmons, [1988] 2 SCR 495; LCDSCC, no. 50.

[107] Regina v. Smith (Edward Dewey), [1987] 1 SCR 1045; LCDSCC, no. 27.

[108] Regina v. Strachan, [1988] 2 SCR 980; LCDSCC, no. 52.

[109] Regina v. Therens et al., [1985] 1 SCR 613; LCD, 5th ed., no. 44; LCDSCC, no. 7.

[110] Regina v. Thomsen, [1988] 1 SCR 640; LCDSCC, no. 37.

[111] Regina v. Tremblay, [1987] 2 SCR 435; LCDSCC, no. 30.

[112] Regina v. Turpin, [1989] 1 SCR.

[113] Regina v. Vaillancourt, [1987] 2 SCR 636; LCDSCC, 33.

[114] Regina v. Vermette, [1988] 1 SCR 985; LCDSCC, no. 40.

[115] Regina v. Whyte, [1988] 2 SCR3; LCDSCC, no. 43.

[116] Reynolds v. A.-G. of B.C., [1984] 4 CRD 325.30-01 (B.C. Court of Appeal), on appeal from [1983] 2 CRD 325.30-01 (Supreme Court of B.C.)

[117] Robertson and Rosetanni v. The Queen, [1963] SCR 651; LCD 4th ed., 396.

[118] Roe v. Wade (1973), 410 U.S. 113.

[119] Roncarelli v. Duplessis, [1959] SCR 121.

[120] Rothman v. The Queen, [1981] 1 SCR 640.

[121] RWSDU v. Dolphin Delivery Ltd., [1986] 2 SCR 573; LCD, 5th ed., no. 47; LCDSCC, no. 18.

[122] RWSDU v. Saskatchewan, [1987] 1 SCR 460; LCDSCC, no. 23.

[123] Saumur v. Quebec and A.-G. Que., [1953] 2 SCR 299.

[124] Scott v. A.-G. Can., [1986] 8 CRD 325.30-02.

[125] Singh et al. v. Minister of Employment and Immigration, [1985] 1 SCR 177; LCD, 5th ed., no. 41; LCDSCC, no. 4.

[126] Société des Acadiens du Nouveau-Brunswick Inc. et al. v. Association of Parents for Fairness in Education et al., [1986] 1 SCR 549; LCD, 5th ed., no. 57; LCDSCC, no. 14.

[127] Storey v. Zazelenchuk, [1983] 2 CRD 325.20-01 (Saskatchewan Queen's Bench).

[128] Switzman v. Elbling and A.-G. Que., [1957] SCR 285.

[129] The Queen v. Oakes, [1986] 1 SCR 103; LCD, 5th ed., no. 46; LCDSCC, no. 12.

[130] Tiny R.D. Sep. Sch. Trustees v. Regina, [1928] A.C. 363.

[131] Union Colliery Co. of B.C. Ltd. v. Bryden, [1899] A.C. 580 (P.C.)

[132] Valente v. The Queen et al., [1985] 2 SCR 673; LCDSCC, no. 11.

[133] Virginia State Board of Pharmacy v. Virginia Citizens Consumer Council Inc. (1986), 425 U.S. 748.

[134] Walter v. A.-G. Alta., [1969] SCR 383.

[135] Weremchuk v. Jacobsen, [1987] 9 CRD 325.30-01.

Index

Aboriginal rights (section 25), 41, 58-59, 87, 167

Abortion, 4-5, 7, 152-61, 175-81, 210, 216, 220. *See also Morgentaler* case

Administration of justice into disrepute, whether proceedings would bring (section 24 [2]), 140-44

Adversary system, 65-66

Affirmative action programs, 50, 51, 163

A.-G. Man. et al. v. A.-G. Can. et al. [5], 42

A.-G. Que. v. A.-G. Can. [7], 43

Alberta Act, 187

Alberta Court of Appeal, 71, 86

Alberta Court of Queen's Bench, 117-18

Alberta Labour Reference, 86-91

Alberta Press Bill, 19-20

Alberta Youth Court, 221

Alliance Against Abortion, 180

Amnesty International Quebec, 106

Andrews case, 11, 165-71, 184-85, 213

Assembly, freedom of (section 2[c]), 10, 24, 44, 70, 86, 119

Association, freedom of (section 2[d]), 10, 24, 30, 44, 70, 87-88, 90, 108-9, 119, 219, 224

Badger case [13], 113

Basile v. A.-G. Noiva Scotia [14], 47

Bayefsky, Anne, 164

B.C. Civil Liberties Association, 123-24

B.C. Court of Appeal, 82, 117, 166

B.C. Elections Act, 116

B.C. Motor Vehicle Act case [69], 63, 144-48, 153, 214

B.C. Municipal Act, 118

B.C. Supreme Court, 47, 112, 116, 123-24

BCCEU case [21], 85

Beetz, Mr. Justice Jean, 32, 79, 84, 88, 120-21, 132-33, 157-58, 160, 189, 191-93, 197, 199, 203

Bennett, W.A.C., 30

Bhinder case [16], 183

BigM case [82], 26, 70-75, 171

Bilingual/bireligious heritage, 14-15

Bilingualism, 193-94, 211-12

Bill of Rights (Alberta), 31, 34, 118

Bill of Rights (Canada), 11, 15-17, 24-26, 34, 36, 74, 132, 135-36, 139; in contrast to Charter, 35, 71, 108, 171; equality rights in, 49, 163-64, 166-67, 170-71; as interpreted by courts, 25-29, 33-34, 44, 61-62, 177, 211, 213, 218; notwithstanding clause in, 24-25, 27; origins of, 23; precedents, 140; section 1# (rights and freedoms), 24, 26, 28, 35, 48; section 2 (legal judicial rights), 24, 35, 48, 65, 131-133, 190, 200; section 133 (language rights), 51-52

Bill of Rights (U.S.), 12-13, 15, 21, 50-51, 72, 123, 137-38, 182; amendments to, 225; "due process" clause in, 145-46; implied limitations clause in, 56; as precedent in Charter cases, 63

Bill 22 (Official Language Act — Quebec), 187-88

Bill 30 (Ontario), 173-74

Bill 63 (Act to Promote the French Language in Quebec), 187

Bill 101 (Charter of the French Language — Quebec), 43, 57, 94-97, 99, 101-2, 104-8, 186-89, 195, 206, 210, 212, 216. *See also* Quebec clause

Bill 178 (Quebec), 106

Bilodeau case [17], 187, 196-202, 204, 207